An object-oriented environment:
Principles and application

D. COLEMAN, P. ARNOLD, S. BODOFF,
C. DOLLIN, H. GILCHRIST, F. HAYES
AND P. JEREMAES
Object-Oriented Development: The Fusion Method

D. HENDERSON-SELLERS
A Book of Object-Oriented Knowledge

K. LANO AND H. HAUGHTON
Object-Oriented Specification Case Studies

J. LINDSKOV KNUDSEN, M. LÖFGREN,
O. LEHRMANN MADSEN AND B. MAGNUSSON
Object-Oriented Environments: The Mjølner Approach

M. LORENZ
Object-Oriented Software Development: A Practical Guide

D. MANDRIOLI AND B. MEYER (eds)
Advances in Object-Oriented Software Engineering

B. MEYER
*Reusable Software: The Base
Object-Oriented Component Libraries*

B. MEYER
Eiffel: The Language

B. MEYER AND J.-M. NERSON
Object-Oriented Applications

P. J. ROBINSON
Hierarchical Object-Oriented Design

R. SWITZER
Eiffel: An Introduction

An object-oriented environment: Principles and application

Bertrand Meyer
ISE, Santa Barbara
SOL, Paris

Prentice Hall

New York London Toronto Sydney Tokyo Singapore

First published 1994 by
Prentice Hall International (UK) Limited
Campus 400, Maylands Avenue
Hemel Hempstead
Hertfordshire, HP2 7EZ
A division of
Simon & Schuster International Group

Printed and bound in Great Britain by the
University Press, Cambridge

Library of Congress Cataloging-in-Publication Data

Available from the publisher

British Library Cataloguing in Publication Data

A catalogue record for this book is available from
the British Library

ISBN 0-13-245507-2

---

2 3 4 5   98 97 96 95 94

Short table of contents

Preface   vii

Contents   xi

1   Getting started   1

2   A guided tour   7

3   Environment principles   41

4   General interactive mechanisms   53

5   Controlling a session the Project Tool   75

6   Compiling systems: the Melting Ice Technology   81

7   The System Tool: describing a system   113

8   Class Tools: browsing through software   123

9   Feature Tools, Execution Object Tools, and symbolic debugging   139

10 Using the workbench outside of the graphical environment   165

11 Obtaining the best possible performance   171

12 Building GUI applications: an introduction to EiffelBuild   177

Index   225

The full table of contents starts on page xix.

Short table of content

Preface

Given the bearing they exert on all aspects of software construction, it is not surprising that the principles of object technology should change the way we envision and design development environments. This book attempts to show how the consistent application of these principles can yield an environment that helps produce the quality results that we have come to expect from object-oriented software construction.

Although "object-oriented environment" has become a catchprase, generously bestowed at times on any product that uses as much as an icon or pulldown menu, in reality little significant innovation has occurred in software development environments since the appearance of the Smalltalk system two decades ago. This lack of progress has been somewhat obscured by advances in the underlying technology: faster machines, larger memories, new window systems, hardware and software support for interactive graphics. The resulting benefits, however, are not specific to software development; they exist in all application areas of computers. The software-specific aspects of today's environments do not differ much from what their predecessors offered; the available tools, in particular, are still the conventional ones — a compiler, an interpreter, a debugger, a pretty-printer and so on. Modern interaction techniques improve the appearance of these tools but do not change their nature.

It is also common to see an environment being labeled as object-oriented simply because it supports an object-oriented programming language. But this is of course abusive: the concepts of the target language do not magically spread to the environment.

To get the real benefits of object technology we must base the design of the environment itself, and the way it interacts with its users, on the same principles that the method defines for software construction, starting with the idea from which everything else follows: data abstraction.

This book explores what object-oriented principles mean for software development environments and describes in detail the ISE Eiffel 3 environment, which from the ground up was designed as the application of these principles.

Three major themes run throughout the book: consistency, ergonomics, and support for professional software development. It is useful, before you read about their consequences in the following chapter, to take a first look at each of them in turn.

CONSISTENCY

Consistency is essential in making an environment easy to learn and pleasant to use. Again and again in the discussion you will note that whenever two of the facilities offered by the environment are conceptually similar the way in which users access them is the same, even if they appear in quite different contexts. This principle has guided hundreds of design decisions, which individually are sometimes of little consequence but together cover most of the users' interaction with the environment. It affects everything from window layouts to textual messages and interaction techniques.

The principle of consistency goes far beyond the user interface. As already noted, the starting point for this book is that the environment should derive from the same object-oriented concepts that presided over the design of the method and of the language. Again and again in the presentation you will notice ideas and notations that the environment directly borrows from these two sources. For example a tool of the environment is either void or *targeted* to a development object, just as in the language an entity (a variable) is either void or *attached* to an object; and in the same way that you can instantiate a class (an object type) to yield an object, using a creation instruction written **!! x**, the interactive application builder offers a mechanism for instantiating a command type to yield a command, using a button whose graphical appearance ▐▲ directly recalls the syntax of creation instructions.

On targeting a tool see chapter 4; on the interactive application builder and the notion of command see chapter 12.

ERGONOMICS

The second major thread of the book is ergonomics, also known as human factors analysis. The goal pursued here is well captured too by the term "user-friendly" — yet another catchprase, but one that denotes a noble concept: turning the environment into a faithful and unobtrusive developer's assistant. This is easier said than done. One of the challenges is how to satisfy a wide range of users, from novices to experts; another is to use techniques that will look good not just during a five-minute demonstration but during day-in, day-out use for large developments. One year is not an unusual duration for someone's assignment to a project; at eight hours a day, this means about two thousand hours spent in front of a terminal using the environment's mechanisms. How many times, having been initially attracted to a new tool, were you still enamored of it two thousand hours later?

This book cannot promise eternal love. But the environment it describes was specifically designed for long-term usage by demanding developers. In particular, while we of course embraced the concepts of modern interactive graphical environments — what is sometimes called WIMP: Windows, Icons, Menus, Pointing device — we had grown dissatisfied with some of the techniques they commonly use, and took a critical look at some of the widely accepted ideas. This is the reason, for example, why you will find no keep-button-down dragging operations (stressful and error-prone), few operations requiring double clicking (inconvenient) and almost no pulldown menus (better techniques are available); but you will learn new interaction mechanisms such as typed drag-and-drop, application building through visual association, tool format selection, the Focus Area technique and universal clickability.

The last two items in this list provide good examples of why it is necessary to look beyond common WIMP techniques:

- The notion of Focus Area addresses an issue raised by graphical icons, a staple of modern environments. For novices, or for a demonstration, it seems better to have large icons each equipped with a text legend indicating its meaning. But as soon as you have learned the basics and started to use the environment, good use of screen space becomes a major concern: icons should then be small and if (as should be the case) they are not too numerous you will remember their meanings; the space they take up is stolen from your work, and legends detract your attention from your own texts. The Focus Area technique solves the dilemma by using small, clear icons, but reserving a common text area to display the meaning of each icon as you move the mouse cursor over it.

- Clickability (a new term and apparently a new concept) is a consequence of the environment principles studied in chapter 3, in particular semantic consistency and direct manipulation. It enables the environment's users to grab just about any representation of a development object (class, feature or otherwise) wherever it appears in a textual or graphical representation. The result is an effective way of traveling through a possibly complex software system, replacing many of the functions of browsers and other exploration tools.

Ergonomics is not an exact science, and the self-imposed challenge of building a system that will still look good to its users after 2000 hours of constant usage is a tough one. While I cannot promise that we have not left or introduced some source of inconvenience, I can at least offer as evidence the observation that the environment's developers do use that very environment for all of their own work, and so did not have to travel very far to put themselves in the users' shoes. (Using your own tools is of course only a necessary condition, not a sufficient one; you still have to find out very actively what *other* users have to say about them. Such external input has been essential in bringing the environment to where it is today.)

Just as importantly, this book does not just describe the environment's interaction techniques but also, just as the book *Object-Oriented Software Construction* analyzed the pros and cons of many method and language design choices, discusses their rationale in detail, especially in areas where they differ from commonly accepted ideas. So even if you do not agree with all of our decisions you will at least be able to appreciate the intellectual path that led to them, and perhaps come up with your own solutions.

PROFESSIONALISM

The last of the three major themes listed above was the ability to support professional development. Although not all software is (or should be) developed by professional software developers, a very important class of software requires professionals. It includes large systems, mission-critical systems, systems that must be around for a long time — often having to undergo many successive changes in the process — and in general all systems for which quality is a major requirement.

In such cases, the overall quality of the environment and its ergonomics remain as important as ever, but must be complemented by the certainty that the developers will have access to all they need to deliver to their customers the best possible results.

This goal has several consequences. One of them is the attention that the environment's design devoted to performance. Although object-oriented technology is initially targeted at increasing other software qualities, in particular extendibility, reusability and reliability, it also has much to contribute to efficiency — without which the approach could not reasonably succeed in practical industrial developments. Efficiency includes two aspects:

If performance is an important consideration for your developments, be sure to read chapter 11, which is specially devoted to this topic.

- Development time, for which, as you will discover in this book, a novel approach to compilation, the *Melting Ice Technology*, makes it possible to achieve the same instantaneous turnaround commonly associated with interpreter-based environments, without sacrificing the security and run-time performance of compiler-oriented environments.

- Execution time, which thanks to the environment's compilation mechanisms is comparable to what can be obtained by programmers using traditional languages such as C.

Another aspect of the focus on professional development will be particularly apparent in the presentation of Graphical User Interface application building in chapter 12, which contains a combination of visual and textual interface techniques. For many tasks a visual mechanism, such as drag-and-dropping a graphical object, is the best solution; but when it comes to adding a new command with non-trivial semantics, nothing beats writing the corresponding routine text. Even though the application builder makes it possible to develop an application without typing a single line of text — a possibility that will be of interest to novices and professionals alike — if it can entirely be expressed in terms of existing reusable elements, professionals will not resent having to add some textual elements of their own when the novelty of the task justifies it.

THE ROLE OF OLDER TECHNOLOGY

The goal of supporting professional software development also has a consequence regarding the underlying technology. Although the environment is fully and enthusiastically object-oriented, it internally relies on the software technology that comes closest to a universally available machine-level language: C.

We disagree here with the hybrid approach embodied in C++ or Objective-C, and its attempt to merge two incompatible views: the object-oriented method, which is all about abstract reasoning and the rational structuring of software systems, and C, which is all about bytes, words, addresses, pointers and other low-level concepts. But even though it is in most cases unfit for direct consumption by humans, C is an acceptable vehicle as a target language for compilers, and is used in this role by the environment described in this book.

This approach has yielded a number of advantages. The most obvious one is portability: the environment is available on many different development platforms. Another is cross-development: you can take the output of a development and port it to a platform that has a C compiler. Yet another is the ease with which you can use the language and environment to interact with existing tools, many of which are C-based. In particular you can write "wrapper" classes that provide an object-oriented encapsulation of existing facilities or access to external devices.

This use of C is an example of what I believe to be a general model for evolution in the software field. We cannot reject older technology overnight; but we should not, as has so often be done by the industry, use this obvious observation as an excuse for maintaining the status quo or neutering new ideas in the name of compatibility. Instead, we should implement the new ideas fully and remorselessly; but in this implementation effort we may internally rely on the older technology as a stepping stone to achieve this goal quickly and effectively.

SELF-APPLICATION

A property of the environment, already mentioned briefly, deserves to be emphasized: the ISE Eiffel 3 environment is written in Eiffel, self-developed, and self-compiled.

A C program of a few thousand lines, part of the "run-time system", encapsulates the interface to the operating system, in particular for such aspects as memory allocation, signal handling and license management. Everything else — currently about 3000 classes totaling several hundred thousand lines — is in Eiffel. The versions that run on the many supported platforms are generated, *via* C, by the environment's compiling facilities, applied to the environment itself.

The original bootstrap process involved two principal steps. The first compilers, which started to appear in 1986, and culminated in 1990 with ISE Eiffel 2.3, were written in C. (Obviously, one must start somewhere, and you will not go very far unless you select in the first iteration a language for which an implementation exists!) ISE Eiffel 3 was designed as a new product, and was written in Eiffel from the start. Intermediate versions were checked, compiled and tested using the 2.3 compiler. Then when the first version was felt complete and stable enough it was used to compile itself. (As anyone who has gone though such a process can testify, this first self-compilation is a momentous event.) From then on each successive version or intermediate release served to compile the next one, which was then immediately applied to itself to verify that the process had reached what mathematicians called a fixpoint — the result must be exactly the same!

This self-application process was not just a question of principle; more important was the realization that a system of the scope, difficulty and ambition of ISE Eiffel 3 could only be done in a reasonable amount of time by using Eiffel. It is indeed thanks to the full application of the method and the language that we were able to implement all that we had initially envisioned, and more.

But self-application is also, particularly for users of the environment, an irreplaceable guarantee of seriousness. Discovering that the manual for a text processing system was not written with the system itself would probably make you suspicious. Similarly, a software development environment that is claimed to help develop ambitious software systems with a certain method and language is itself an ambitious software system; it is hard to take its claims seriously if you discover that it was produced using another method, language or environment.

Self-application is never a sufficient condition of quality, since there is no guarantee that the set of facilities which the environment uses for its own purposes covers everything that other developments will need. It is, however, a necessary condition, and a good sign. That the environment successfully compiles its own 3000 classes does not prove it will process yours properly, but does make such an event much more likely.

Self-application also helps the quality assurance process: developers cannot ignore deficiencies, since they are the first to suffer from them. For the user or prospective user, it provides an existence proof, a model, and a way to ascertain the claims made on behalf of the environment. Efficiency is an example. Seeing how fast the environment processes user requests, and knowing that it is entirely written in itself, is the best way for a new user to realize that the performance fo the generated code is indeed as high as asserted.

CONTENTS OF THE ENVIRONMENT

ISE Eiffel 3 is a complete development environment intended for the development of quality software. The structure of the environment is described by the figure on the facing page. It includes the following elements, of which the present book describes only the core subset:

- **EiffelBench** is the development environment supporting fast compilation, editing of software texts, browsing, debugging, and production of C packages for cross-development. The normal mode of interaction with EiffelBench is through a Graphical User Interface (GUI); a non-graphical version, callable from the command line, is also available.

- **EiffelBase** is the library of reusable components covering the needs of many applications in the area of fundamental data structures and algorithms.

- **EiffelVision** is the library of toolkit-independent GUI facilities for building interactive graphical applications that will run on many different platforms. All the graphical components of ISE Eiffel 3 were built with EiffelVision; you may use the library to equip your own components with similarly convenient interactive interfaces.

- **EiffelBuild** is the GUI application builder applying visual techniques to the construction of graphical applications — not just their interface, but the entire applications. EiffelBuild generates maintainable Eiffel classes, including calls to EiffelVision features for the graphical aspects.

- The **EiffelLex** and **EiffelParse** libraries support lexical analysis and parsing of languages.

- **EiffelStore** is the persistence library, which supports the storing of Eiffel objects on various media (files, relational databases, object-oriented databases). EiffelStore offers a number of interfaces, or *handles*, to various commercially available database management systems, and automactically maps a single Eiffel source text to these various systems, in the same way that EiffelVision maps a single source text to various GUI toolkits.

- The **EiffelShelf** is a repository of user-contributed reusable components in various application areas.

- **EiffelCase** is the set of tools for seamless analysis and design of object-oriented software, supporting the BON (Business Object Notation) analysis method and enabling a seamless transition to the later stages of software development through the generation of Eiffel classes.

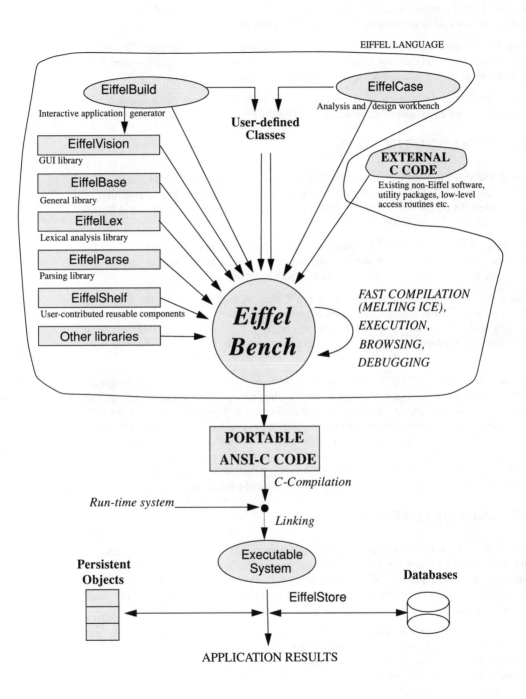

This list will grow as the environment develops. In particular, more libraries are being designed and will be added to those listed above, furthering the central goal of the approach: building an industry of quality reusable software components.

All the components of the environment are designed to work together. The tools' consistency follows from their use of a common method and language — Eiffel — and from a consistent set of user interface principles described in chapter 3.

This book provides a detailed description of EiffelBench — the centerpiece of the environment — and an extensive introduction to EiffelBuild.

THE MANUAL AND THE BOOK

The project behind this book was to write a single text that would serve both as a manual, of interest to users of ISE Eiffel 3, and as a presentation of the principles and application of object-oriented environments, of interest to readers who want to learn about the topic but do not necessarily have access to the environment itself.

The two versions have indeed remained almost identical, although the manual comes with information on product installation, a description of the license manager and release notes that are of no immediate interest to readers who are not users.

Retaining the hands-on style of a manual ("Click on the **OK** button; the following window appears...") was a conscious decision, meant to convey to the reader a concrete grasp of how the environment works. If you do not have access to the environment, you should view this approach as a pedagogical device intended to make the discussion more lively.

In the same way that *Eiffel: The Language* included in a single thread a language tutorial, a language manual and a language reference, the present book merge two genres that are usually considered separate, the conceptual introduction and the user's manual. As with its predecessor, the risk exists that it will be disappointing on both counts: too conceptual for the environment user in search of concrete information, and too practical for the general reader in search of concepts. The wager, of course, is that the reverse will happen: that users will appreciate the presentation of the concepts, and general readers will enjoy seeing the environment at work, almost as if they were sitting in front of a terminal.

FONTS AND CONSISTENCY

A note on a small point — cosmetics, really, but very visible — is in order for readers familiar with the Eiffel literature. The officially recommended typographical conventions for the language use bold italics (previously just bold) for keywords, such as *class*, italics for developer-defined names for classes, features and entities, such as *LINKED_LIST*, and roman for comments.

Unfortunately, these conventions, while appropriate for the printed page, do not transpose well to screen formats, where some of the results would not be visible enough. The environment uses by default a bold font, as in **class LINKED_LIST**, for everything. Although users can define other font settings, the figures of this book naturally use the default convention, which corresponds to what a beginning user will see on the screen.

The existence of separate screen and paper styles presented a dilemma for the preparation of this book. The method and the supporting literature show a constant obsession with consistency. But consistency with what: the paper standard or the screen format?

For the short software extracts that appear in the text, it was felt necessary to depart from the usual conventions so that the appearance would be the same as in figure. So you will indeed see **class LINKED_LIST** rather than *class LINKED_LIST*. (A few discussions are not connected to any figure do use the standard conventions.) This will be surprising at first if you are familiar with other presentations of the language, but the alternative — using a different font in the figures and in the text — would have been worse.

SUPPORTED PLATFORMS

You will probably notice a Unix-X-Motif flavor in the screenshots that serve to illustrate the environment throughout the text. Do not attach too much importance to this style; the environment runs on many different hardware-software platforms where, thanks to the versatility of EiffelVision, it adapts to the underlying toolkits — just as systems developed with it can be easily ported to different environments.

In particular, versions for Microsoft Windows, NEXTSTEP and VMS are also available, as well as versions for other environments. Please check with ISE if you need more details.

OTHER DOCUMENTATION

This book is the fourth in a series. Previous volumes covered the method, the language, and the base libraries; addressing the environment issue was the logical next step. Here are the precise references to the three predecessors: *All the books cited here are published by Prentice Hall*

- *Object-Oriented Software Construction* describes the object-oriented method, starting from the software engineering issues and principles that lead to it.

- *Eiffel: The Language* covers the language in detail. It also includes (in appendix D) a presentation of the Lace language, used to specify how to assemble a system from a set of classes.

- *Reusable Software: The Base Object-Oriented Component Libraries* discusses the principles of library design and their application to EiffelBase, EiffelLex and EiffelParse. It also serves as reference for these three libraries.

A book tentatively titled *Eiffel: The Graphics* is planned; it will cover EiffelVision and EiffelBuild. Shorter documents distributed by ISE with the software cover these two components as well as EiffelStore.

The BON analysis and design method which, as noted above, serves as the conceptual basis for EiffelCase, is presented and discussed in detail in *Seamless Object-Oriented Software Architecture: Analysis and Design of Reliable Software* by Jean-Marc Nerson and Kim Waldén.

Introduction to the Theory of Programming Languages, although covering a different area of computing science (the formal syntactic and semantic description of languages), introduces a number of related theoretical concepts, useful in particular to understand the ideas behind EiffelBuild.

CONTENTS OF THE BOOK

Chapter 1 is a road map which briefly shows how to approach ISE Eiffel 3 and this book. Make sure you read it, and everything else it says you should read, even if you are eager to get your hands on the environment itself. It focuses on the needs of the first-time user, of the first-time installer, and of the hurried reader.

Chapter 2, entitled "A guided tour", is a step-by-step demonstration of some of the principal facilities of EiffelBench. It will quickly enable you to get familiar with some of the basic mechanisms.

Chapter 3, "Environment principles", explains the novel environment and interface concepts that were applied throughout the design of all the environment's components in an attempt to make them easy to use, powerful and consistent.

Chapter 4, "General interactive mechanisms" describes the conventions and techniques used in all the individual elements, or *tools*, of the environment.

Chapter 5 describes the Project Tool, which serves as control panel of any EiffelBench session, used in particular to trigger the compilation commands.

Chapter 6 is entitled "Compiling systems: the Melting Ice Technology". It describes the combination of compilation facilities — melting, freezing, precompiling and finalizing — intended to reconcile two goals that are often considered incompatible: very fast turnaround after a change, and production of highly optimized, portable object code.

Chapters 7 and 8 describe two types of tool that play a central role in compiling and browsing: System and Class Tools. Class Tools in particular, based on the principal abstraction of the Eiffel method, the notion of class, provide the mechanisms for exploring the structure of a system and seeing what happens to its components in the various transformations which they incur because of inheritance.

Chapter 9 describes the Feature and Execution Object Tools, the principal vehicles for the symbolic, object-oriented debugging facilities of the environment. Particularly interesting is the possibility they offer of catching an exception *before* it occurs, and using all the browsing mechanisms of the environment to explore the complete static and dynamic context that leads to the exception.

Chapter 10 explains how to use the major facilities of EiffelBench without relying on its graphical facilities — for example how to compile a system from a command line rather than from within the environment, or to apply browsing tools from within a shell script.

Chapter 11 discusses **optimization tips**, explaining how to produce the most efficient possible code. Make sure you read it if run-time performance is important to you.

Chapter 12 is a detailed introduction to EiffelBuild; although not an exhaustive reference, it will enable you to start producing advanced Graphical User Interface applications. It also shows that the environment and interface principles underlying the environment and described in chapters 3 and 4 can be beneficial to many different applications besides EiffelBench.

FUTURE DEVELOPMENTS

The publication of this book marks a milestone: the completion of the technological base for our view of what the software industry should be.

Although the need will undoubtedly arise both for new tools and for improvements to the existing ones, the environment as it stands today is a proven and robust construction, which has already been used to develop (besides itself) a number of large and difficult systems.

Building on that basis, much work of course remains. Foremost in the coming years will be the effort to develop thousands of reusable components to cover the major needs of the software industry. The mechanisms described in the following pages will, I hope, provide a powerful help to achieve this goal.

Santa Barbara   B.M.
February 1994

AUTHOR'S ADDRESS

ISE, 270 Storke Road Suite 7
Goleta, CA 93117 USA
Telephone 805-685-1006, Fax 805-685-6869, Electronic mail <bertrand@eiffel.com>

TRADEMARKS

EiffelBench, EiffelBuild, EiffelCase, EiffelStore and "More than a pretty interface" are trademarks of Interactive Software Engineering Inc.

SOFTWARE CREDITS

ISE Eiffel 3 is the result of the work of many people over many years.

The development of EiffelBench proper was brought to completion by Frédéric Deramat (precompilation, environment, debugging mechanism), Xavier Le Vourch (compilation, incrementality) and Dino Valente (environment, compilation), aided by Didier Dupont (environment) and building on a foundation laid by Frédéric Dernbach (compilation, incrementality), Raphaël Manfredi (run-time system, debugging mechanism, license manager, portability) and Philippe Stephan (interface principles, environment, debugging mechanism, overall system architecture). Further important contributions were made by David Morgan (parsing) and Glen Smith (run-time system, license manager). The support of Darcy Harrison and Annie Meyer throughout the project was also essential.

The principal contributors to EiffelBuild have been Frédéric Deramat, Xavier Le Vourch, Glen Smith and Dino Valente. Bruno Puchault wrote an early version.

A complete picture must also include the preceding versions of ISE Eiffel. Version, as noted, was initially bootstrapped from a compiler written in ISE Eiffel 2.3, and was made possible by the accumulated work on all the earlier releases. The project leader for all these releases was Jean-Marc Nerson. Key contributions came from Reynald Bouy (libraries), Denis Caromel (exception handling), Vince Kraemer (graphics), Philippe Lahire (graphics), Frédéric Lalanne (compilation), Olivier Mallet (compilation), Bernard Nieto (optimization), Jean-Pierre Sarkis (compilation, run-time system), Hervé Templereau (compilation) and Deniz Yuksel (compilation), as well as others too numerous to list here.

ACKNOWLEDGMENTS

The development of ISE Eiffel 3 benefited from the help of several companies, through equipment loans or otherwise. We are grateful in particular to Altos Computers, the Bank of New York, Data General, IBM, MIPS Corporation, Prentice Hall, Pyramid Corporation, Reynolds and Reynolds, the Santa Barbara Bank and Trust, the Santa Cruz Operation, Sony, and Sun Microsystems. Among the individuals who helped we are particularly thankful to Joel Crosby, the Gibault family, Helen Martin, and the Mendelsohn family. Tom Morrisette provided useful comments on a draft of the book. Raphaël Meyer helped prepare the final version.

Prior to its official release ISE Eiffel 3 was for many months available in pre-release form. The feedback of the pre-release users was invaluable. Again there are too many people to acknowledge here, but one should definitely mention Marc Bousse from IRISA (Rennes, France), Satoshi Fushimi from IMSL (Tokyo, Japan), John Kersholt from Hogeschool Enschede (The Netherlands), Andrew MacGaffey from Reuters (Chicago), James McKim from the Hartford Graduate Center (Hartford), David Quarrie from Lawrence Berkeley Laboratory (Berkeley), Michael Ryba from the University of Stuttgart (Germany), Richard Wiener from the University of Colorado (Colorado Springs) and all the members of the Eiffel support teams at ISE distributors Cromasoft (Mexico City, Mexico) and SRA (Tokyo, Japan) — a very international group indeed.

A particular note of thanks, for exceptional services rendered, is due to David Hollenberg from the Information Sciences Institute of the University of Southern California. A software developer's dream user, he performed a sharp, critical and systematic exploration of successive versions of the pre-release, submitting countless problem reports and suggestions which directly led to a considerably improved environment.

Contents

Preface   vii

    CONSISTENCY   viii

    ERGONOMICS   viii

    PROFESSIONALISM   ix

    THE ROLE OF OLDER TECHNOLOGY   x

    SELF-APPLICATION   xi

    CONTENTS OF THE ENVIRONMENT   xii

    THE MANUAL AND THE BOOK   xiv

    FONTS AND CONSISTENCY   xiv

    SUPPORTED PLATFORMS   xv

    OTHER DOCUMENTATION   xv

    CONTENTS OF THE BOOK   xvi

    FUTURE DEVELOPMENTS   xvii

    AUTHOR'S ADDRESS   xviii

    TRADEMARKS   xviii

    SOFTWARE CREDITS   xviii

    ACKNOWLEDGMENTS   xviii

Contents   xix

1 Getting started   1

    1.1 OVERVIEW   1

    1.2 FOR THE FIRST-TIME USER   1

    1.3 SETTING UP YOUR ENVIRONMENT   2

        1.3.1 Environment variables   2

        1.3.2 Path   3

    1.4 CONTENTS OF THE DELIVERY DIRECTORY 4

2 A guided tour   7

2.1 OVERVIEW   7

2.2 COPYING THE EXAMPLE   7

2.3 STARTING EIFFELBENCH AND OPENING A PROJECT   8

2.4 THE NOTION OF PROJECT AND THE FILE SELECTOR   10

2.5 SPECIFYING AN ACE   11

2.6 COMPILING   13

2.7 THE USER INTERFACE MECHANISM   16

2.8 EDITING AND BROWSING THROUGH CLASSES AND FEATURES   19

2.9 A LITTLE MORE ABOUT BROWSING   28

2.10 MODIFYING AND MELTING   31

2.11 SYNTAX ERROR MESSAGES   33

2.12 A VALIDITY ERROR   34

2.13 EXECUTING AND DEBUGGING   36

3 Environment principles   41

3.1 OVERVIEW   41

3.2 METHOD SUPPORT   41

    3.2.1 Consistency   41

    3.2.2 Object-orientation for the software and its developers   42

    3.2.3 The perspective of the environment's user   44

    3.2.4 The Data Abstraction principle   45

3.3 DIRECT MANIPULATION   45

3.4 SEMANTIC CONSISTENCY   46

3.5 STRONG TYPING   47

3.6 ERRORS: PREVENTION RATHER THAN CURE   49

4 General interactive mechanisms   53

4.1 OVERVIEW   53

4.2 TOOLS AND THEIR TARGETS   53

    4.2.1 Creating a new tool   54

    4.2.2 Retargeting an existing tool through drag-and-drop   54

    4.2.3 Retargeting through keyboard entry   56

    4.2.4 Retargeting and formats   57

    4.2.5 Void tools, targeted tools, and the target's visual representation   58

4.3 THE TYPED DRAG-AND-DROP MECHANISM   59

    4.3.1 Drag-and-drop steps   59

4.3.2 Why drag-and-drop works the way it does: a human factors analysis   59

4.3.3 Quick Retargeting   60

4.4 GENERAL TOOL ORGANIZATION   62

4.4.1 General layout   62

4.4.2 Quit button   63

4.4.3 Window border, holes, and resynchronization   63

4.4.4 Focus area and text input areas   63

4.4.5 Button areas   64

4.4.6 Text window   64

4.4.7 Format area and Shell button   64

4.4.8 Tool-independent operations   64

4.5 APPLYING OPERATING SYSTEM COMMANDS
     TO DEVELOPMENT OBJECTS   65

4.5.1 Editing a class with vi   65

4.5.2 Changing the shell command   65

4.5.3 Changing the default command   66

4.6 EDITING DEVELOPMENT OBJECTS   67

4.6.1 Adjusting the font   67

4.6.2 Searching for a string   68

4.6.3 Modifying text   69

4.6.4 Saving text   69

4.6.5 Reinitializing text   70

4.7 THE FILE SELECTOR   70

4.7.1 File Selector layout   71

4.7.2 Using the File Selector   72

4.8 TYPED HOLES AND PEBBLES   73

5 Controlling a session: the Project Tool   75

5.1 OVERVIEW   75

5.2 OPENING A PROJECT   75

5.2.1 Starting EiffelBench   75

5.2.2 Choosing the project directory   76

5.2.3 Directory requirements and trouble-shooting   76

5.3 PROJECT TOOL OPERATIONS   78

5.3.1 Tool window setup   78

5.3.2 The holes   78

5.3.3 Iconifying the Project Tool window   79

5.3.4 The buttons   80

6 Compiling systems: the Melting Ice Technology   81

    6.1 OVERVIEW: FROM COMPILERS TO CASE TOOLS   81

        6.1.1 Beyond programming language compilers   82

        6.1.2 Incrementality   82

        6.1.3 An automatic process   82

    6.2 THE MELTING ICE TECHNOLOGY   83

        6.2.1 Why three compilation modes?   83

        6.2.2 The Melting Ice Principle   84

        6.2.3 Distinguishing between the three modes   85

    6.3 USING THE THREE COMPILATION MODES PROPERLY   87

        6.3.1 Melting   87

        6.3.2 When melting is not appropriate   87

        6.3.3 Freezing   88

        6.3.4 Finalizing   89

        6.3.5 Command-line interface   89

        6.3.6 Compiling an entire universe   90

    6.4 EXECUTING A COMPILED SYSTEM   90

        6.4.1 Executing from within the graphical environment   91

        6.4.2 Specifying the arguments under the graphical environment 91

        6.4.3 Running a frozen or melted system outside of the environment 92

        6.4.4 Executing the result of a finalized system   95

    6.5 PRECOMPILATION   96

        6.5.1 Precompilation concepts   97

        6.5.2 Using precompiled libraries   98

        6.5.3 Producing precompiled libraries   100

        6.5.4 Moving precompiled libraries   101

    6.6 COMPILATION ERRORS   102

        6.6.1 Syntax errors   102

        6.6.2 Validity errors   103

        6.6.3 The state of a system after an interrupted compilation   107

    6.7 FINALIZATION   107

        6.7.1 The finalization directory   107

        6.7.2 Porting to a different platform; the configuration file 108

        6.7.3 Finalization and precompilation   109

        6.7.4 Assertion checking in final mode   110

        6.7.5 Run-time assertion monitoring: the methodological perspective 111

        6.7.6 Not your usual software development context   112

        6.7.7 Generating optimal code: a summary   112

7 The System Tool: describing a system   113

  7.1 OVERVIEW   113

  7.2 HOW EIFFEL SOFTWARE IS ORGANIZED   113

      7.2.1 The notion of system   113

      7.2.2 The root and its needed classes   114

      7.2.3 The universe   114

      7.2.4 Lace   115

  7.3 CREATING THE ACE FOR A NEW PROJECT   116

  7.4 SYSTEM TOOL OPERATIONS   117

      7.4.1 Tool window layout   117

      7.4.2 Text format   118

      7.4.3 Clusters format   119

      7.4.4 "Not in system" classes   121

8 Class Tools: browsing through software   123

  8.1 OVERVIEW   123

  8.2 CLASS TOOL OPERATIONS   123

      8.2.1 Tool window organization   123

      8.2.2 Retargeting to a class or a feature   125

      8.2.3 Class Tool retargeting through name input   126

      8.2.4 The format button row   128

  8.3 CLASS FORMATS   129

      8.3.1 Saving and editing   129

      8.3.2 Basic representations of the class text   130

      8.3.3 Short, flat and flat-short forms   132

      8.3.4 Information about related classes   133

      8.3.5 Information about features of the class   135

9 Feature Tools, Execution Object Tools, and symbolic debugging   139

  9.1 OVERVIEW   139

  9.2 BROWSING WITH FEATURE TOOLS   140

      9.2.1 Tool window layout   140

      9.2.2 Feature Tool formats and commands   141

      9.2.3 Retargeting a Feature Tool   142

      9.2.4 Textual retargeting vs. abstract retargeting   143

      9.2.5 Obtaining information about the callers of a feature   145

      9.2.6 Finding out about the history of a feature   145

9.3 STOP POINTS   148

9.4 EXECUTION OBJECT TOOLS   150

9.5 USING THE DEBUGGING MECHANISM   155

  9.5.1 The classes   155

  9.5.2 Setting up stop points   157

  9.5.3 Executing   158

  9.5.4 Catching an exception before it occurs   161

  9.5.5 From debugging to run-time exploration   164

10 Using the non-graphical interface   165

10.1 OVERVIEW   165

10.2 A REMINDER: EXECUTING FROM OUTSIDE EIFFELBENCH   166

10.3 COMPILING AND BROWSING   166

  10.3.1 Using **es3**   166

  10.3.2 The options   167

  10.3.3 Using the options   168

  10.3.4 Using a precompiled library under **es3**   168

  10.3.5 Producing a finalized system with **es3**   169

  10.3.6 The interactive mode: **–loop**   169

11 Obtaining the best possible performance   171

11.1 OVERVIEW   171

11.2 COMPILATION PERFORMANCE   172

  11.2.1 Compilation speed   172

  11.2.2 Disk space used by a large system   173

11.3 HOW TO ASSESS SPEED OF EIFFEL-GENERATED CODE   173

  11.3.1 Using final mode   173

  11.3.2 Assertions   173

  11.3.3 A non-problem area: polymorphism and dynamic binding   174

  11.3.4 The case of garbage collection   174

11.4 EFFICIENT ARRAY OPERATIONS   175

11.5 OTHER HINTS   176

12 Building GUI applications: an introduction to EiffelBuild   177

12.1 OVERVIEW   177

12.2 GUI APPLICATION BUILDING: THE CONCEPTS   178

  12.2.1 More than a pretty interface   178

  12.2.2 Seamlessness   178

12.2.3 No need for simulation   179

12.2.4 The graphical and the textual   179

12.2.5 The model: Context-Event-Command-State   180

12.2.6 Reuse and extension, tools and catalogs   182

12.2.7 Direct manipulation and conventional wisdom   182

12.3 THE EXAMPLE SYSTEM   183

12.4 SETTING UP AND STARTING EIFFELBUILD   184

12.4.1 Setting up the environment   184

12.4.2 Libraries   185

12.4.3 Starting EiffelBuild   185

12.4.4 Opening a project   186

12.4.5 The basic windows   187

12.5 DRAWING THE INTERFACE   188

12.5.1 Context categories   188

12.5.2 Creating a permanent window   188

12.5.3 Adding, moving and resizing contexts   189

12.5.4 Adding and modifying a button   191

12.5.5 Editing contexts   192

12.5.6 The Context Tree and semantic consistency   194

12.5.7 Duplicating objects   196

12.5.8 The Context Tree and the Base Tool   198

12.5.9 Adding color   198

12.6 THE HISTORY MECHANISM   200

12.6.1 The history window   200

12.6.2 Undoing and redoing   200

12.6.3 Unrolling and replaying an entire session or session slice   201

12.6.4 Undo-redo for your own systems   201

12.7 SPECIFYING BEHAVIORS AND COMMANDS   201

12.7.1 The Behaviors format   201

12.7.2 The notion of behavior   203

12.7.3 Dropping an event   203

12.7.4 The command catalog   204

12.7.5 Command types and command instances   205

12.7.6 Building a behavior pair   207

12.7.7 Building system by visual association   208

12.7.8 A complete command class   208

12.7.9 Defining a command by inheritance   211

12.7.10 Making a command undoable   215

12.8   THE STATES   216
  12.8.1   The concept of state   216
  12.8.2   Are states bad?   216
  12.8.3   Taking the state into account   217
  12.8.4   States for the editing system   217
12.9   APPLICATIONS   218
  12.9.1   The transitions   220
  12.9.2   Finishing the system   222
12.10 GENERATING AND EXECUTING   222
  12.10.1 Generating an Eiffel system   222

Index   225

1

Getting started

1.1 OVERVIEW

This chapter introduces no fundamental concept but simply describes the practical set-up necessary to use the environment. It is written, like the rest of this book, under the pretense that you are actually sitting in front of a computer where the environment has been installed; but if that is not the case just consider this assumption as a literary device meant to make you understand the ideas in a direct and concrete way.

1.2 FOR THE FIRST-TIME USER

If this is your first use of ISE Eiffel 3, here is what you need to do.

1 • Before anything else, read the present short chapter in its entirety. (You should also have read the Preface to know the overall structure of the environment.)

2 • Check with your system administrator whether the environment has been installed. If so, note the path name of the directory in the file system where the installation has been made; you will need to know it to set up your working environment as explained below. This path name always ends with **Eiffel3**; a typical value might be **/usr/local/ Eiffel3**, although every computer installation has its own conventions.

3 • Set up your working environment (path, environment variables), as described below.

4 • If you want to know the principles of the environment in some detail before starting to use it, read chapters 3 to 11.

5 • If you prefer to get hands-on experience first, read the next chapter (*A guided tour*) which takes you, step by step, through a demonstration of the environment and invites you to try some of the principal facilities on an example system. This will enable you to get a direct grasp of the concepts and facilities of the environment.

1.3 SETTING UP YOUR ENVIRONMENT

To use ISE Eiffel 3, you will need to assign appropriate values to two environment variables, and set up your "path" properly.

1.3.1 Environment variables

An environment variable is a name with an associated value, which the operating system passes to all commands — in particular to the Eiffel commands. You may find out what environment variables have been set, and to what values, by typing (depending on the platform that you use) one of the commands **printenv**, **setenv** (with no arguments) or **env**.

ISE Eiffel 3 needs two environment variables: **EIFFEL3** and **PLATFORM**. The value of **EIFFEL3** is the path name of the directory where ISE Eiffel 3 has been installed. As already noted above, this name is of the form */a/b/c/.../***Eiffel3**, where the last element is always **Eiffel3**. The value of **PLATFORM** is the name assigned to the platform (hardware-software architecture) of the machine on which you will be running Eiffel. This has to be one of the supported values; ask you system administrator which one applies to your machine. The platform is indicated on the label of the tape or other media on which ISE Eiffel 3 was delivered. Some possible values are the following

```
alpha alphavms apple aviion fujitsu
hp9000 ibm6000 mips
mswindows nextstep os2
pyramid sco sgi solaris
sonyrisc sony68000 sparc ultrix
vms vmsalpha
```

Note that platform names only contain lower-case letters and digits (no intervening blanks, underscores or dashes).

The "shell" (command language) that you use has an instruction that enables you to set the value of an environment variable. For example if you are using the "C-shell", you can use the **setenv** command to set up the two environment variables as in the following example:

```
setenv PLATFORM ibm6000
setenv EIFFEL3 /usr/local/Eiffel3
```

If you are using a shell other than the C-shell and do not know the command for setting up an environment variable, consult the operating system's manual or your system administrator.

In any case you will need these values to be set up properly not just for the current session but for any session in which you intend to use ISE Eiffel 3. This means that you should include the two variable setting commands (such as the above) in a file that is read each time you start a session. Under the C-shell the file **.cshrc** in your home directory, which is consulted every time the shell starts its execution, is the appropriate place for these commands. Other shells have similar conventions.

To check that the values of the environment variables have been properly set, you may at any time use the shell command **printenv** or **env** as mentioned above, or simply display their values through the shell command

```
echo $EIFFEL3 $PLATFORM
```

1.3.2 Path

Next you must set up your path. The path is the value of a special variable called **path**; that value is the list of directories which will be searched for files containing the commands that you want to execute. This list will need to include the directory where the executable commands for ISE Eiffel 3 reside.

The principal directory to include in your path is

```
$EIFFEL3/bench/spec/$PLATFORM/bin
```

where **$EIFFEL3** and **$PLATFORM** are the values defined above (make sure they have been set before you update the path). To update your path under the C-shell, use the two commands

```
set path = ($EIFFEL3/bench/spec/$PLATFORM/bin  $path)
rehash
```

This assigns to **path** the previous value of the variable (written as **$path**), concatenated with the name of the new directory. Here too, other shells have slightly different conventions to achieve the same effect. The **rehash** command makes sure the new path takes effect immediately. (On many platforms the **rehash** is not necessary, but it cannot hurt.)

As before, you should include the above path assignment (the first instruction, without the **rehash**) in your **.cshrc** file or equivalent to be able to use the Eiffel tools in future sessions.

In the path assignment, you are not required to use the environment variables: you could instead use the exact path name, for example **/usr/local/Eiffel3/bench/spec/ibm6000/bin**. We recommend the above form, however, for two reasons:

• If your system administrator moves the Eiffel installation to a new directory, you will only need to update the **EIFFEL3** variable.

• If you are using Eiffel from computers with different architectures (for example an IBM RISC 6000 and a Sun Sparc), your path will be correct on each platform without manual intervention on your part if you make sure that the **PLATFORM** environment variable is always properly set up.

If you do use the above **set** command or its equivalent, do not forget to check that **EIFFEL3** and **PLATFORM** are properly set up prior to any execution of the command, whether from the command line or as part of a script.

1.4 CONTENTS OF THE DELIVERY DIRECTORY

One more piece of information is useful before you start: how the delivery — the **$EIFFEL3** directory — is organized.

The full structure is depicted by the figure which appears on the following page. The exact contents of your delivery directory will only be a subset of this figure, depending on what exact tools you have ordered; it is useful, however, to know the overall organization. The file *VERSION* indicates the number and date of the current version. The main subdirectories are:

- **bench**: EiffelBench.

- **build**: EiffelBuild.

- **library**: the various libraries. Subdirectories include **base** for EiffelBase, **lex** for EiffelLex, **parse** for EiffelParse, **store** for EiffelStore, **vision** for EiffelVision. Most of these libraries consist of several clusters, which in turn occupy subdirectories.

- **shelf**: the EiffelShelf — reusable software components and tools distributed as part of ISE Eiffel 3 but originating from various companies and universities. (We hope you will contribute to this directory for future releases.)

- **install**: files used by the installation process and the license manager.

- **precompiled**: precompiled versions of libraries shared by many users. This directory contains libraries that are delivered in precompiled form, as well as templates for precompiling other libraries at installation time or later.

See "PRECOMPILING LIBRARIES", A.4, page 235.

- **examples**: ready-to-run examples. This is further subdivided into subdirectories such as **bench** and **base**.

- **2.3.migration**: tools to help ISE Eiffel 2.3 users convert their software to the version 3 level.

- **case**: EiffelCase.

- **Bug_reports**: instructions and pre-arranged forms for reporting problems and bugs.

- **products**: information on ISE's products and services.

- **Release_notes** (not shown on the figure): version-specific and platform-specific information.

Each of these directories contains a *README* file containing explanations and guidelines.

Many of the directories listed above include (directly or a few levels below) subdirectories with the following standard names:

- **help**: directories containing help files, defaults, and error messages.

- **bitmaps**: directories containing bit-maps for icons and other graphical symbols.

- **spec**: directories containing binary (platform-specific) files. The name **spec** stands for "specific".

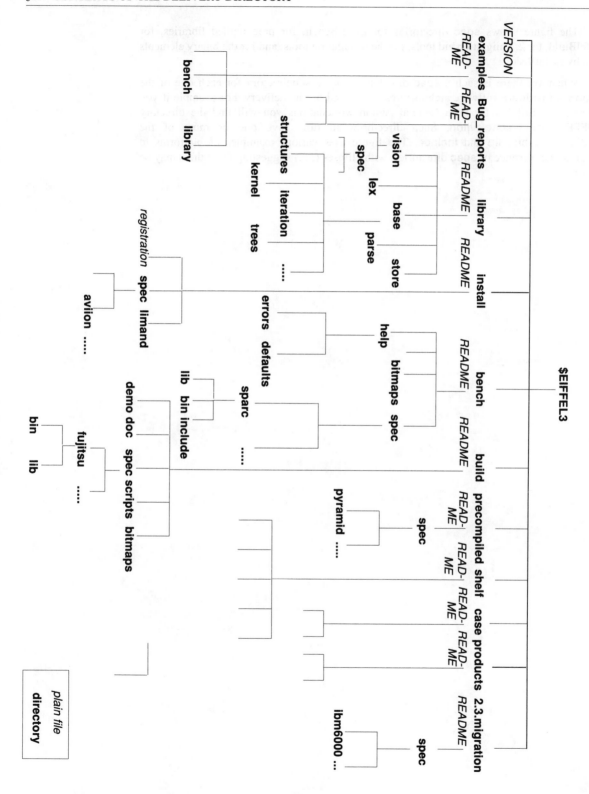

The figure shows **spec** directories for EiffelBench, for precompiled libraries, for EiffelBuild, for 2.3 migration aid tools, for the installation tools, and for the binary elements used by EiffelVision.

Whenever there is such a **spec** directory, it has a subdirectory for each one of the platforms (hardware-software architectures) supported by the delivery. For example if you ordered ISE Eiffel 3 for Data General Aviion workstations you will find the directory **$EIFFEL3/bench/spec/aviion**. Such directories in turn have one or more of the subdirectories **bin, lib** and **include**. The figure uses various examples of platforms to illustrate the presence of **spec** directories, with ellipses (.....) suggesting that others may be present.

2

A guided tour

2.1 OVERVIEW

This chapter introduces the essential properties of EiffelBench. It will take you through a tour of the environment, using a preexisting example system.

Although not a complete reference, the presentation will help you become familiar quickly with the way you can use the environment for your work.

2.2 COPYING THE EXAMPLE

The installation directory contains a small example which we suggest that you use for your first brush with the environment. If you have access to EiffelBench as you read this chapter, the best way to take the guided tour is to execute all the suggested operations as you read about them: learning by doing.

To run the example, you must have set up your environment as explained in the previous chapter. In particular, make sure that your path is properly set and that the environment variables **EIFFEL3** and **PLATFORM** have the proper values. Throughout this chapter, **$EIFFEL3** refers to the directory where ISE Eiffel 3 has been installed, with a path name that ends with **Eiffel3**.

Since you will be invited to edit and modify some aspects of the example, you should work on a copy, not on the original, so as not to affect future users. Choose or create a directory of your own; let *YOURDIR* be its path name. To copy all the files of the example into directory *YOURDIR*, use the shell command

```
cp  $EIFFEL3/examples/bench/tour/*    YOURDIR
```

Once you have fully compiled the example, the contents of *YOURDIR* will take up about 1.7 megabytes, assuming that you are relying on precompiled EiffelBase (the default). Without precompiled EiffelBase you would need about 5.5 megabytes.

2.3 STARTING EIFFELBENCH AND OPENING A PROJECT

To launch Eiffel Bench, change directory to *YOURDIR* and, from the command line, type

ebench

EiffelBench first comes up in the form of two overlaid windows similar to the following. (In later sessions, when you restart a previously compiled project, only the back window will appear.)

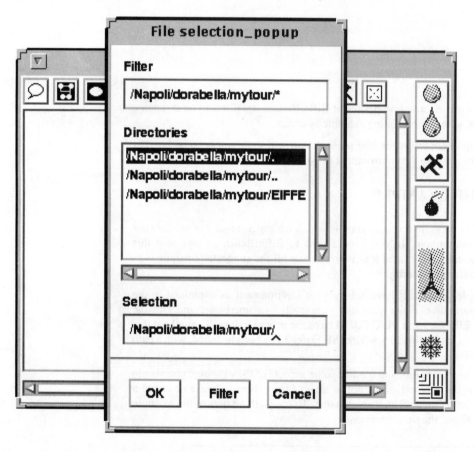

Note that depending on the graphical toolkit and window manager that you use the exact appearance of these windows, and of all other screen views shown in the figures of this book, may be somewhat different on your computer. Also, **/Napoli/dorabella/mytour/**, which appears in the **Filter** and **Selection** fields, is the directory that was used to prepare this chapter; it will be replaced in your case by the name of your chosen directory, *YOURDIR*.

The back window is for the Project Tool, which we will explore in a little while. The one that partially obscures it is the **file selector**, which you can use to select a project.

The file selector (which comes from the underlying graphical toolkit) will enable you to travel through the file hierarchy when you need to. For the moment, however, you can stay right where you are since you launched **ebench** from *YOURDIR*, which you can use as project directory. So you should just click on the bottom-left button that says **OK**; this will select the current directory.

*To "click" means to press a mouse button and release it imme- diately. In this book, unless otherwise specified, the button to use for clicking is the **leftmost** button on your mouse.*

The file selector disappears and only the Project Tool remains:

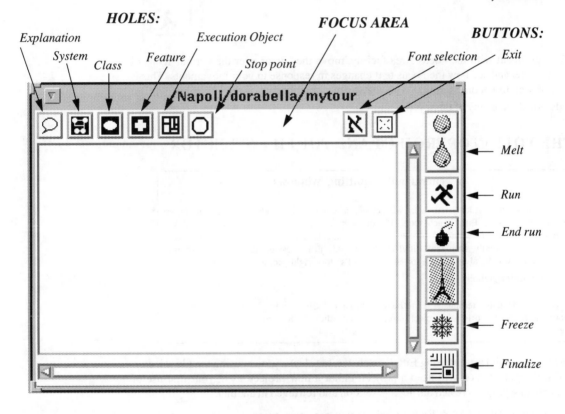

The Project Tool will serve as the basic control panel throughout your use of EiffelBench.

To avoid wasting precious screen real estate, the icons (buttons and holes) of all ISE Eiffel 3 tools contain no explanatory text, but thanks to the **focus area** technique that will not stop you from learning quickly what they mean, or refreshing your memory if you later forget one of them.

Whenever the cursor is on a meaningful region, the Focus Area in the middle of the top border of the Project Tool serves as a mini-help facility by showing the type of the corresponding region. The short text which appears in the Focus Area is called the current

Focus of the EiffelBench session. For example if you bring the cursor to the third icon from the left on the top row (without clicking) the focus area will indicate that it is a Class hole:

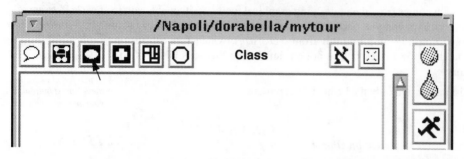

To experiment with the Focus Area facility, move the cursor over the various icons of the control panel and see how the Focus text changes in response to your movements. This is also a good way to become familiar with the various components of the control panel. But please do not click on any of them yet!

2.4 THE NOTION OF PROJECT AND THE FILE SELECTOR

> **A general note: quitting windows**
>
> In the rest of this guided tour you will create a number of windows corresponding to the various types of EiffelBench tools. If you want to get rid of one of these windows, do **not** use the "kill window" or "quit window" mechanism of your window manager, as this would actually terminate EiffelBench. Instead, just click on the Terminate button of the tool, which always appears at the tool's top right corner, and has a shape suggesting disintegration: ⊡.
>
> If you accidentally terminate EiffelBench through "kill window" or otherwise, just restart it from the original project directory and click "OK" immediately in the file selector.

The first thing you did after starting EiffelBench was to select a project using the file selector. Every EiffelBench session will need a project: either a new project, as in your first use of EiffelBench, or a project created during one session and retrieved in another.

A project is defined by a directory where you can store some of your project-related files, and where the compiler will also store its own internal files, using a subdirectory called **EIFFELGEN**.

For your first session, the project directory is whatever directory you chose for *YOURDIR* — the directory where you made a copy of the example according to the instructions at the beginning of this chapter. Then, when you clicked on **OK** in the file selector, EiffelBench created the **EIFFELGEN** subdirectory.

In future sessions you will be retrieving an existing project, and **EIFFELGEN** will already exist, containing all the information about that project; you will be able to use the file selector to retrieve the project. But that is for later.

2.5 SPECIFYING AN ACE

Once you have selected a project directory you must load an Ace, which you will use to specify the various directories where needed Eiffel classes appear and to set the appropriate compilation options. As you will recall, Ace means Assembly of Classes in Eiffel; an Ace is written in Lace, a simple Eiffel-like notation.

For details on Aces and Lace see "Eiffel: The Language", Appendix D, pages 513-534, "Specifying systems in Lace".

Whenever you open an existing project, an Ace is already associated with it; but for a new project you must provide your own Ace. To do so, you can either select an existing file or build a new Ace from a standard template. If you do not load an Ace now you will be asked to do it when and if you request a compilation of some form.

To continue the guided tour and load an Ace, click on the System hole. As you may remember from the figure on page 9, this is the second icon from the left on the top border of the Project Tool. A panel comes up, offering you the choice between selecting a file or loading the template:

*As noted above, the button to use for clicking in all operations so far is the **leftmost** mouse button.*

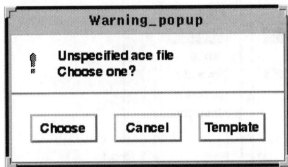

The usual choice for a new project is **Template**, which gives you a prefilled template with the most commonly used options and libraries. Here, however, it will be simpler to use the model that has been prepared specifically for the Guided Tour. Click on **Choose**. You get the file selector again:

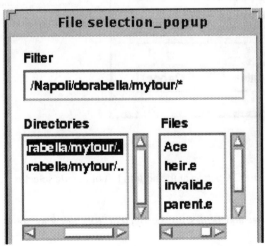

In the central part of the file selector window, the left column lists directories (only its rightmost part is visible above); the right column lists the files in the current directory. The first of these files is called **Ace**; it contains a simple Ace file which is exactly what you need for the example.

Click on the name of that file; it appears in reverse video:

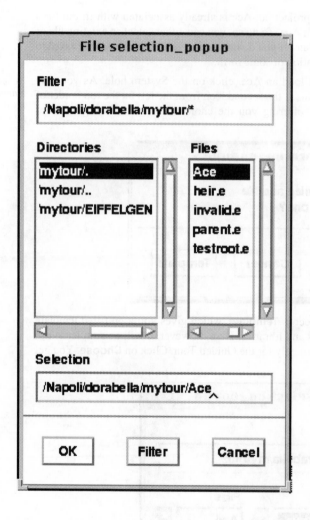

Then press the Return key (or click on the **OK** button at the bottom left of the file selector window).

This dismisses the file selector window and brings up the System Tool showing the contents of the Ace file:

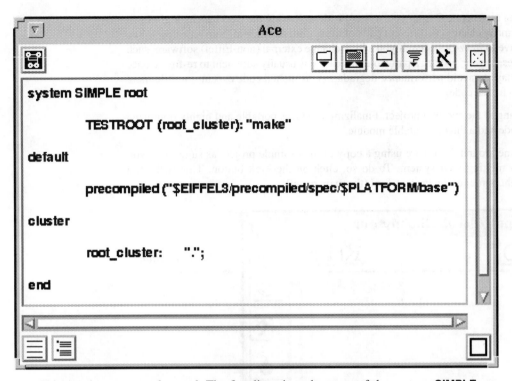

This Ace is easy to understand. The first line gives the name of the system, **SIMPLE**. The second gives the name of the root class, **TESTROOT**, the name of the cluster to which it belongs, **root_cluster**, and the name of the root's creation procedure which must be executed: **make**. The **default** clause indicates that this system is relying on a precompiled version of the EiffelBase library, stored in the directory shown (which is the normal place for precompiled EiffelBase). Finally the **cluster** clause lists the clusters of the system; here the root cluster is the only one explicitly listed, although the system actually includes many others, available as part of the precompiled EiffelBase library. The entry for a cluster lists the cluster name, followed by a colon and by the name of the associated directory enclosed in double quotes. Here the single cluster entry lists **"."**, denoting the current directory, for **root_cluster**.

> In general, we will prefer giving the full directory name for each cluster, so that we can start a session from an arbitrary directory. For this guided tour, however, using "." makes things easier, and having to start the session from the example directory is not a problem.

2.6 COMPILING

The Eiffel Bench compilation mechanism relies on ISE's **Melting Ice Technology**. It offers three forms of compilation: melting, freezing and finalizing, serving complementary purposes:

- Use melting after making a few changes. Melting is much faster than the other two mechanisms: melting time is proportional to the size of the changed parts and affected classes, whereas the time needed to freeze or finalize is in part proportional to the size of the full system. Typically, melting will take but a few seconds after small changes.

• Use freezing to generate C from your system without leaving the workbench, or after you have made many changes to different parts of the system and melted them repeatedly. You will also have to freeze a system if you add or change external (non-Eiffel) software, such as C routines, to your system. Apart from this case it is usually sufficient to re-freeze once every few days to avoid performance degradation, as melted code executes a little more slowly than frozen code.

• Use finalizing at the end of a project. Finalizing produces portable and highly optimized ANSI-C code and a final executable module.

The first time around, if you are using a copy of the example project as suggested, you should begin by melting your system. To do so, click on the Melt button. This is the top button on the right border of the Project Tool (the main panel):

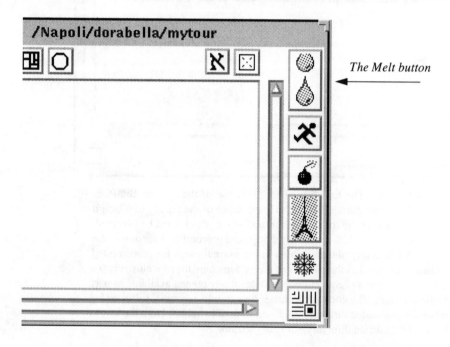

The Melt button

Remember that if you are ever in doubt about what a button does you can always move the cursor over the button, without clicking of course, and look at what the Focus Area shows.

During the compiling process, if you bring the cursor to the Project Tool or any other EiffelBench window, the cursor icon will have the form of a little clock, indicating that EiffelBench is busy and will not let you perform any EiffelBench action until the compilation operation (melting in the present case) terminates.

EiffelBench now starts exploring your system to determine what needs to be recompiled — in principle all classes, since you are starting from scratch with a new system. The compilation messages appear in the window from which you launch EiffelBench (not in a window of the environment proper), where they will look like this:

```
┌──────────────────────────────────────────────────────────┐
│ ▽            An ISE Eiffel 3 session                       │
│ [Napoli] Dorabella 1030 - Degree 6: cluster root_cluster   │
│ Degree 5: class TESTROOT                                   │
│ Degree 5: class HEIR                                       │
│ Degree 5: class PARENT                                     │
│ Degree 4: class TESTROOT                                   │
│ Degree 4: class PARENT                                     │
│ Degree 4: class HEIR                                       │
│ Degree 3: class TESTROOT                                   │
│ Degree 3: class PARENT                                     │
│ Degree 3: class HEIR                                       │
│ Degree 2: class TESTROOT                                   │
│ Degree 2: class PARENT                                     │
│ Degree 2: class HEIR                                       │
│ Degree 1: class HEIR                                       │
│ Degree 1: class PARENT                                  ▲  │
│ Degree 1: class TESTROOT                                   │
│ Melting changes                                         ▼  │
└──────────────────────────────────────────────────────────┘
```

The guided tour system actually includes many more classes than what the messages suggest; but most of them are part of EiffelBase and have been precompiled. So EiffelBench only compiles the classes of the **root_cluster** directory: **TESTROOT, HEIR** and **PARENT.** For each class it goes through degrees 5, 4, 3, 2 and 1, then "melts changes" at degree zero (which in the Celsius scale is where water turns to ice). There is also an initial Degree 6 operation, which examines the cluster as a whole. After the message **Melting changes** the Project Tool window displays the message **System recompiled**, returning control to you.

The process is automatic: all the information the compiler had, from the Ace, was the name of the root class and the directory where **root_cluster** is located. The compiler takes care of the rest, in particular of finding all the classes that must be compiled.

The process is also quite fast. On a typical middle-of-the road workstation, lightly loaded, the elapsed time between the click on the **Melt** button and the message **System recompiled** is about 15 seconds. Of course the exact time on your system will depend on how powerful your computer is and what else it is doing; accessing files through the network rather than locally also introduces a penalty.

The precompilation mechanism is quite important in achieving this performance. Although here EiffelBench has compiled only three classes, the real size of the system — that is to say, the number of classes on which the root class depends directly or indirectly, including **STD_FILES** which is used for input and output, and its own ancestors and suppliers — is 61 classes. So although the example system is still small it is not trivial; compiling it without using precompiled EiffelBase would take about 15 minutes, including C compilation and linking, on the typical workstation mentioned above.

When assessing EiffelBench's compilation speed you are actually assessing its execution speed too, since the environment is written in Eiffel and produced using its own compilation mechanism.

After having compiled the system, you will need to resynchronize the System Tool — bring it up to date with the result of the compilation. The system tool is the window whose top border reads **Ace**; it is also identified by its top-left icon, which is a System hole, appearing as this: ▣.

If for some reason the System Tool is not visible, bring it up by clicking on the System hole that also appears, represented by an almost identical icon ▣, in the Project Tool (the main control panel).

2.7 THE USER INTERFACE MECHANISM

Now that you have a compiled system, you can start exploring its properties by launching Class Tools and Feature Tools, which also enable you to modify the classes of the system.

As all the other components of ISE Eiffel 3, EiffelBench relies on the typed drag-and-drop interface principle. You work with **development objects** such as classes, features, run-time class instances and systems. The basic operation consists of picking a development object, identified by its name appearing in one of the EiffelBench tool windows, and dragging it into a matching **hole** of some tool (the same or another). As you are dragging a development object, its type is represented by the shape of the corresponding **pebble**: oval disk for a class, cross for a feature, cluster graph for a system. The pebble can only be dropped into a hole of a matching type. This is one of the properties that make the ISE Eiffel 3 environment typed — as is only fitting since the Eiffel language and method are themselves strongly typed.

Now that you have a compiled system you can start using typed drag and drop.

Select a development object, for example the name of the root class, **TESTROOT**, in the System Tool. To start dragging it, click on the place where its name appears in the System Tool window, using the **rightmost** mouse button. Do not maintain the button pressed; instead, just press it and release it immediately:

*In the rest of this book, clicking with the rightmost mouse button is called **right-clicking**. To click, with no further qualification, means to left-click.*

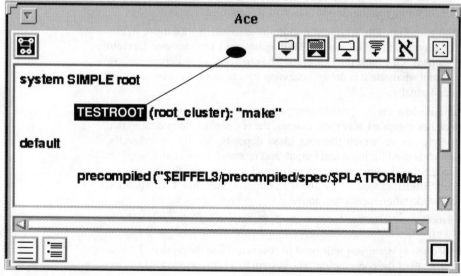

As you start moving the mouse around, a pebble tracks the cursor position, and a line continuously connects the pebble to the object's original position The pebble's shape indicates the type of the development object that you picked; for a class it is an oval disk:●. The possible pebble shapes correspond to the shapes of the holes at the top left of the Project Tool:

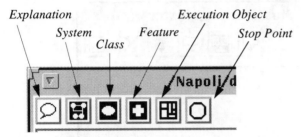

Back to drag-and-drop. Until you click a button, you are in the "Drag step", where the pebble and line track the cursor movement. You may terminate this situation in either of two ways:

- If (as will normally be the case) you want to drop the selected object into a hole of matching shape, bring the pebble to the hole and right-click — using the same button that you used to pick the object in the first place. (Right-clicking the button on a non-matching hole, or outside of any hole, will terminate the Drag step.)

- If, however, you change your mind for any reason, left-click anywhere. This cancels the object's picking and gets you back to the state that prevailed before you selected the development object.

In the first case, if you drop a pebble into a matching hole in the control panel, this will launch a new tool window of the appropriate type (Class Tool, Feature Tool, Execution Object Tool...) on the selected development object. If the hole is in a previous tool window, that existing tool will now provide information and operations on the newly selected object. We say that this object is now the **target** of the tool, or that the tool is **targeted** to that object.

Since the development object that you have selected, **TESTROOT**, is a class, you should bring the corresponding pebble to the Class Hole of the Project Tool; this hole is easy to spot since its shape, an oval, matches that of the pebble representing the selected class:

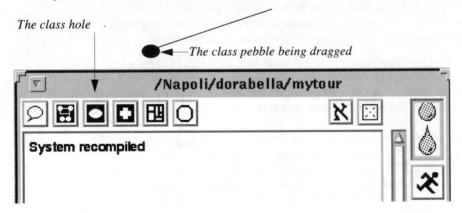

Dropping the pebble into the hole will start up a new tool of the appropriate type — in this case a Class Tool, which shows the beginning of the text of class **TESTROOT**. Here is how it looks:

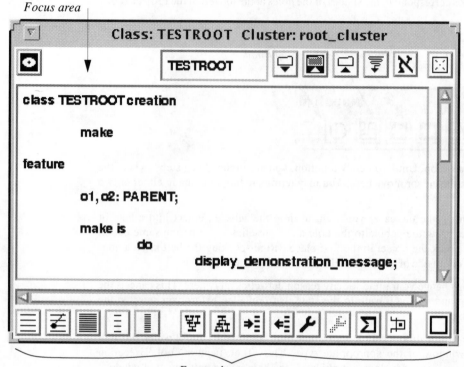

Focus area

Format button row

The top border gives the names of the class and of the cluster to which it belongs. On the next line, you find the class hole ⬛ into which, as you may have guessed, you will be able later on to drag-and-drop new class pebbles. The text field that follows contains the name of the class; we will soon see that it is editable. Then come a few more buttons; to find their meaning, use once again the Focus Area facility by moving the mouse cursor over these buttons without clicking. The buttons' captions appear not in the Project Tool as before but in the Class Tool's own Focus Area, to the left of the text field containing the class name.

The bottom row of the Class Tool contains another set of buttons, which can be used to change the Format of the class display and obtain various elements of information on the class. We will review them shortly, but you may get a preview of their purposes now by moving the cursor over them and looking at the Focus Area text.

A small point may have caught your attention: why does the class hole appears as ⬛ in the top border of the Project Tool and as ⬛ in the top corner of the Class Tool? The answer is simply that the tiny dot in the second case indicates that the tool is "occupied": it has been targeted to a certain development object — class **TESTROOT** in the example. The dot represents this development object; so you can use it to drag-and-drop class **TESTROOT** exactly as you would do with the class name.

2.8 EDITING AND BROWSING THROUGH CLASSES AND FEATURES

By now you have a System Tool and a Class Tool, and you have access to all the browsing facilities of the environment. Here are some examples that you can start trying.

Bring up the System Tool; if it is not visible just click on the System Hole ▦, in the Project Tool. The format button row at the bottom left appears as ▤ ▤, offering just two formats: Text, the default, and Clusters. Click on the second format, Clusters, to see a list of all the system's clusters and their classes:

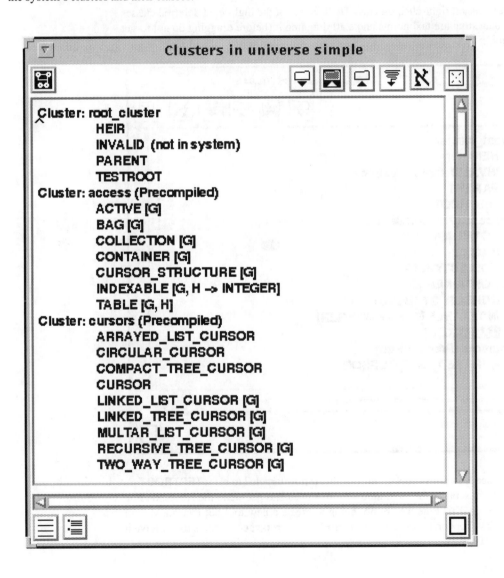

Under this format the System Tool shows all the classes of the universe (the set of directories), cluster by cluster. Here because you have been relying on precompiled EiffelBase all the clusters of that library are included, plus the **root_cluster** which comes at the beginning of the list. One of the classes of that cluster, **INVALID**, has not been compiled; it contains an error and will be used below to illustrate the reporting of compilation errors.

All of the class names in the list are clickable. This means that you can drag-and-drop them to a Class Tool; in other words, that the development objects that they represent — classes — are available for you to apply all the facilities of the environment. Let us experiment with this notion of clickability.

In the **access** cluster, right-click on class **TABLE**, one of the high-level deferred classes of the EiffelBase data structure taxonomy, and start dragging it (before dragging do not forget to release the button):

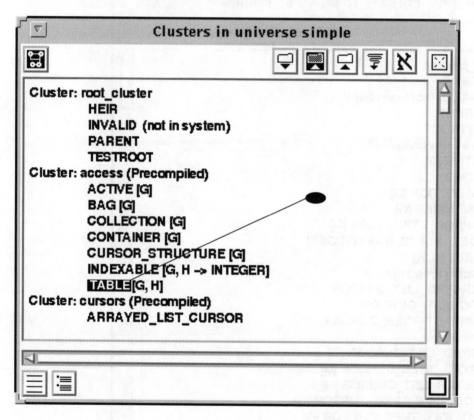

When we first needed a Class Tool — the one that is now targeted to class **TESTROOT** — we had to create it from scratch; the technique was to drag a class pebble to the corresponding hole in the Project Tool. This time we are not going to create a new tool but instead we will reuse the existing Class Tool or, to use the proper terminology, **retarget** it, that is to say, give it a new target: class **TABLE**.

To do so bring the pebble to the top-left corner of the existing Class Tool, and drop the pebble into the Class Hole 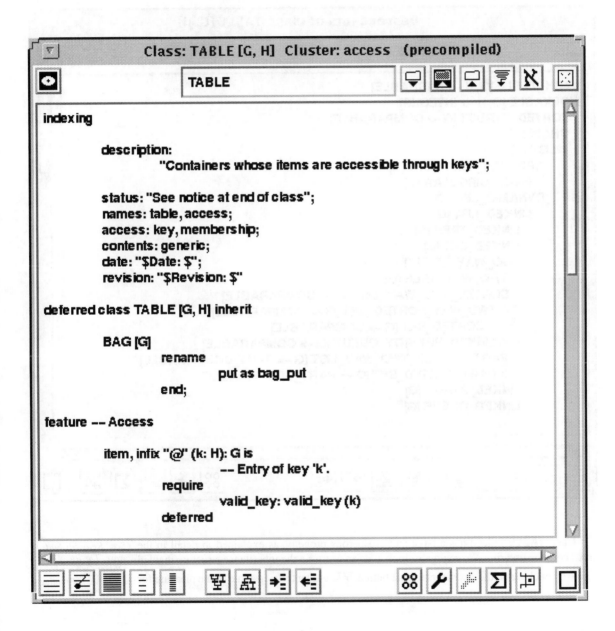 by right-clicking. This replaces the current target of the Class Tool, **TESTROOT**, by the class that you have just selected, **TABLE**. As a result, the tool will now show the beginning of the text of **TABLE**:

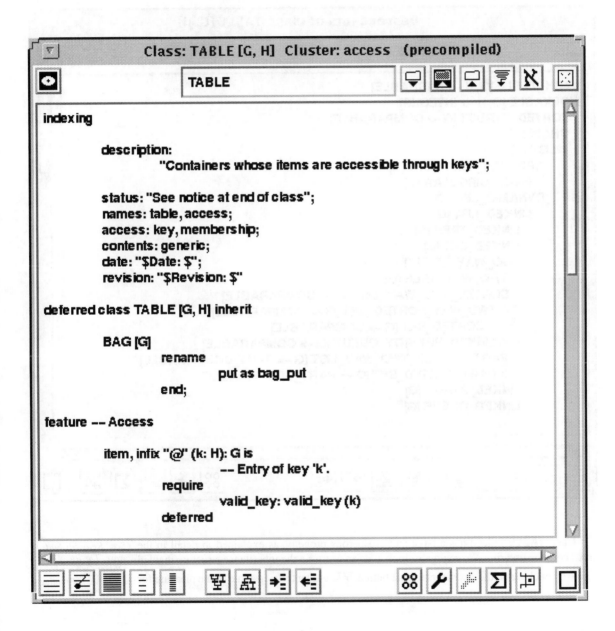

The bottom row of icons in this tool lists all the formats under which you can display a class. The format by default, used to display **TESTROOT** before and **TABLE** now, is the Text format, corresponding to the bottom-left format button: ☰. Another interesting format is the Descendants format, 🏛, under which you will see not the class text but its inheritance hierarchy. Click on the Descendants button to see the descendants of **TABLE**:

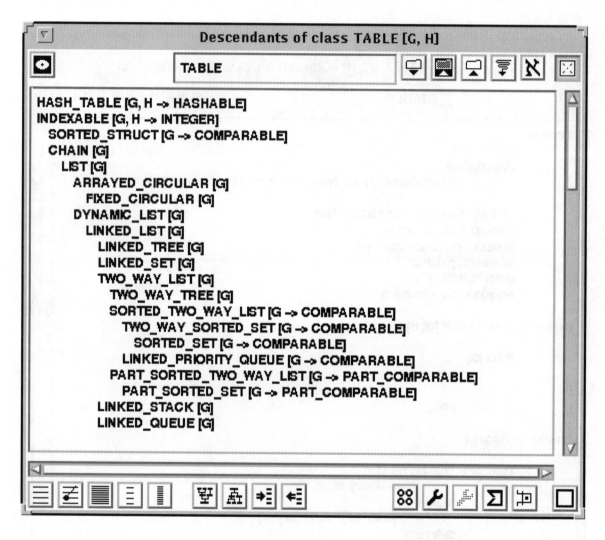

Class **TABLE** indeed has a large and prosperous progeny, as explained in detail in the book about the libraries. We could also look at its ancestry — the inheritance structure that led to it — by clicking on the Ancestors format button 👥, but let us keep some of the pleasure for later.

See "Reusable Software: The Base Object-Oriented Libraries", Prentice Hall, 1994.

For now, we come back to the Text format (just click on the leftmost format button, ☰, for Text) and start experimenting with the Feature Tool. In class **TABLE** there is a feature called **valid_key** which, as the name suggests, determines whether a key is usable for a certain table. To find its declaration, use the scrollbar of the Class Tool and go about half-way through the class text (to line 31 out of 65, to be precise); alternatively, you could use the Search button ☰ on the top-right part of the Class Tool window, which will bring up a self-explanatory search panel. Either way, you get to the feature declaration:

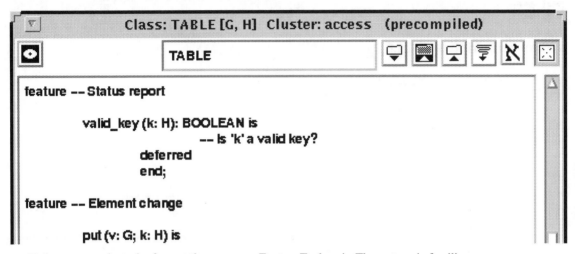

To learn more about the feature, let us start a Feature Tool on it. The pattern is familiar: typed drag and drop. As you right-click on the name **valid_key** the cursor takes the shape of the pebble representing a feature, a cross:

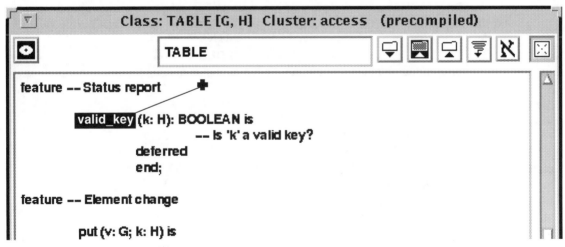

You do not have a Feature Tool yet, so you need to create a new one; do so by dropping the pebble into the Project Tool. Actually, this is time to see a shortcut: although in principle you are supposed to drop the pebble into the matching hole 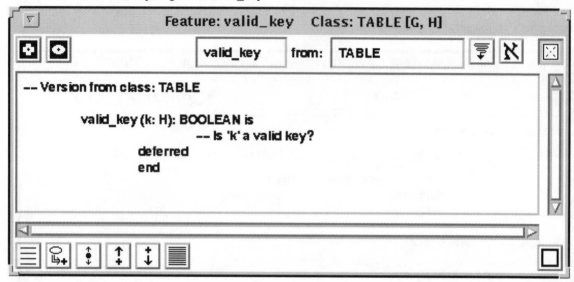 of the Project Tool, you may in fact drop it anywhere in the Project Tool window. This technique, which also works for other pebbles, amounts to treating the window as a large hole of the appropriate type. It enables you to rely on typed drag-and-drop without making the effort to shoot straight at a small target.

A Feature Tool comes up, targeted to **valid_key**:

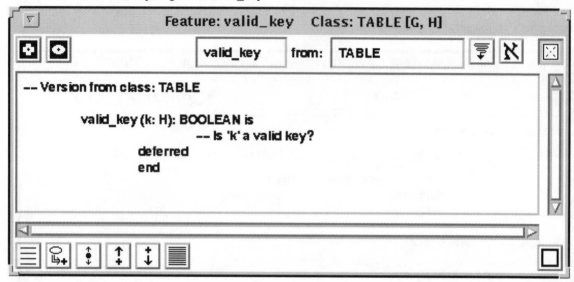

The default format is Text, using the same icon (the one at the bottom left) as for Class Tools. So all we see for the moment is the feature text again. You will experiment with the other formats later, but to see just one of them try Descendant Versions by clicking on the corresponding button: ↕ , the second from the right. Here is the result:

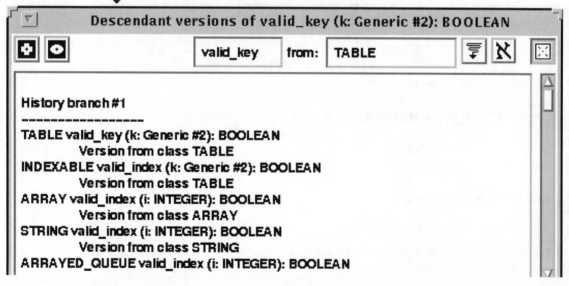

Under this format we see the successive adventures of feature **valid_key** in the descendants of **TABLE**, which as we already know from having looked at the Descendants format of this class are numerous. In **TABLE** the feature is deferred; in descendants it is variously effected (that is to say, provided with a non-deferred implementation) and renamed. The Descendants Versions format shows all these versions. Note that there are many more than fit on the above figure; you may use scrolling or the Search button to find the rest.

We see for example from the second entry that class **INDEXABLE** renames the feature **valid_index**, but that the version it uses is still from **TABLE**: in other words it does not redeclare it, keeping the deferred version. **ARRAY** and **STRING**, for their part, both rename and redeclare the feature.

All the feature and class names that appear in this format are clickable. So if you want to know more about any of the feature's versions you can get to it directly by drag-and-drop. Assume for example that you want to know what the version for **STRING** is. Just right-click on its name, **valid_index**, as it appears in the fourth entry, and start dragging it:

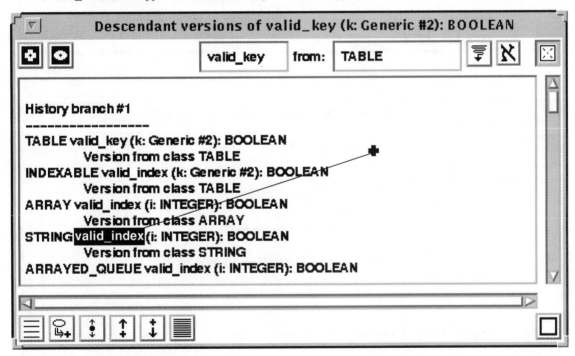

But you do not actually need to go anywhere; it suffices to retarget the current Feature Tool. You can do it by dropping the pebble into the Feature hole at the top-left; but as we saw above this is not necessary: just dropping the pebble anywhere in the window will have the same effect. So in a case such as this one just right-clicking twice on **valid_index** does the job: the first click drags; the second click drops. Unlike with traditional double-clicking mechanisms, however, the two clicks do not need to occur within a particular time interval.

The Feature Tool is still in the Descendant Versions format; so the retargeting shows that format for **valid_index**, the **STRING** version of our original feature:

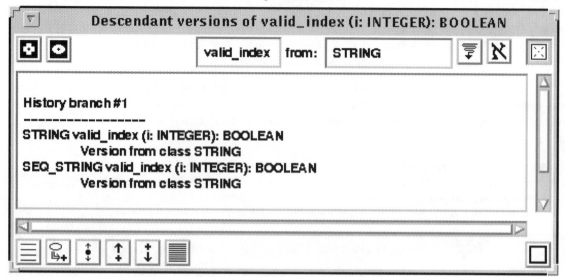

To see the text of the feature, click on the Text format button ≡ at the bottom left:

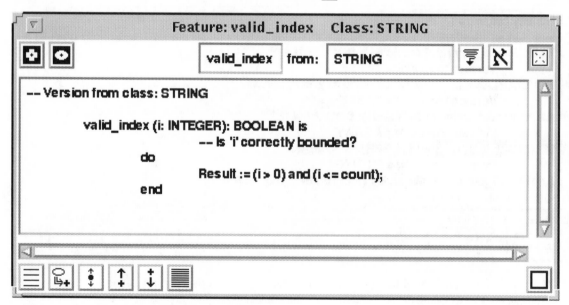

The text of the feature's version in class **STRING** appears.

Let us explore one more operation with this example. Assume you now want to know what the feature looks like in class **ARRAY**. It is not difficult to obtain this information quickly using the preceding mechanisms; but here is one technique that we have not yet encountered.

You may have noted that the top-left corner of the Feature Tool shows not one but two holes: ⬕ ⬕. The first represents the feature to which the Feature Tool is currently targeted; the second represents the class to which that feature belongs. You may drop pebbles of the appropriate types in both of these holes. In particular, you may drop a class into the class hole.

To do so, go back to the System Tool, which must still be in the Clusters format. (If it is not visible, click on the System hole of the Project Tool; if it is in the wrong format, click on the Clusters format, the second one on the bottom row.) Find class **ARRAY** in the clusters; it appears in the cluster **kernel**. (You may use the Search button to find it; or just scroll through the text). Then right-click on it and start dragging it towards the class hole of the Feature Tool:

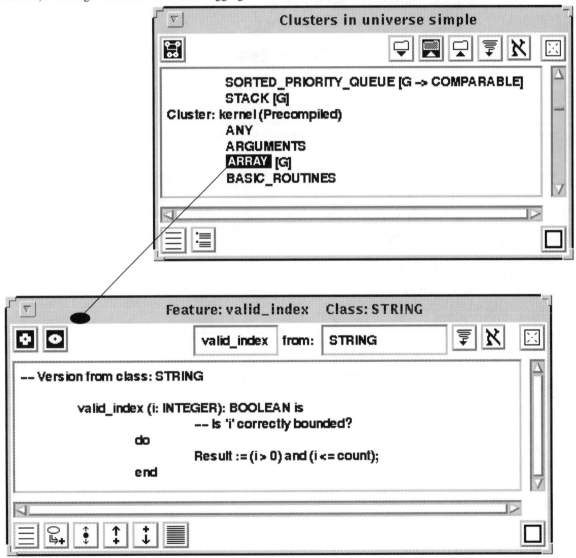

Here too you may drop the class pebble anywhere in the window, not just in the class hole.

The result is to show the version of **valid_index** for the newly selected class, **ARRAY**:

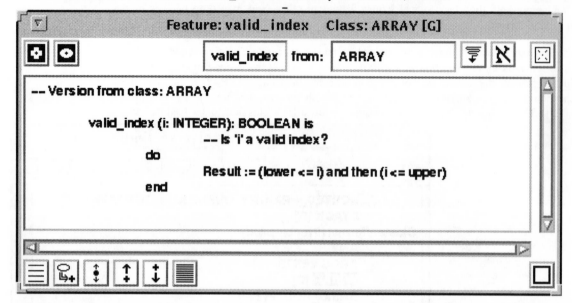

If you have had some experience with object-oriented software construction, you will by now have realized how important these facilities are. In particular, given the power and versatility of feature redefinition, polymorphism and effecting, it is essential to be able to find out quickly the answer to questions such as:

- What does feature *f* become in class *C* ?

- What are the descendants of *C* ?

- From what class does the version of *f* in *C* come?

- What was the original version of *f* ?

With the facilities seen so far it is already possible to answer such questions in many cases. Many more possibilities are offered, detailed in the following chapters.

2.9 A LITTLE MORE ABOUT BROWSING

To complement the preceding introduction and preview the full explanations of the following chapters, here are a few important possibilities that you should find useful as you start using the environment.

One shortcut that we have not seen serves to create a new tool targeted to a selected development object. Rather than dragging the object to the Project Tool, you may simply control-right-click (click with the rightmost mouse button while holding down the CONTROL key) while the mouse cursor is on the object.

It is also possible to create a tool without targeting it. To do this, simply click on the corresponding hole of the Project Tool, used here as a button. You may target the resulting tool later, using any of the available techniques.

To target or retarget an existing tool, the most convenient method is usually to drop a pebble into one of its hole as illustrated above. But sometimes you just know the name of the new target and do not have it readily available for dragging on the screen. Then you can just type the name of the new target. For example, in the last figure, the Feature Tool has two fields at the top showing the feature name, **valid_index**, and the class name, **ARRAY**. These two fields are editable. So you can for example see the feature **count** from **ARRAY** by typing its name in the first editable field, replacing **valid_index**. (Before typing characters into a field, you may have to click with the leftmost mouse button somewhere in the field, to make the field responsive to keyboard input. You can use the Backspace key to erase the original characters, or double-click on the original name and type the new one over it.) Then press the Enter (or Return) key; this retargets the tool to show the desired feature:

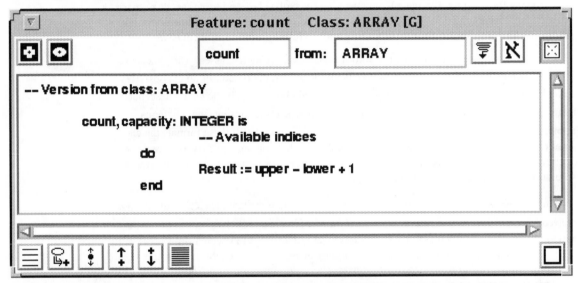

This technique also applies to Class Tools. So for example if you quickly want to see the text of a class whose name is not otherwise visible on the screen just proceed as follows: click on the Class Hole ⬤ of the Project Tool; this gives you an untargeted Class Tool:

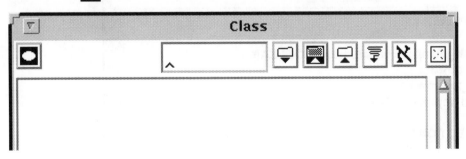

You can then simply type the name of the desired class, followed by Enter, in the text field in the middle. This will target the tool to that class.

Another essential set of mechanisms is provided by the various formats of the Class Tool. We have seen a few; here is a preview of the others.

The first group of formats on the format button row provides various views of a class. The basic view is the default Text format ☰, which shows the class text. The Clickable format ⇌ is similar to Text but has more clickable elements; in particular you can click on a feature name in a feature call (not just in a declaration) so as to see what exact feature will be called. The Flat format ☰ shows a developed form of the class, with all inherited features put alongside the immediate features defined in the class itself. The Short format ☰ shows an abstracted version of the class, in which all implementation properties are removed, keeping only the signature, header comment and assertions of each exported feature. The Flat-short format ☰ is the short view of the flat form; it provides the official client interface of a class and serves as the primary form of class documentation, especially for libraries. Note that Flat and Flat-short take significantly longer to display than the other formats, so you may want to try them last.

Formats of the second group give information about related classes. The Ancestors format ⵚ, which will list the ancestor hierarchy all the way to the mother of all classes, **ANY**. Its complement the Descendants format ⵚ, already used above, which shows the descendant hierarchy. The Clients format ➡☰, shows all classes that use the current one as clients; the Suppliers format ⬅☰, shows all the classes of which it is a client. In all these formats the class names that appear in the resulting lists are all clickable, so that you may quickly explore a class structure by going from class to class. (I find it particularly convenient for this kind of exploration to keep **two** Class Tools, drag-and-dropping names from one to the other.)

The last set of formats gives information about the features: attributes ∷, routines 🔧, deferred features ⁀, external routines ⊡. Everything of interest is clickable, as in this extract from the Routines format applied to the EiffelBase class **LINKED_LIST** which shows for each feature of the class (clickable) the list of its argument types (all clickable), its result type (clickable) if it is a function, and the ancestor class (clickable) where it was defined:

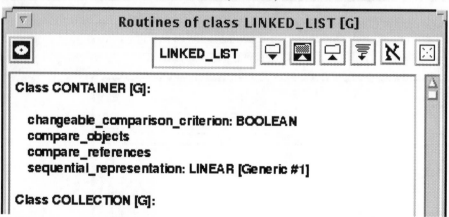

The Shell button ☐ , the rightmost one on the bottom panel, enables you to start an editor session on the class or feature being edited. By default this will be the **vi** editor, but we will see in a later chapter how to substitute any other editor. Actually, as the name of the button implies, you can use it to apply any outside command (any shell operation) to a class or feature.

See "APPLYING OPERATING SYSTEM COMMANDS TO DEVELOPMENT OBJECTS", 4.5, page 65.

2.10 MODIFYING AND MELTING

The next fundamental aspect of EiffelBench is the facility for modifying one or more classes and recompiling the system quickly through the melting mechanism.

Let us use class **HEIR** as the class to be modified. By now you know how to get a Class Tool targeted to it: take an existing Class Tool and retarget it by typing the name of the class in the top text field; or use proximity drag-and-drop, starting for example from the System Tool in Clusters format, where you will see the class listed among those of **root_cluster**.

To select a format or otherwise click on a button, always use left-clicking.

Here is the beginning of the class text:

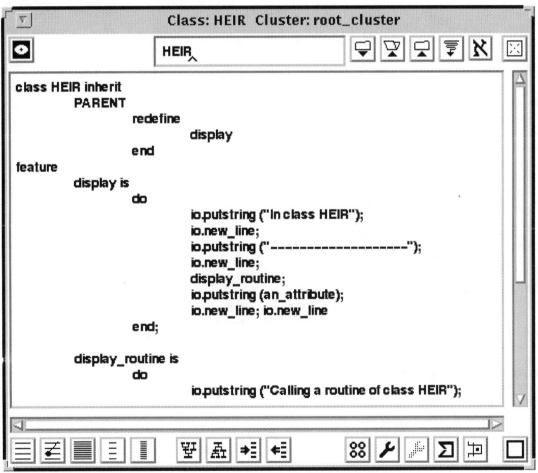

The change that you are asked to make is to add after procedure **display**, just before **display_routine**, a procedure **new_ message** that reads as follows:

```
new_message is
    do
            io.putstring ("Message added later");
            io.new_line
    end;
```

Then at the very beginning of **display** add a call to the new procedure, so that the first four lines of the **display** procedure now read:

```
display is
    do
            new_message;                    ◄─────────────  The new line
            io.putstring ("In class HEIR");
```

(It does not matter if you forget the semicolon after **new_message**.) To do these modifications just left-click at the place where you need to insert text, and type it. The Class Tool gives you access to the editing facilities provided by the underlying toolkit. You can use Backspace and arrow keys; you can also replace text by selecting it with the mouse (or double-clicking) and typing the replacement over it.

As soon as you start typing anything into the text the Save button ▨ in the top row of buttons changes into a different icon ▽ to indicate that the text has been modified. Once you have finished the changes click on that button to save the modified text; the button goes back to the original icon ▨.

Having saved the new text of the class, you may perform a quick recompilation. Just click on the Melt button of the Project Tool as you did for the first compilation. The melting process starts; during that process, as during a freeze, the cursor icon in any EiffelBench window will have the form of a small clock and you are prevented from doing any actions. (The change above is simple enough that you should not make any mistake, but if you do and the correction is not obvious check the next two sections.)

After a short while (typically a few seconds), the system will be ready to use again, with your modifications taken into account. During the melting process, a few messages (again of the form "**Degree** *n*: **class** *XXX*") will appear in the window from which you started EiffelBench, but there will be fewer such messages: EiffelBench automatically determines the smallest possible set of classes that must be recompiled. For this particular change, this set only includes **HEIR**, so all that happens is degrees 5, 4, 3, 2 and 1 on this class, then "Melting changes" and we are done.

Just to see the process at work, click again on the Melt button. EiffelBench looks at the system to see what has happened since the last melting or freezing, sees that nothing has changed, and returns control to you. The process takes only a few seconds. There is never any need to tell EiffelBench about what you have changed, or to specify class dependencies through Make files or similar traditional techniques; the analysis of changes and class relations is entirely automatic.

2.11 SYNTAX ERROR MESSAGES

For the example system you probably will not run into any errors. But it is important to know what happens if you do make a mistake.

When the compiler detects an error, either in the Eiffel code or in the Ace, it will display a message in the main window. Some elements of this message, such as class names or error codes, will be clickable; in other words, you may drag-and-drop them to the appropriate hole to get more detailed help.

To see what happens in the case of a syntax error, replace the keyword *is* by *ist* in the first line of routine **display_demonstration_message** of class **TESTROOT**. Save the file and push the Melt button. Compilation stops and the Project Tool shows the following message:

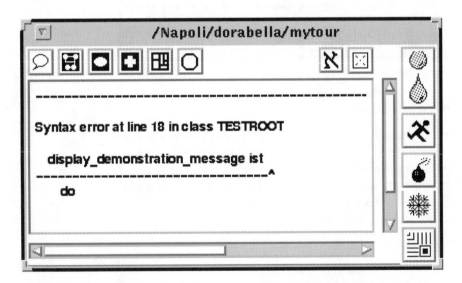

The character cursor ^ indicates the place of the error. To find out what the error is (assuming of course that you did not already know, as here), you may edit the class — by using either a Class Tool of the EiffelBench or some other editor of your choice — and go to the given line number. But there is a better way.

As you may have guessed, the class name as it appears in the error message, **TESTROOT** in our example, is clickable. So you may drag-and-drop it to any Class Tool, which will show the text of the erroneous class. In this case the text shown is not the beginning of the class but the point of the error, with the offending text highlighted in reverse video:

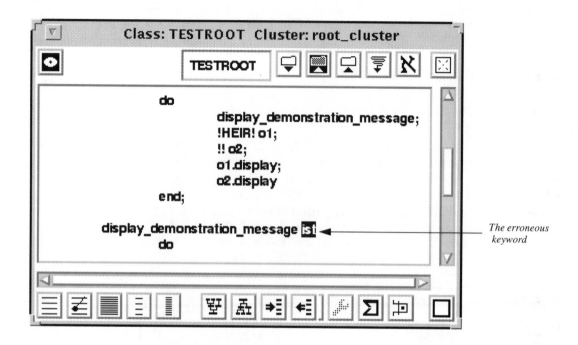

The erroneous keyword

Correct the mistake, save, and melt again.

You may wonder why the syntax error messages are not a little more verbose than just **Syntax error**. The reason is merely that Eiffel's syntax, being simple and regular, does not require sophisticated error messages; almost all syntax errors result from trivial oversights. If you make a syntax error and the reason is not immediately clear, you may use for a quick check the four-page Eiffel syntax handbook distributed with the release.

2.12 A VALIDITY ERROR

The only errors of substance in Eiffel are those which cause violations of one of the validity constraints given in the language definition. Each one of these constraints is identified by a four-letter code of the form **V***XXX* (the first letter is always **V**). A validity violation will produce a precise error message, which includes the validity code. Although short, the error message is usually sufficient to find out what the error is. If not, you can right-click on the error code and drag-and-drop it to an Explanation Tool, which will show the full text of the violated constraint, straight from the book *Eiffel: The Language*.

To see this mechanism on an example, let us introduce a validity error. There is in fact one ready for you: at the end of class **TESTROOT**, just before the final **end**, you will find the following comment line:

> **-- inv: INVALID**

If uncommented, this is a declaration of a feature of type **INVALID**. A class called **INVALID** indeed exists in file **invalid.e** of the root cluster, but it contains a validity error. To see what it is, remove the initial double-dash **--** in the above line from class **TESTROOT** so that it is not a comment any more, save, and melt again. The compiler executes degrees 5, 4 and 3 on **TESTROOT** and **INVALID**, but here is what appears in the Project Tool at the end of degree 3:

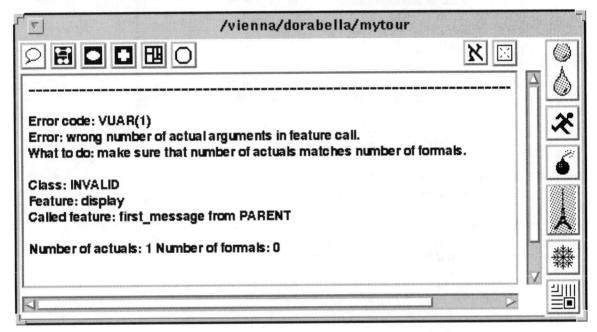

Class and feature names are clickable, so you may easily find out for yourself what went wrong: procedure **display** of class **INVALID** calls **first_message** from **PARENT** with one argument, but the procedure actually takes no argument.

Something else was also clickable in the above window: the error code itself, **VUAR**. Assuming the message was not sufficient to understand the error, you could drag-and-drop the code, for which the pebble is of the Explanation shape 🗩, into the corresponding Explanation hole ◯ of the Project Tool. This will display the complete text of the violated rule from *Eiffel: The Language* as shown below. Note that since the code appears as **VUAR(1)** the clause that is violated is the first one; this convention of showing the clause number in parentheses applies to all multi-clause validity constraints.

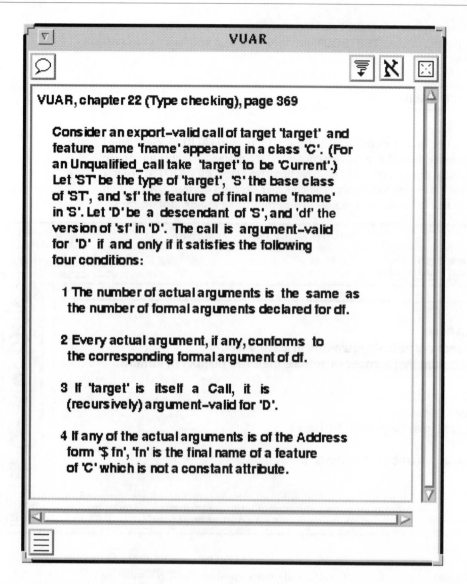

VUAR, chapter 22 (Type checking), page 369

Consider an export-valid call of target 'target' and
feature name 'fname' appearing in a class 'C'. (For
an Unqualified_call take 'target' to be 'Current'.)
Let 'ST' be the type of 'target', 'S' the base class
of 'ST', and 'sf' the feature of final name 'fname'
in 'S'. Let 'D' be a descendant of 'S', and 'df' the
version of 'sf' in 'D'. The call is argument-valid
for 'D' if and only if it satisfies the following
four conditions:

   1 The number of actual arguments is the same as
     the number of formal arguments declared for df.

   2 Every actual argument, if any, conforms to
     the corresponding formal argument of df.

   3 If 'target' is itself a Call, it is
     (recursively) argument-valid for 'D'.

   4 If any of the actual arguments is of the Address
     form '$ fn', 'fn' is the final name of a feature
     of 'C' which is not a constant attribute.

2.13 EXECUTING AND DEBUGGING

So far we have compiled our example system and browsed through it and through the
libraries, but not executed anything. Let us now see how to execute a system — and to debug
it if somethings does not appear right.

   Since you were treacherously led to introduce a validity error in the previous section,
you must first make sure it is removed. The simplest way is to remove the argument to

first_message in the last line of procedure **display** in class **INVALID** so that the line just reads:

> p.first_message

(Alternatively, you can change the declaration of **invalid** in **TESTROOT** back to its original comment form.) Save and melt again.

To run the system you may use the Run button 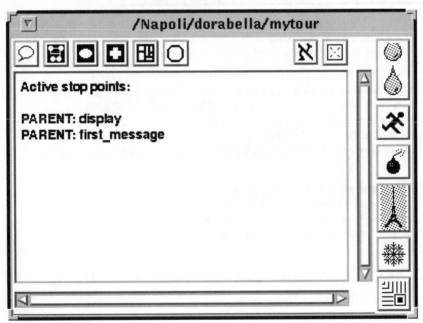 on the right border. As you will have noted from looking at the class texts, all that the example system does is to print a few messages. The output appears in the window from which you started EiffelBench. You can run the system as many times as you wish; do not, however, click repeatedly on the Run button in rapid succession.

To finish this tour it is appropriate to get a first glimpse of the debugging facilities, which are better characterized, bugs or not, as facilities for watching what goes on at execution time and exploring the object structure. The only new notion is that of stop point. To put a stop point on a routine, pick the routine anywhere — by now you know several ways to do that — and drag-and-drop it to the Stop Point hole ◯ of the Project Tool (yes, the routine's cross fits). Right now perform this operation on the two procedures **display** and **first_message** of class **PARENT**. After each drop the Project Tool window shows the list of active stop points; here is the display after you have put both stop points:

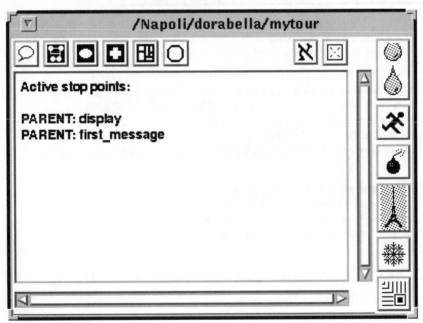

(To remove a stop point, drop the routine again into the Stop Point hole, which acts as a flip-flop switch.)

Now press the Run button again. The application will stop on the first stop point:

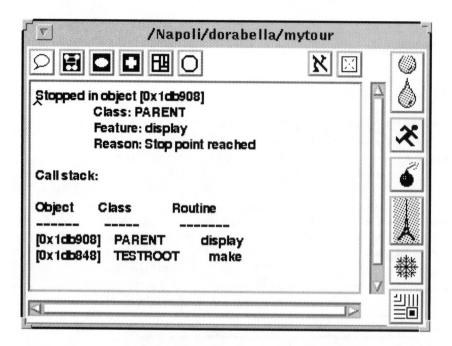

Once again everything of interest in this window is clickable. The main novelty corresponds to the last major kind of developer abstraction that we have not seen yet: execution objects.

The **Call stack** field shows the execution path. Reading from bottom to top: the first call applied procedure **make** to the root object, an instance of class **TESTROOT** identified as **0x1db848**. This triggered a call to procedure **display** of class **PARENT** applied to an object identified as **0x1db908**; if you look at the text of **TESTROOT** you will find out that this must be the object attached to the attribute **o2** and resulting from the second creation instruction in the procedure **make**.

The numbers identifying objects are internal codes (which, by the way, will probably have different values when you run this example on your computer) and do not mean much by themselves, except to determine whether two objects are the same. But they represent abstractions: execution objects. So you can click on any of them to see the corresponding run-time object and its fields.

The pebble for an execution object looks like this: ▓▖. You may drag-and-drop it into an object hole ▓ such as the one in the Project Tool. The resulting Object Tool will show the fields of the object and their values.

Here for example is the result for the object **0x1db848** on the last line — the root object of our system, of type **TESTROOT**:

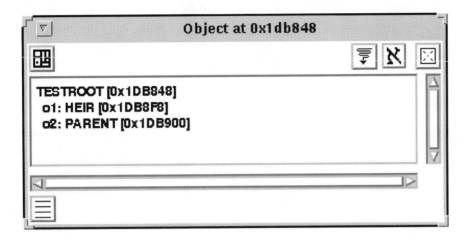

This object only contains fields that are references to other objects; you can follow these references and see the other objects by using the usual drag-and-drop mechanism. In more elaborate examples, objects will also have fields containing values such as integers, real numbers and characters, which you will be able to see and check directly. Such an example appears in the chapter specifically devoted to debugging.

On symbolic debugging, Feature Tools and Execution Object Tools see chapter 9.

These facilities make it possible to traverse the run-time object structure in a fast and convenient way.

As you have probably guessed, the class names that appear as types of the fields — **HEIR** and **TESTROOT** above — are clickable. So you can go directly from an object to its generating class to see how the attributes are declared and what the routines do. If you are looking for a possible bug in your system, the combination of all these exploration mechanisms makes it possible to examine the context of the error and go directly to the source of the problem.

Of particular interest is the debugging mechanism's ability to stop on an exception **before** the exception occurs. You are notified of an impending exception (assertion violation, call applied to void reference, operating system signal or other) and have the opportunity to use all the facilities of EiffelBench to analyze the exact conditions that lead to this exception, and the surrounding object structure. This will be studied as part of the more general discussion of debugging.

Beyond debugging, these are precious mechanisms to understand your software better by following step by step what happens at execution time and exploring the run-time object structures — often sophisticated, and hence sometimes complex — made possible by the method, the language and the libraries.

***

By now you should have a good general grasp of the flavor and power of EiffelBench. You will be able to change the example project as you please, as well as to create, execute and test your own systems — not demonstrations any more, but useful software to solve real problems. The following chapters will help you towards this goal by providing more details about the concepts and practice of the environment.

3

Environment principles

3.1 OVERVIEW

A good object-oriented environment should use a common and consistent set of principles and conventions. In the previous chapter we have seen some of the most important practical aspects at work; this chapter explains the underlying concepts.

We will successively examine the following five key rules:

- The *data abstraction* principle: what objects does an object-oriented environment handle?

- The *direct manipulation* principle: defining a proper relation between the environment and its interface.

- The *semantic consistency* principle: how to ensure uniformity.

- The *typing* principle: how to avoid errors by prevention rather than cure.

- The *redemption* principle: how to provide constructive feedback when an error does occur.

Together, these principles define the conceptual basis of the environment.

3.2 METHOD SUPPORT

The first principle follows from the decision to ensure full consistency between the development method and the supporting tools. It affects both the design of the environment's mechanisms and the user interface under which it offers them.

3.2.1 Consistency

Any ambitious method of software development, good or bad, enforces a certain view of the world, or at least of the software world. The role of the environment is to support that view, but the environment should go further and provide its users — the software developers — with concepts, techniques and interaction principles that directly reflect the notions which they use to develop their software. Not satisfying this condition would mean that we expect software developers to have a split personality, switching constantly between the method's and the environment's views of things.

Nowhere perhaps is this requirement of consistency between the method and the environment more applicable than in object-oriented software construction, which represents such a bold departure from previous ways of developing software. Many of the techniques and mechanisms that are appropriate for a CASE tool supporting structured analysis, or for a programming environment supporting C or Pascal, are not applicable in an object-oriented environment.

A fresh view of environment principles and interaction techniques is particularly necessary in the approach of this book, based on a method and a language that are wholly and uncompromisingly object-oriented. They are so for a reason, of course: because this is the best known way to obtain the highest levels of quality and productivity in software development. To let the method yield its full realization, we should make sure that the supporting environment uses the same concepts.

The result, as described in this book, is an environment that strives to bring out the best in object-oriented technology — and is even pleasant to use.

3.2.2 Object-orientation for the software and its developers

What does it mean to have a wholly object-oriented method and language? Other books discuss this question at length, but if we need an answer that will fit a single paragraph it should be something like the following: in this approach your software is defined by a set of **data abstractions**, each represented by a **class**. For example a system which manages a book library may be based on classes representing such data abstractions as **BOOK**, **BORROWER**, **CATALOG** and **TRANSACTION**. At execution time, the software will manipulate objects: individual instances of these classes, for example individual books, borrowers, catalogs, transactions. There is more, of course — assertions, static typing, covariance, exception handling, garbage collection, inheritance, redefinition, polymorphism, dynamic binding, information hiding — but everything more or less follows from the foundational idea of data abstraction.

See the books "Object-Oriented Software Construction" and "Eiffel: The Language".

To discuss the environment we need to be a little fussy about the terminology used to discuss objects. For what is usually called objects, as just defined — run-time instances of classes, for example objects representing books — we may use the more precise term **execution objects**. The data abstractions describing these objects, in other words the classes, may be called **execution abstractions**. These longer expressions are useful because we will soon encounter another level of data abstractions.

The method is object-oriented; so should the environment be. Based on the above observation, this means that the units of interaction between developers and the environment are of the same nature as the units of software development: in other words, they are data abstractions too.

The developers' data abstractions, however, are one level of abstraction higher. Where classes (execution abstractions) had, as their instances, such execution objects as books and transactions, the abstractions directly relevant to software developers are those which describe, as their instances, the software artefacts that developers create, use and modify.

What are these artefacts? Chief among them in Eiffel stand the classes themselves, of course; but there are also others, which you will all find in EiffelBench:

- Systems: assemblies of classes, the object-oriented analog to what is called *programs* in more traditional approaches.

- Projects.

- Features, in particular routines.

- Explanations: help elements, which developers will use to obtain more information, or in case of error.

- The execution objects themselves, since during execution you may want to access them from the environment, especially for debugging purposes.

- Stop points, for testing, debugging and monitoring system execution.

To distinguish such artefacts from the execution objects, we may call them **development objects**. The last item in the preceding list indicates that execution objects, as accessed through EiffelBench, are a special case of development object.

In the same way that execution objects are instances of software abstractions (classes), development objects are instances of **development abstractions**. The above list gave us the six categories of development abstraction in EiffelBench: Class, Project, System, Feature, Explanation and Execution Object.

The following figure summarizes the relationship between development abstractions, development objects, execution abstractions and execution objects. The arrow ➡️ represents the relation "is an instance (an example) of". Example development objects are represented by their EiffelBench symbols, such as the cross for a routine.

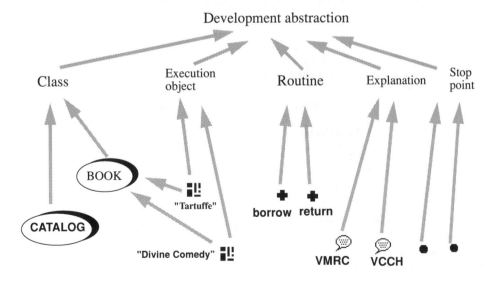

These principles may be applied to tools other than the basic development workbench. Each tool in the environment will introduce its own development abstractions. For example EiffelBuild has Application, State, Behavior, Context and Event. In EiffelCase, Cluster is an important development abstraction.

The conceptual basis for the environment, and a major difference with most of its predecessors, is that everything that you ever manipulate is a development object. As a result, the user-accessible tools are not *function-oriented* tools such as may be found in most environments: editors, compilers, debuggers, browsers and the like. Instead, they are *object-oriented* tools, each based on a development abstraction: Class Tools, System Tool, Project tool, Feature Tools, Explanation Tools, Execution Object Tools. A Class Tool provides EiffelBench users with all the operations available on classes; a Feature Tool, with the operations available on features; and so on.

In the correspondence between the concepts of the method and those of the environment, tools are the environment's counterpart to the language's entities. An entity (similar to the variables of more classical approach) is a name that provides a handle on one or more potential execution objects. For example if you declare an entity as

last_borrowed: BOOK

the name **last_borrowed** denotes a run-time value which, at any time during execution, will be either void (attached to no object) or **attached** to some instance of class **BOOK**. Similarly, a tool of the environment will be either void or **targeted** to a development object of the corresponding type. For example a non-void Class Tool may be targeted to a particular class such as **BOOK**; this means that it provides ways to display the text of that class under various formats, to discover properties of the class (such as its routines, its attributes, its ancestors, its clients), and to apply various other operations to it.

The analogy with an entity attached to an execution object goes further:

• You may retarget the tool to any other development object of the appropriate type — as with an Eiffel assignment instruction that reattaches an entity to a different object.

• You may instead create a new tool and target it to a specified development object — as with an Eiffel creation instruction that creates a new object and attaches it to the target entity.

• The applicable operations may be divided into queries, which return information about a development object (for example the list of its routines if it is a class) and commands (for example, saving the text into a file). The same distinction applies to features that may be called on an entity, and is indeed an important principle of the Eiffel method.

3.2.3 The perspective of the environment's user

The decision to use for the environment a set of concepts and techniques that mirror those of the method and language was justified above on the grounds of consistency. This is indeed a great benefit to the environment's users: not having to switch personalities between your roles as software developer and environment user — to play Dr. Object and Mr. Function.

But consistency is not the only benefit. Some of the other advantages are very practical and quickly visible to the users. The set of facilities that results from the principles developed in this chapter and applied throughout the book is, as I hope you will find out for yourself, more pleasant to use and more powerful than what is offered by earlier environments.

Part of the reason for this improvement is that the environment largely frees its users from having to worry about **states**.

States are also known as modes. A critique of this notion was part of the presentation of the original Smalltalk environment in the August 1981 special issue of Byte Magazine.

Function-oriented tools such as a debugger or a browser lock you in one state at a time: you are using one tool at each step and expected to follow the script that someone else — the tool's author — devised for you.

Instead, object-oriented tools built along the principles of this book enable you to go from development object to development object and, at each step in the process, provide you with all the relevant operations on the objects at hand. *You* write the script. The result is a considerable increase in flexibility and convenience.

For example:

- Rather than a debugger in the functional sense of the term, the environment offers debugging operations in Feature and Execution Object Tools. You are not stuck in debugging state: you execute your software as you wish, putting and removing stop points and examining execution object structures; whenever you like you can pick classes and features and apply browsing and documentation operations to them.

- Rather than a browser, EiffelBench offers a powerful set of operations for exploring and document development objects as you spot them. Some are operations available in Class Tools, for example finding the parents of a class; others apply to Feature Tools, for example finding all the classes where a given feature is redeclared.

The presentation of EiffelBuild in a later chapter discusses the notion of state further. Through its State development abstraction, EiffelBuild makes states explicit and enables application developers to control their number and complexity.

See "Are states bad?", 12.8.2, page 216.

3.2.4 The Data Abstraction principle

The following principle, which determines the organization and interface of all the tools described in this book, summarizes the concepts reviewed so far:

> **Data Abstraction Principle**
>
> An object-oriented environment must be defined by a set of development abstractions, each modeling a type of development object.
>
> For each fundamental development abstraction the environment must provide a corresponding tool, enabling its users to apply queries and commands to development objects of the associated type.

3.3 DIRECT MANIPULATION

The notion of direct manipulation was introduced by Ben Shneidermann in "Direct Manipulation: A Step Beyond Programming Languages" in IEEE Computer, 16, 8, August 1983, pages 57-69.

A good interactive environment should apply the technique of "direct manipulation": it will show on the screen the visual representations of some application objects, and will let the users perform various operations on these objects by performing visual operations on their representations. In other words, it fosters the illusion that each representation **is** the underlying application object. To manipulate the representation is to manipulate the object.

You may wish to apply this principle to the object-oriented applications that you develop (with the help of the environment). For example a visual library management system might show books, borrowers, borrowing transactions and other execution objects under suitable visual representations, and allow its users to perform various operations on them in a convenient visual fashion.

The environment itself should use the same approach, applied one level of abstraction higher: not to execution objects but to development objects. (You will use these development objects to produce execution objects, which may themselves have direct-manipulation visual representations.)

Direct manipulation in the environment described in this book relies on a uniform interaction technique, introduced in chapter 2 and described in full detail in the next chapter. The basic way of performing an operation on a development object is to click on a button of a tool of the appropriate type — Class Tool for a class, and so on — targeted to the object; if no tool is currently targeted to the object, you will first have bring it to a tool of a matching type through the typed drag-and-drop mechanism explained later in this chapter. Both of these fundamental operations, applying an operation button and drag-and-dropping an object, are based on the principle of direct manipulation.

The following principle summarizes this mechanism used throughout the environment to ensure direct manipulation of execution objects:

> **Direct Manipulation Principle**
>
> An object-oriented environment should support the direct manipulation of development objects.
>
> A powerful technique for achieving this goal is to associate with each development object a pebble, which can be drag-and-dropped into matching holes of a corresponding object tool, and to use the tool's buttons to apply operations to the object.

3.4 SEMANTIC CONSISTENCY

Another key principle helps give their full meaning to some of the preceding rules.

During a session of the environment the screen may contain several different representations of a given development object. For example a class name C may appear in several texts displayed in various Class Tools, Feature Tools and Execution Object Tools. (An Execution Object Tool shows the fields of a certain object, captured during execution; for each field, it shows the type of the corresponding attribute, which may be C.) In a targeted tool, the tool's target also appears as a little dot in the top-left hole of the tool. In addition, the class may appear in the form of a pebble for the drag-and-drop mechanism.

It is essential to a proper application of the Direct Manipulation principle that all these representations, whether textual (the class name) or graphical (the dot, the pebble) be absolutely equivalent from the perspective of the environment's users. In other words, if you see a development object in any tool under any representation and want to perform some operation on it, you should be able to do so regardless of the representation that you have seen and of the places where it appears in the visual interface.

This property enables users to feel that they are in control of the environment: they pick the objects which they want to query and modify, and can apply all meaningful operations to any object regardless of the tool tin which they chose to pick it.

Here is the principle that summarizes this requirement:

> **Semantic Consistency Principle**
>
> An object-oriented environment should enable its users, for any symbol (textual, graphical or otherwise) representing a development object in the user interface, to select the object through the symbol and apply any operation that is semantically valid for the object, regardless of the symbol's context — tool, location, format, representation.

3.5 STRONG TYPING

Another idea that plays a central role in the method and language and can be fruitfully transposed to the environment is the concept of type.

In the typed approach to object-oriented software construction, every object has a well-defined type, which results from the declaration of the corresponding entity in the software text. In such declarations the specification of the type is a required component. The benefits of typing are discussed in detail in the references mentioned at the beginning of this chapter; they include in particular the following three:

T1 • Making the software safer by enabling compilers to detect many errors that, with other approaches, would be detected much later or not at all.

T2 • Improving the readability of the software: by declaring every entity with the corresponding type you give a strong and immediate indication to the software reader about what the entity is intended for and how it will be used.

T3 • Helping compilers generate efficient code.

The general theme of this chapter — consistency between the method and the environment — suggests that the environment should be typed too, and indeed an object-oriented environment will benefit from strong typing. For environments too strong typing will be beneficial. Like execution objects and the corresponding entities, development objects and the corresponding tools will have clearly defined types. The advantages are the counterparts of T1 and T2 above: safety (helping users avoid errors) and readability (which here means ease of use).

Regarding errors, recall that for a user of the environment there are only two fundamental operations:

O1 • Click on a button of a tool, to apply a certain operation to its target object.

O2 • Drag a pebble into the corresponding hole in a tool.

This leaves room for only a few possible user errors. With O1, a button might be inapplicable to the development object; in such a case an error message may pop up (following conventions discussed in the next section), or the environment may do nothing and remain silent. With O2, the pebble might not be a valid new target for the tool.

This is where strong typing helps. Every development object has a type: Class, System, Project, Feature, Explanation or Execution Object. Every tool also has a type: Class Tool, Feature Tool and so on. When a tool is targeted to a certain object, the tool clearly indicates the object's type. When you are dragging an object, the pebble's shape serves to visualize the types of development objects; and a pebble of a certain shape can only be dropped into a hole of a compatible shape. For example you cannot drop a class pebble into a feature hole. (If you try it, the environment will not perform any operation but will take you out of drag-and-drop mode, as if you had clicked a button other than the rightmost one.)

The basic typing rule of the environment, then, is similar to the basic typing rule of the language: as you may only attach an entity declared of a certain type to an object of a compatible type, so you may only target a tool of a certain type to an object of a compatible type.

The only significant difference is that the environment is an interactive mechanism with immediate feedback; in other words you cannot, as a user, rely on a compiler to flag your type errors for you. You need ways to avoid errors in the first place. Here the graphical conventions are essential: each tool clearly displays its type, in particular through the shape of its holes; each development object's type is also clearly visible, as soon as you start dragging the object, through the shape of the pebble that represents it; and the type compatibility requirement is represented visually by the requirement that the pebble must match the hole.

In both the language and the environment the rules for reattachment or retargeting leave some room for flexibility: they require compatibility of source to target, not identity. The language's type system achieves this flexibility through inheritance and polymorphism, allowing reattachment of an object of a specific type to an entity of a more general type. For example you may attach an object of type **RECTANGLE** to an entity of type **FIGURE**, assuming the second of these classes is an ancestor of the first. The environment provides similar tolerance (although it is less systematic about it) by letting pebbles match holes in some cases when they are not of identical shapes.

For example you may drop a feature pebble into a Class hole; the new target of the Class hole will then be the class in which the feature appears, positioned at the feature, with the entire feature text highlighted.

> This is a nice and easy way to obtain the context of a feature: you select the feature at a place where its name appears and bring it to a Class hole. From then on you can move to ancestors of the feature's class, to its clients, descendants and so on.

A general property of these techniques is that in many cases they make errors impossible — as opposed to an approach focusing on techniques for *correcting* errors a posteriori.

For example if you are dragging a class you are naturally encouraged to bring it to a Class hole since it has the same shape; if you bring it to a routine hole it will not fit; and if in spite of all this you drop it there anyway, the environment will simply not do anything.

A more traditional approach might be able to detect an erroneous operation only after it has been attempted, and might then have to produce an error panel reading **YOU MAY NOT COPY A CLASS ONTO A ROUTINE!** and requiring the user to take some action to get out of the error mode.

These various observations lead to the fourth of our foundational rules:

> **Strong Typing Principle**
>
> An object-oriented environment should associate a type with every development object, ensure that each object's type is immediately apparent from the object's visual representation, define simple rules as to what operations and combinations are permitted on objects and tools of each possible type, and enforce these rules through interaction techniques that favor error avoidance over a posteriori detection and correction

3.6 ERRORS: PREVENTION RATHER THAN CURE

The advice to favor detection over correction is not limited to type errors, but may be applied to all potential errors. The environment should use prevention and feedback rather than cure and reproach.

A common example of the opposite approach is provided by the "Gotcha" error panels used extensively by so many interactive systems. A Gotcha panel is a window that pops up when the user has made some error, but offers only one way out; it usually looks somewhat like this:

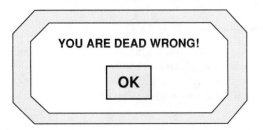

Gotcha panels do not leave users any other choice than clicking "OK", presumably after repenting for their sins, but without being even given a chance to mend their ways. The view of interaction which presided to the design of such "interactive" tools seems rather one-directional.

A popular workstation text processing software shows an interesting kind of Gotcha panel. After using the "capture graphics on screen" command you are not allowed to proceed until you have clicked on **OK** in an "alert" panel that indicates successful completion of the operation and stores the contents of the captured screen area into a file, replacing any previous contents of that file.

At first this seems innocuous if a bit absurd (success is not normally a cause for alert!) and irritating (one feels treated like a child whom parents will not let open a gift package without saying "thank you, sir" first). But in fact the flaw is more serious. During the screen capture part of the operation, you must maintain the button pressed throughout; as discussed in the next chapter, this is a stressful and error-inducing technique. It is therefore very easy to make a mistake, for example to release the pressure inadvertently and have the operation capture only part of the intended area. In such a case what one looks for is a "Cancel" operation, which would restore the earlier version of the file, if any. But it is too late! Only **OK** is offered. The poor user has no other choice than to click on this button, thereby signing an act of surrender without conditions: the file has already been irreparably overwritten.

On the drawbacks of keep-button-down mouse operations see "Why drag-and-drop works the way it does: a human factors analysis", 4.3.2, page 59.

EiffelBench has few error panels thanks to the techniques mentioned above. For those that proved necessary, the principle was, whenever possible, to give user a **choice** in the proper sense of the term: two or more possibilities. One of these possibilities is usually to give up the requested operation, through a "Cancel" button; but there is at least one other that provides a chance to correct the problem and try again.

Here is a typical example. We saw in the previous chapter that it is possible to retarget a Class Tool simply by typing its name in the editable class name field at the top. What happens if what you type, say **MY_CLASS**, is not the name of a class in the system?

See "A LITTLE MORE ABOUT BROWSING", 2.9, page 28.

A Gotcha panel telling you **No such class!** might at first seem appropriate but the environment knows better:

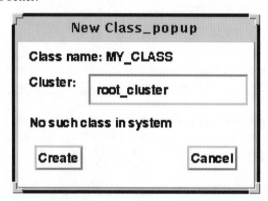

If the name is indeed an error, you can choose **Cancel**. But the environment also offers to create the class for you in the current cluster, here **root_cluster**, or another (which you can select by typing the cluster name in the corresponding field). In this case the environment will generate a template for the class, and give you the corresponding Class Tool so that you can edit the template.

This example is an illustration of our last principle:

Redemption Principle

When a user attempts an erroneous operation and the error can only be detected after the operation has been requested, the environment should not just report the error and enable the user to cancel the request, but also, whenever conceptually possible, provide the user with at least one other choice which transforms the request into a valid operation.

With all these ideas it is a rare situation indeed that justifies the use of a Gotcha panel.

In fact only one case seems to make a Gotcha panel inevitable: catastrophic termination. This case arises when an irrecoverable problem (due to some external, uncontrollable event) prevents the environment from proceeding in any reasonable way. Then it is appropriate, before giving up, to announce the bad news and make sure the user receives it. Needless to say, a well-designed system will have very few if any such cases. EiffelBench has one, mentioned in a later chapter.

See "Directory requirements and trouble-shooting", 5.2.3, page 76.

Although EiffelBench uses no other true Gotchas, it includes a small number of Gotcha-like panels, but with a difference. Here is one such "pseudo-Gotcha". Thanks to precompilation it is possible to deliver a library to your customers without delivering the source code of classes in that library. But then a developer using the environment at one of your customer sites can still drag the name of one of these classes (although one could argue that they should be made non-clickable). What happens if that user of the environment then drops the name of such a class, say **TWO_WAY_LIST**, it into a Class Tool? The only response that seems to make sense is to display a panel:

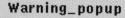

> **Warning_popup**
>
> ❗ **File: /base/common/Eiffel3/library/base/structures/list/two_way_list.e cannot be read**

This is at first sight a Gotcha panel of a sort, but it does not take long to see the difference: the panel does not have an "OK" button!

Unless you believe in punishing users, there is no need for such a button. Having to click on "OK" — which really means being forced to plead guilty — is not a very constructive way to interact with the environment. The EiffelBench approach is more friendly, although paradoxically and sadly it will at first seem bizarre to people used to the Gotcha panels of older environments: they will fumble around for a button to click on, thinking perhaps that it is there but some bug in the display mechanism prevents them from accessing it.

You may look around: there is no such button. But it is not a bug. Your first significant action — typically, dragging and dropping a development object, or typing a name into a text field — will make the panel and with it all memory of the error vanish forever, like a bad dream that the body's first stir chases away at the start of a bright new day.

4

General interactive mechanisms

4.1 OVERVIEW

The various tools of the environment — Class, System, Feature, Explanation and Execution Object Tools, as well as the tools of EiffelBuild and those of EiffelCase— support specific operations, associated with the individual semantics of the corresponding development object types and described in the following chapters.

The tools of Eiffel-Build—Context, Command, State and others—are studied in chapter 12.

Some of the operations, however, are common to all tools. They are described in this chapter. We will successively explore: the notions of tool and tool target; the typed drag-and-drop mechanism; the general layout of tool windows; how to escape from the environment to apply operating system commands; editing facilities; how to use the file selector to traverse the file hierarchy; and what holes and pebbles are available

4.2 TOOLS AND THEIR TARGETS

At each stage during its existence, an active tool is either **void** or **targeted** to a certain development object, called the tool's **target**.

If the tool is targeted, its target's type will always match the tool's type: it will be a class for a Class Tool, a feature for a Feature Tool and so on. This means that the tool shows information about the object and allows you to perform all permissible operations on that object. For example a Feature Tool will be targeted to a certain feature, and will enable you to perform various operations on that feature, such as showing its text and showing its ancestor versions.

With two exceptions, you can have as many tools of each type as you wish — limited only by the number of windows you are willing to allow on your screen. The exceptions are the Project Tool and System Tool, since during an EiffelBench session you work on just one project and one system.

Assume you want to work on a certain development object, for example a class, and need a tool of the corresponding type, a Class Tool in this example. You have a choice between two possibilities: you can create a new tool; or, if a tool of the appropriate type exists but is currently targeted to another object, you can retarget that tool to the object you want. Let us see how to take care of both cases.

4.2.1 Creating a new tool

To create a new tool targeted to a given object, you may use either of four mechanisms:

C1 • Drag-and-drop into a Project Tool hole

C2 • Drag-and-drop elsewhere in the Project Tool.

C3 • Control-right-click.

C4 • Create a void tool and retarget it.

Using C1, you may drag-and-drop the chosen object into a matching hole of the Project Tool. (The details of the drag-and-drop mechanism are given later in this chapter.) The Project Tool has holes for Class, System, Feature, Explanation and Developer Object.

You may also, using C2, drag-and-drop the object anywhere into the text part of the Project Tool's window, not just into the selected hole. This is in fact a variant of the preceding solution; in general EiffelBench is quite tolerant as to where you can drop a pebble: the dropping point can be outside a hole if there is no ambiguity. Conceptually you may view the entire text part of a tool as a big hole of the corresponding type. In the Project Tool the type of the tool that will be created is determined by the type of the pebble that you dropped. This is similar to an Eiffel creation instruction of the form $!T!\ x$, which will create an object of type T even if the type declared for x is a more general one.

You may also use technique C3 to create a new tool by control-right-clicking on the desired development object. This means bringing the mouse cursor to any place where the object's name appears, for example the name of a class or feature appearing in some tool, and clicking with the rightmost mouse button while holding down the CONTROL key. Control-right-clicking will create a new tool of the appropriate type targeted to the selected object, without a need for drag-and-drop.

Finally, technique C4 enables you to use the Project Tools's holes to create a void tool for later retargeting. The holes of the Project Tool double up as buttons, giving a new meaning to the word *buttonhole*. Clicking on any of them except System and Stop Point will create a tool of the corresponding type, initially not targeted to any object. You may target it later using any of the techniques described below. This is useful, for example, if you want to examine a class text and you do not have an immediately usable Class Tool: you can just click on the Class buttonhole of the Project Tool, which gives you a void Class Tool; then retarget the tool to the desired class by typing the class name into the top text field, or through any of the other retargeting mechanisms explained next.

4.2.2 Retargeting an existing tool through drag-and-drop

If a tool of the appropriate type already exists, you can easily retarget it to an object. Just find the identifying hole of the tool; this is the hole that appears at the top-left corner of the tool window. Then drag-and-drop the selected object into that hole.

For example in the Class Tool whose top part appears next is currently targeted to class **GENERAL** from EiffelBase; its class hole appears at the top left of the window:

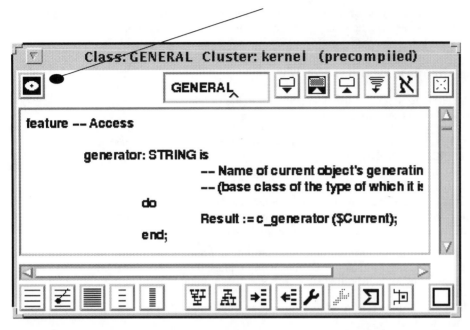

A class pebble is in the process of being dragged; this means that a class was picked in some other tool. Let us assume that class was **CHAIN**, also from EiffelBase. Dropping the pebble into the class hole retargets the Class Tool to **CHAIN**:

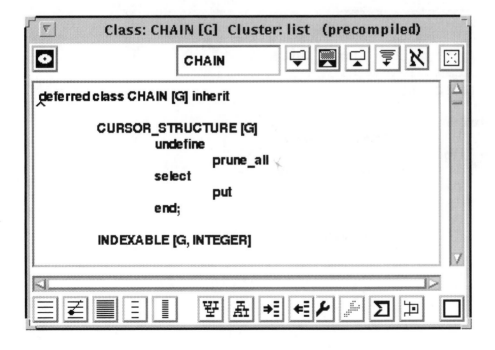

Here too there is some tolerance: you can actually drop the pebble anywhere in the tool window; just look at each tool as one big hole of the tool's type. As explained below, this makes a simple shortcut possible in some cases.

See "Quick Retargeting", 4.3.3, page 60.

4.2.3 Retargeting through keyboard entry

Another very useful retargeting technique is also available in the case of Class and Feature Tools: you can simply type in the name of the desired of the new target.

At the top of every Class Tool there appears a text field which gives the class name (shown as **GENERAL** and **CHAIN** in the preceding two figures). To retarget the tool to another class, you may just bring the mouse cursor to that field, click with the left button to make the text field active, type in the name of the desired class, and press Enter. For example starting from the first one of the preceding two Class Tools, targeted to **GENERAL**, we could have obtained the second one by erasing the name of the class in the top text field and typing the name **CHAIN** instead, then pressing Enter. A simple way to do such a replacement is to double-click on the original name, which then appears in reverse video, **GENERAL** in the example; then if you type a new name, for example **CHAIN**, it will replace the previous one. You can also use the Backspace key to erase individual characters of the original name.

This technique, which may also be used to add a new class to a system, will be seen in more detail in the study of Class Tools.

See "Class Tool retargeting through name input", 8.2.3, page 126.

In the case of Feature Tools there are two text fields, one for the class name and one for the feature name, as in this Feature Tool obtained from the last Class Tool by control-right-clicking on the name of feature **first** of class **CHAIN**:

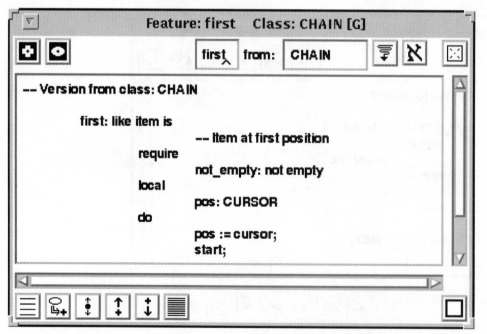

In this case you can use the keyboard to change either the feature name (to look at another feature of the same class) or the class name (to see a feature of the same name in another class) — or both. More details in the discussion of Feature Tools.

See "Retargeting a Feature Tool", 9.2.3, page 142.

4.2.4 Retargeting and formats

A tool targeted to a development object will show information about that object in some format, selected through one of the tool's bottom buttons. When you retarget the tool to another object, the format does not change.

For example, the following Class Tool is targeted to **CHAIN** as above, but now the Ancestors format has been selected, so that the window shows the beginning of the multiple inheritance hierarchy which leads to **CHAIN**. (You would have to enlarge the window or use its scrollbar to see the whole hierarchy.)

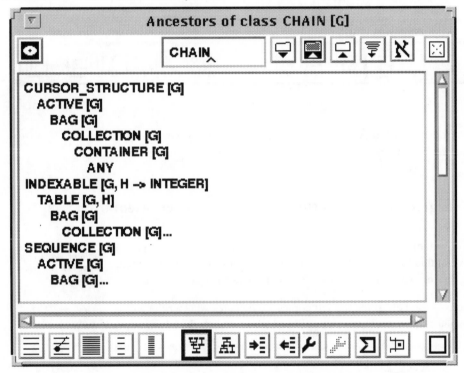

Note how the selected format (the first button in the second group of format buttons on the bottom row) is highlighted through a special frame.

Now assume that you retarget the tool to another class, such as **SEQUENCE** (one of the ancestors of **CHAIN**), using any of the retargeting mechanisms studied above. The format will remain the same — Ancestors — so that the tool will now show the ancestors of class **SEQUENCE**:.

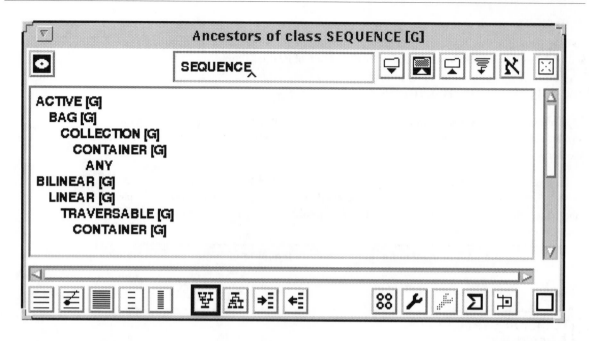

If you want to see some other format, click on the appropriate button. For example, click on the Text button, the bottom-left one in the Class Tool, to display the text of class **DYNAMIC_CHAIN**.

4.2.5 Void tools, targeted tools, and the target's visual representation

At most times a tool will be targeted to a development object of the corresponding type. A tool may, however, be void; this happens when you initially create it through the technique labeled C4 above: using the corresponding hole of the Project Hole as a button.

Technique C4 was explained in "Creating a new tool", 4.2.1, page 54.

The tool's input hole — the hole at the top-left corner — indicates whether the tool is targeted or not. If it is targeted, the hole contains a tiny dot which represents the target; this is the case with the above Class Tool, whose top-left Class hole appears as ⬤. For a void Class Tool, the hole would just appear as ⬤.

In a targeted tool, the dot that appears in the middle of the input hole truly represents the target development object. This means in particular that you can use it for a drag-and-drop. In the situation illustrated by the above figure, for example, class **SEQUENCE** is available (as a development object) through that dot. So you can right-click on the input hole to drag-and-drop class **SEQUENCE** anywhere. The effect will be the same as if you had picked the name of the class in a tool where it appears.

4.3 THE TYPED DRAG-AND-DROP MECHANISM

Typed drag-and-drop is the fundamental interaction technique of the environment. We became familiar with it in the Guided Tour; let us now explore all of its details and see how it naturally yields a quick retargeting mechanism.

4.3.1 Drag-and-drop steps

A better although somewhat longer name is: Pick, Drag and Drop. The mechanism works in three steps:

D1 • Pick step: select an object to be dragged. You will identify the object by its name, which may appear anywhere in any tool; positions where such objects appear are said to be **clickable**. To pick the object, right-click on it; that is to say, move the mouse cursor to the object's name, press the mouse's right button, and release it immediately. Do **not** maintain the button down; the click will have no effect until it is followed by a release.

D2 • Drag step: move the pebble around. As soon as you have picked the object, the mouse cursor changes into a pebble whose shape indicates the type of the selected object: oval disk ● for a class, graph 🖳 for a system, cross ✚ for a feature, balloon 💬 (as in comic books) for an explanation, multi-field rectangle ⧉ for an execution object. As you move the mouse, the pebble follows; in addition, a solid line continuously links the pebble to the originally selected object, tracking the pebble as it moves, for example ──────────────✚ if you are dragging a feature.

D3 • Drop step: drop the pebble. Move the pebble to a valid dropping point; normally this is a hole of the matching type (empty oval hole ⬭ for an oval pebble, empty cross ✚ for a cross pebble and so on) but, as noted above, there is some tolerance and you may actually go to any place in the text window of an appropriate tool. Then right-click again as in step 1, that is to say, click the rightmost mouse button, the same one that you used for picking the object in the first place, and release it immediately.

The first right-click, in the Pick step, picks the object; the second one, in the Drop step, releases it.

If at any time during the Drag step you change your mind and decide not to drop the pebble in any hole, just **left-click** anywhere (that is to say, click the leftmost button and release it immediately) at any time. This takes you out of drag-and-drop. With a three-button mouse, middle-click will have the same effect.

In Drop step (D3) a right-click executed outside of a valid drop position, for example on a non-matching hole or outside of any EiffelBench window, will do the same as left-click: taking you out of drag-and-drop.

4.3.2 Why drag-and-drop works the way it does: a human factors analysis

If you are used to more traditional forms of drag-and-drop, you may be at first tempted to maintain the mouse button pressed in the drag step (D2). This is indeed the more common approach in earlier interactive environments. Careful examination and experimentation quickly shows, however, that this traditional mechanism causes three unacceptable problems: user stress, error-proneness and inadequate support for cancellation.

The mechanism quickly leads to stress and muscle fatigue, as you must maintain pressure during a possibly long trip to the destination. This is unacceptable for any system — but would be even more so for the environment of this book, where drag-and-drop is the basic operational mechanism, so that a user may well spend the better part of a working day dragging pebbles into holes.

The traditional mechanism is also error-prone. You are supposed to maintain the button pressed during the entire drag step, but it is all too easy to release it accidentally. If this your day of bad luck, the cursor could be at a position, other than the intended one, where it is valid to perform a "drop". One shudders at the potential consequences.

Finally, what happens if you start to drag and then change your mind — deciding that the whole drag-and-drop was not appropriate after all? With the traditional approach the only solution is to try to find a place where dropping is *not* valid, and so will have no bad effect. But this assumes that you know for sure where dropping is valid and where it is not; and if you do find a safe spot, it may be quite far from the starting point, causing a long mouse trip and more muscle fatigue. With the cluttered state of many displays (the downside of the "desktop metaphor"), it is in fact quite possible to encounter a situation where no such safe spot exists; what will happen then?

> Old user interface designers still talk in hushed tones, when no layperson is present, of a nuclear plant operator who started a potentially catastrophic drag-and-drop, then realized his mistake, but could not find a safe place for dropping. It is said that specially trained mouse-pushers, known in the business as "fat cats", had to take one-hour shifts, twenty-four hours a day for a period of two years, to hold the fateful button down until the problem was finally solved using techniques which, unfortunately, were only documented in a report that to this day remains classified.

The drag-and-drop technique described above avoids these problems. Once you have right-clicked on an object it is yours; you can keep it for as long as you like without having to do anything. In fact you can go and have lunch if you like; the object will still be in the Drag step when you come back. As you move the mouse, the pebble follows. If you change your mind at any time, just left-click and everything will be as if nothing had happened. If, on the other hand, you are ready to drop, just pick the target and right-click again.

There may remain a small role for keep-button-down operations other than drag-and-drop if displacements are small and an accidental release may not cause any damage. (In particular there should be an "undo" mechanism for every action.) A typical example is resizing a graphical object. There are no such operations in EiffelBench but EiffelBuild uses them in a few cases, dictated in part by the underlying window system. EiffelBuild has an arbitrary level undo-redo mechanism, which further limits potential damage.

On button-down operations in EiffelBuild see "Adding, moving and resizing contexts", 12.5.3, page 189 and "Duplicating objects", 12.5.7, page 196.

4.3.3 Quick Retargeting

A consequence of the above conventions and shortcuts is that two successive right-clicks will often allow you to retarget a tool quickly, without performing any actual dragging.

This quick-retargeting technique is particularly useful for Class Tools. Assume a Class Tool targeted to class **CHAIN**, in Text format, somewhere towards the middle of the class, as shown on the first figure on the facing page.

The function **index**, appearing at the current top position, returns a result of type **INTEGER**. Although a basic type, **INTEGER** is defined by a class of the Kernel library in EiffelBase. Assume you fancy looking at the definition of **INTEGER**. This is possible from within the environment, although you should definitely not try to modify this class.

*On basic classes such as **INTEGER**, see "Eiffel: The Language", chapter 32, "Basic Classes".*

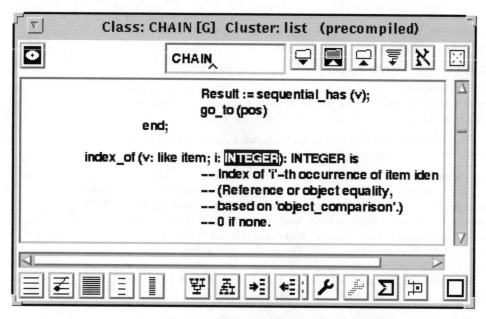

To retarget the current Class Tool to **INTEGER**, you could drag the occurrence of this class name to the class hole at the top left corner of the window. But remember that the entire Class Tool window is like a big class hole, so you may drag the class name anywhere in it.

Since the name already appears in the class tool, you will not need to drag at all. Just right-click twice on **INTEGER**, and the Class Tool retargets itself to this class:

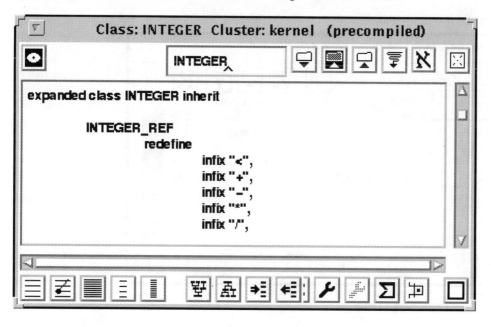

As you may have guessed, there is no new mechanism involved here, but simply an application of the previous techniques — drag-and-drop without the drag. Here is the sequence of events:

- The first right-click picks the object, putting you in the Drag step (step 2 above).

- You do not move the pebble, however, and may not even have the time to see it; instead you right-click again to drop the pebble. Because of the tolerance indicated above, this drop operation is successful since the pebble is indeed in a class tool.

- The drop operation retargets the class tool (previously targeted to class **CHAIN** in the above example) to the selected development object (class **INTEGER**).

You may think of this mechanism as double click. ISE Eiffel 3, however, does not rely on any double click operation in the traditional sense. Double-clicking as used in many interactive systems requires users to click on a button twice within a specified interval, typically a half second or so. Along with traditional drag-and-drop, this is one of the mechanisms that make the expression "mouse fatigue" immediately evocative to extensive users of common Graphical User Interface applications. The need to obey a short inter-click interval causes undue stress. The mechanism just described does not suffer from these drawbacks since it merely requires two successive clicks, without imposing any requirement on how fast they should occur.

Double-clicking is still required by some mechanisms of the underlying toolkit to overwrite a name; see for example "Using the File Selector", 4.7.2, page 72.

4.4 GENERAL TOOL ORGANIZATION

All tools in EiffelBench and other components of ISE Eiffel 3 have the same general organization.

4.4.1 General layout

The figure below shows the layout which, in its general form, is common to all tools.

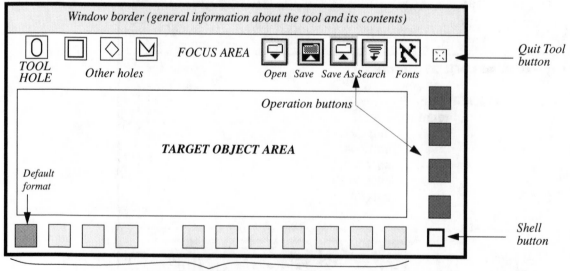

4.4.2 Quit button

The first standard component to be noted is the Quit Tool button ⊡ at the top-right corner (below the window border). By clicking on it you will exit the tool. For the Project Tool, this means quitting EiffelBench, so in this case a panel will show up and ask you to confirm or cancel.

Note: how to quit a tool

As already noted in the Guided Tour, you should always use the Quit Tool button to terminate a tool. Using the window manager's "Quit Window" or "Kill Window" mechanism will terminate EiffelBench.

4.4.3 Window border, holes, and resynchronization

Let us now look at the other areas from top to bottom and from left to right.

On the upper border of the window (provided by the underlying window manager) EiffelBench displays general information about the target; for example a Class Tool will show the target class and the cluster to which that class belongs.

Below the window border comes the first line of the tool proper. Its top left part contains one or more holes, into which pebbles may be dropped. The first of these holes, at the top-left corner, is the tool's **input hole**, used for retargeting and indicating the tool type: class hole for a Class Tool and so on. It has two further applications:

- When the tool is targeted, the input hole will contain a small dot representing the target. As already noted, you may right-click on the hole to drag-and-drop the dot, representing the associated development object.

- To start using a preexisting tool (System, Class or Feature) again after a compilation step that may have affected the underlying development object, you must **resynchronize** the tool so that the environment can work again properly on its target. This is done by left-clicking on the input hole. This operation is equivalent to dropping the associated object into the tool again; it could also be achieved by right-clicking twice on the input hole's dot.

4.4.4 Focus area and text input areas

The second part of the top line is the Focus Area, which is empty by default but, as you move the cursor over any of the icons (buttons and holes) of the tool, will display short messages highlighting the meaning of the icon at the mouse cursor's current position.

The Focus Area technique makes it possible to satisfy the needs of novice users, who require a quick and easy way of refreshing their memory about the meaning of the various icons, as well as those of experts, who want all the screen space they can use, and do not like it to be taken up by captions for icons with which they became familiar long ago.

After the Focus Area there may be an extra zone (not shown on the last figure, but appearing on the Class Tools reproduced earlier): a text field which holds the name of the target object, and into which you may enter a new name to retarget the tool.

The editable text field is present only in Class and Feature Tools.

4.4.5 Button areas

The last (rightmost) part of the first line contains a number of operation buttons. They represent standard operations — read from file, save, search, change fonts, quit — whose icons are the same for all applicable tools. They are reviewed in the next section, except for Quit (always the last button on the right) which has already been seen.

In some tools the rightmost part of the window contains a column of tool-specific operation buttons. This is for example where you will find the compilation buttons (Melt, Freeze, Finalize) in the Project Tool.

4.4.6 Text window

Below the first line of holes, Focus Area and buttons comes the main area of the window: the target object area, which shows information relative to the development object to which the tool is currently targeted. The exact form of that information depends on the development object, the tool's type, and the last format selected.

4.4.7 Format area and Shell button

The last line of the tool window contains the buttons used to set the format for displaying the target object in the text window area. The set of available formats depends on the tool type, but the leftmost button always corresponds to the default format — the format under which a tool comes up when you first create it. For classes, features and systems this is the Text format: the Eiffel or Lace source text.

At the end of the last line, some tools have a Shell Command button ☐, which you can use to apply an arbitrary non-EiffelBench command to the target object, as explained below.

The Shell button is studied in 4.5, page 65.

4.4.8 Tool-independent operations

As noted above, some buttons appear in many or all tools. Along with the Shell button they include the following:

⊡ Quit: terminate the tool, as discussed in the previous section.

▽ Open: reset the contents of the target object from the contents of a file. The file selector (see next section) will pop up so that you can choose the appropriate file.

▣ Save: save contents of the target object to the associated file, if any. This button will appear as ▽ in a tool whose text has been modified since the last Save or Save As.

△ Save As: save contents of the target object to arbitrary file. The file selector will pop up.

≣ Search: look for a specific string in the text of the target object. A self-explanatory panel will pop up, enabling you to type in the string and search for it repeatedly, starting from the current cursor position in the target object area.

א Font: change font for the text representation in the target object area (more about font selection below)

All these buttons except the first provide editing functions on the text of tool targets. Let us first examine the Shell command facility and then the various editing operations.

4.5 APPLYING OPERATING SYSTEM COMMANDS TO DEVELOPMENT OBJECTS

The Shell Command button ☐, which appears in Class and Feature tools, enables you to execute an arbitrary operating system command on the tool's target; one application is to edit the corresponding file using **vi** or some other editor.

4.5.1 Editing a class with vi

If you left-click on the Shell Command button, the effect is to apply the **current shell command** to the tool's target. By default, the current shell command is

> **xterm –geometry 80x40 –e vi +$line $target**

which has the effect of creating a new window ("xterm") and starting a session of the **vi** editor in that window, applied to the file containing the tool's current target (identified by **$target**); the **–geometry** option sets the size of the window, here 80 columns and 40 lines, and the + option of **vi** makes it possible to position the editing window so that it starts at the requested line (identified here by **$line**).

This mechanism provides a convenient way to apply a non-EiffelBench editor to the target's text.

For a Class Tool, the file that will be edited will be the file containing the class. For a Feature Tool, it will also be a class file: the file containing the class to which the routine belongs.

In all cases, make sure that you do not inadvertently perform inconsistent modifications from inside and outside EiffelBench:

> ### Note: using non-EiffelBench editors
>
> If you edit a class with an outside editor such as **vi**, be careful not to modify it concurrently with the EiffelBench editor, as offered in the Class Tool. When you are done with the editor session, resynchronize the Class Tool to the updated target text by clicking on the top-left hole (the class hole).

4.5.2 Changing the shell command

The above shell command using **xterm** and **vi** is just the default. You can use any other editor or, more generally, apply any shell command by clicking on the Command button.

To change the current shell command, **right-click** on the Command button (that is to say, click and release the rightmost mouse button, not the leftmost as when you just want to execute the current shell command).The following panel will appear:

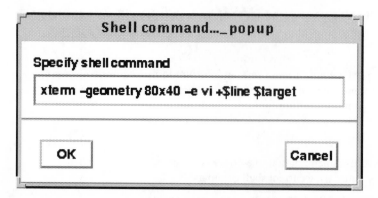

The text shown is the current shell command. You may edit that text and replace it by any command that you wish to be the new default command. Click on **OK** (unless you change your mind, in which case you should click on **Cancel**); this will execute the command that you have typed, and make it the new current shell command.

In the text of the command, you may use two special notations, illustrated above in the default shell command (the one using **xterm** and **vi**):

- **$target** denotes the target file. For a class target this is the file containing the class text; for a routine target this is the file containing the class to which the routine belongs.

- **$line** denotes the line number of the current cursor position in the target file.

Thanks to this facility, you may apply any operating system command to the text of a class — for example have it processed by an operation of a configuration management system, run it to a text processing tool, mail it to colleagues anywhere — from within the environment itself.

4.5.3 Changing the default command

The above default command calling **vi** in an **xterm** window was chosen simply because it is of interest to many users. But you may replace the default shell command prior to executing EiffelBench by setting the value of the environment variable **EIF_COMMAND** to the appropriate text.

For example if you do not normally use **vi**, and want to use as default command a session of your favorite editor *myeditor*, you may include in your initialization file (**.login** or **.cshrc** under the C-shell) a command of the form

```
setenv EIF_COMMAND 'xterm -e myeditor -l $line $target'
```

given here in C-shell syntax (which you may transpose to that of other shells). Do not forget the quotes, without which the **setenv** command would incorrectly try to evaluate **$target** and **$line** as the values of some shell variables.

4.6 EDITING DEVELOPMENT OBJECTS

Let us now review the various operations that are available, through the buttons listed above, to tools of all types or at least, in certain cases, of several types: changing the font, searching for a certain string, saving into a file, reinitializing from a file.

4.6.1 Adjusting the font

When you push the Font button 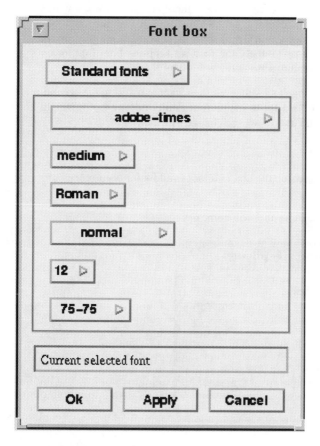, a Font box pops up, looking like this (or something similar):

The Font Box provides you with a list of menus to select the font that best suits your needs. The exact set of fonts, styles and sizes depends on your installation. For each option, the entry shown on the above figure gives the current choice; you may click on it to get a menu of all the available choices and select one of them. Here is the list of options, given in the order in which they appear on the figure, and each identified by the current selection as shown on the figure:

- **Standard fonts**: with this menu you get one other choice, "Non-standard fonts".

- **adobe-times**: this menu will give you the choice of basic font family.

- **medium**: sets the weight of characters; other choices include light, normal and bold.

- **Roman**: sets up character angle; the other choices are italic and oblique.

- **12**: character size; other typical choices are 8 (quite small on the screen), 14, 18, 24. The default, 12, is fine for normal work, but for a demonstration of the environment to be seen by several people you may want to use, for example, 18.

- **75-75**: resolution (there are usually only one or a few values here).

As you try various combinations, the next-to-last line of the Font Box show the words **Current selected font** displayed in the selected font, so that you can see what the font looks like. Click on one of the buttons of the last line: on **OK** to apply the selected font to the current tool and get rid of the Font Box, on **Apply** to apply the font but keep the Font Box, or on **Cancel** to get rid of the Font Box with no other action.

The default font — in case you change to another but then want to revert to the original — is, usually the following: **Non-standard fonts** menu, font family **screen-bold**, weight **nn**, size **nn**, resolution **75-75**. This default may, however, change with the platform.

4.6.2 Searching for a string

The Search button makes it possible to search the text in a tool window for occurrences of a certain string.

If you click on this button you a Search panel will come up:

Type into the text field at the top the string that you want to find in the text of the tool's target. (Before starting to type you may have to left-click into the text field to make it responsive to keyboard input.) Then press the Enter (or Return) key or click on the **next** button. If there is no occurrence of the search string in the target's text this operation will have no effect; otherwise it will highlight the next occurrence of the string on or after the current active position in the target. If that occurrence was not in the part displayed in the window, scrolling will occur as needed to make it visible. Searching is not case-sensitive.

To search for successive occurrences, continue pressing Enter in the Search panel or clicking on **next**. The searching command wraps around the end of the text.

If you need to perform searches in several tools, each will have its own Search panel. In each tool the Search panel stays up until you either click on **cancel** or dismiss the tool.

4.6.3 Modifying text

The text that appears in a tool's window under various formats is in many cases editable.

The editing operations are for the most part those of the underlying toolkit. They include text entry, deletion, cut and paste.

As soon as you have made any modification to a text, the Save As button, which originally appears as 🖼, changes its shape to 🗁, a shape suggesting an open file and indicating that you should at some point (unless you have second thoughts and want to abandon the changes) save the text into a file, using one of the facilities described next.

If you attempt to quit a tool using the Quit button 🔲 or to retarget it, and have not saved your changes, a warning panel will come up to remind you that carrying out the requested operation would cause your changes to be lost:

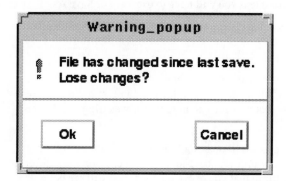

Click on **Cancel** to cancel the quit or open operation; this will give you an opportunity to save the changed text and then restart the operation. Click on **OK** to go ahead with the open or quit if you do not want to retain the result of your changes.

4.6.4 Saving text

To save the current state of the file, you may use the Save button, 🖼 or 🗁, or the Save As button 🖵.

Save will store the text into the file associated with it by default. Classes and Aces are stored in files. Using Save on a class or Ace displayed in Text format will update that file. If another format has been selected, Save will create or update a file whose name is derived from the target's name, with a suffix indicating the format. For example, if a class is stored in file *name*.**e** (the default convention), Save applied to the Ancestors format will write in the file *name*.**ancestors**.

See "CLASS FORMATS", 8.3, page 129.

In general Save is only useful if the button appears in the ▽ form, since otherwise you have not made any change to the text in the current tool. But this is not an absolute rule, as you might have made changes from outside the environment (using for example some external text editor) or from another tool. In such a case clicking on ▨ will override these outside changes and save the tool's current text into the file. Needless to say, such manipulations, where you edit the text of a development object through two or more independent mechanisms, are extremely error-prone and should be avoided.

If you want to save the text into a file of your choice, rather than into a file chosen by the environment, use Save As ⬜. (The white icon, contrasting with the shaded icon of Save, suggests that the file name is not yet decided.) In this case the File Selector, described next, will come up and enable you to specify the appropriate file name.

4.6.5 Reinitializing text

The Open button ⬜ replaces the tool target's current text by the contents of a file, which you will obtain through the File Selector.

This operation only affect the text in the current tool, not the file, if any, associated with the target. If you want to keep the reinitialized text you will have to use Save or Save As.

4.7 THE FILE SELECTOR

t A general-purpose EiffelBench mechanism with which it helps to be familiar is the File Selector, which you will use whenever EiffelBench asks you for the name of a directory or other file required by some operation. We just saw for example that it was triggered by the Open and Save As commands.

The File Selector is not actually an EiffelBench tool; instead, it comes from the underlying window system. As a result, its appearance and precise behavior may differ somewhat, depending on the graphical platform that you use, from what you will see below.

The most common operations that require using the File Selector to provide the environment with a directory or other file include the following:

S1 • Choosing a project; this is needed whenever you start EiffelBench, and was mentioned at the beginning of the Guided Tour.

S2 • Choosing an Ace file.

S3 • Using the Open command ⬜ to load the contents of a file into a tool.

S4 • Using the Save As command ⬜ to save the current state of a tool's target into a file other than the one normally associated with it.

See "STARTING EIFFELBENCH AND OPENING A PROJECT", 2.3, page 8, and "OPENING A PROJECT", 5.2, page 75.

In case S1, what the environment expects from the file selector is a directory name: the name of your project directory. In the other cases, EiffelBench expects the name of a plain (non-directory) file.

The File Selector allows you to traverse the file hierarchy of your computer system, by moving up to the parent directory or down into a selected directory. Then when you spot the file that suits your needs, you select it, exiting from the File Selector.

4.7.1 File Selector layout

Here is the general appearance of the File Selector window, captured at some point during a traversal:

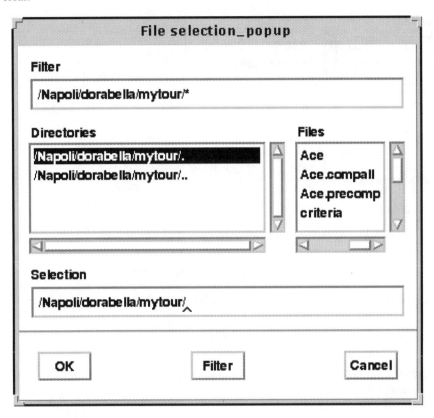

Sometimes the window is too small when it pops up, so that you cannot really see much inside; for example with a smaller window the middle part of the above might appear as:

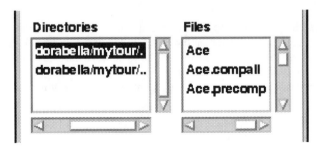

Here the directory names on the left are so truncated as to make it unclear what directories they denote. If this happens, just resize the File Selector window, using your window manager's resizing mechanisms, until the various fields are big enough. Long path names might still not fit; then use the scrollbars to see the left or right part. For example by manipulating the horizontal scrollbar [scrollbar] you can actually show the leftmost parts of the directory names in the narrow window of the last figure:

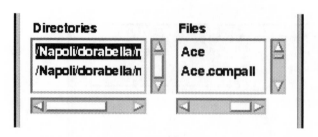

With the first of figures on the preceding page another possible variation occurs when the File Selector is used to select a directory rather than a file (in particular when you open a project). In this case only the **Directories** column appears.

4.7.2 Using the File Selector

Let us now see the various fields of the File Selector and their use. (Refer to the first figure on the preceding page.)

The top field, which reads **Filter**, indicates the current directory, **/Napoli/dorabella/ mytour** in the example, whose files and subdirectories are being offered for consideration. The final asterisk ***** means "all files and subdirectories in the current directory".

The **Files** scrollable list on the right lists the non-directory files in the current directory — **Ace**, **Ace.compall** and so on in the example. The order is alphabetical, but upper-case letters precede all lower-case letters, and digits precede all letters.

The **Directories** scrollable list on the left lists the subdirectories, using the same notion of order. In addition to subdirectories, the list contains a name ending with "/.", representing the current directory, and one ending with "/..", representing the parent directory.

If you click on a name in either the **Directories** or **Files** list, the corresponding directory or file becomes the current selection, and appears in the field that reads **Selection** towards the bottom of the File Selector window.

To move around in the file hierarchy, you may use the Filter mechanism. Click on a directory name to make it the current selection; then click on the **Filter** button at the middle of the File Selector's bottom row. (The window system also allows you to achieve the same effect by double-clicking on the directory name.) If the selected name is that of a subdirectory, this allows you to go into that subdirectory; if it is the parent name, ending with /.., this allows you to move up in the hierarchy.

The **Filter** and **Selection** fields are editable; so if the target of your search is far from your current position in the file hierarchy you may at any time enter a complete directory name in the **Filter** field from the keyboard, and click on the **Filter** button to go directly to the corresponding directory; or you may enter into the **Selection** field the name of the directory or other file that you want to select.

When, as a result of **Filter** operations or direct input, or some combination of these operations, the **Selection** field shows the name of the file or directory that you want to select, click on the **OK** button at the bottom-left corner of the tool. (Pressing the Enter key has the same effect.) This will terminate the File Selector and pass to the environment the name of the directory or other file that it needed to obtain from you.

At any time during the process, you may click on the **Cancel** button at the bottom-right of the screen to terminate the File Selector without passing any file name to EiffelBench; this will cancel the operation for which EiffelBench put up the File Selector. If you were using the File Selector at the very beginning of a session to select a project directory, the effect will be to terminate the session without further notice — since it is impossible to start a session without a project directory.

4.8 TYPED HOLES AND PEBBLES

Most of the holes and pebbles for the various kinds of development object have already been encountered in the Guided Tour or earlier in this chapter.

Here, for ease of reference, is the complete list.

Development object type	Pebble	Hole
Class	●	◖◗
Execution object	⊟⫶	⊞
Explanation	💬	◯
Feature	✚	✚
Stop point		⬡
System	⚏	⚏

The holes have been shown in their untargeted form. The input hole of a targeted tool will contain the dot representing the target; for example, a Class Hole will appear as ◖•◗.

5

Controlling a session: the Project Tool

5.1 OVERVIEW

The Project Tool comes up when you start EiffelBench. It serves as a control panel for an EiffelBench session.

The Project Tool differs from most other tools in that an EiffelBench session can have only one instance of the Project Tool. In contrast, you may create as many Class Tools, Feature Tools, Explanation Tools and Execution Object Tools as you wish. (The System Tool, however, also exists in at most one instance.)

5.2 OPENING A PROJECT

5.2.1 Starting EiffelBench

To start EiffelBench from the command line, type the command

```
ebench &
```

The **&** is not required, but will let you continue executing commands in the window from which you start EiffelBench. It is often convenient, for reasons explained next, to call execute this command from the directory where you want to keep your project.

At this stage the Project Tool comes up, with a File Selector overlaid on top of it.

5.2.2 Choosing the project directory

The form of the initial screen was shown in the guided tour of chapter 2; here it is again:

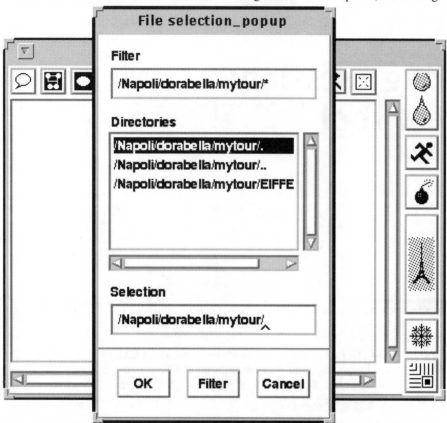

Use the File Selector, as explained in an earlier chapter, to pass to the environment the name of your project directory.

See "THE FILE SELECTOR", 4.7, page 70.

The easiest technique, as noted above, is actually to change directory to the appropriate project directory *before* you start EiffelBench, and type **ebench &** from there. Then when the File Selector comes up it the **Selection** field already shows the proper selection; this is the case above if we assume that **/Napoli/dorabella/mytour** is the desired project directory. Then you do not need to use the File Selector at all except for clicking on the **OK** button (or pressing Enter).

5.2.3 Directory requirements and trouble-shooting

You must keep in mind two requirements that the environment imposes on project directories.

First, even for a new project, the project directory must exist before you start the session; you cannot create it from within the environment.

Second, the environment keeps its own internal files for the project in a subdirectory called **EIFFELGEN** in the project directory. For a new project, the environment will create this subdirectory the first time around. If a directory with that name exists, the environment checks that it is a legitimate Eiffel-generated directory.

If a subdirectory **EIFFELGEN** exists in your project directory but it does not include the expected contents, EiffelBench will refuse to accept your project directory until you correct the problem. In such a case you will see a message of the form

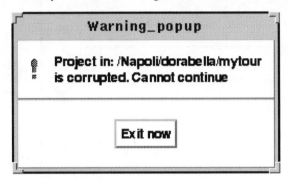

All you can do at this stage is click on **Exit now** (or press Enter). This will terminate the session and enable you to correct the problem in either of two ways:

E1 • If you want to keep the chosen project directory, you must remove the offending **EIFFELGEN** subdirectory from it. From outside of the environment (for example from the window which you used to start the session) move that subdirectory to another location in the file system, or remove it altogether if its contents are not needed. Then click on **OK** and use the File Selector to select the same project directory again.

E2 • If, however, you want to leave the **EIFFELGEN** directory where it is, you will need to select another project directory. Click on **OK** and use the File Selector to find another project directory.

Case E2 is unlikely (it assumes that you have a non-EiffelBench-related directory that absolutely has to be called **EIFFELGEN**). Case E1 is also infrequent; it could theoretically arise if a previous EiffelBench session was brutally interrupted, for example by a machine crash. The situation would have to be truly exceptional, however, since EiffelBench protects itself against such events, so that the next session will simply restart automatically from the state that resulted from the last successful recompilation.

The attentive reader will remember the criticism voiced in an earlier chapter against "Gotcha" panels, which force users into penance without giving them any way to correct their sins. The above panel is indeed a Gotcha — the only one in the whole of EiffelBench, corresponding to the only case that justifies such a panel: detecting a situation that makes it impossible to proceed in any way. Then if all the environment can do is to give up it is appropriate to notify the user first; since there is no continuation in this case the only way to guarantee that the notification reaches its recipient is to request an acknowledgment.

See "ERRORS: PRE-VENTION RATHER THAN CURE", 3.6, page 49.

5.3 PROJECT TOOL OPERATIONS

Let us now review what you can do with the Project Tool.

5.3.1 Tool window setup

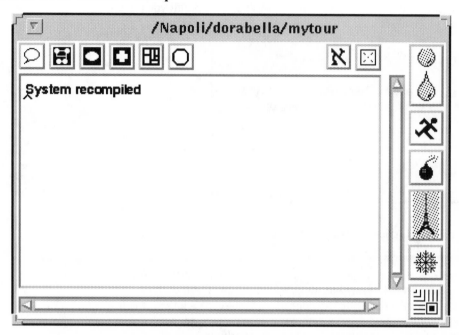

The Project Tool's window is made of three areas:

- The main area (all but the top and right borders) is used by the environment to display messages, in particular compilation errors. This area is scrollable both horizontally and vertically, so that you should not worry if, for example, a compilation produces more messages than will fit in the current window size.

- The top-left icons are holes (Explanation, System, Class, Feature, Execution Object), discussed in the preceding chapter.

- The right column contains the main operation buttons: Melt, Run, End Run, Special, Freeze, Finalize.

As in all tools, the Quit button ⊡ serves to terminate the Project Tool. As here this means exiting EiffelBench, you will be asked to confirm or cancel.

5.3.2 The holes

The icons of the top row are those which are generally applicable to tools and were studied in the previous chapter.

See "TYPED HOLES AND PEBBLES", 4.8, page 73.

As has already been noted, dropping a pebble into a matching hole of the Project Tool, or actually anywhere in the Project Tool's main area, will create a new tool of the appropriate type.

These holes, as noted, are "buttonholes": they also serve as buttons. Clicking into one of them yields a new, not yet targeted tool of the requested type. There are two special cases:

- Since there can be only one System Tool in a session, clicking on the System hole , brings up the System Tool targeted to the system's Ace or, if no Ace has yet been selected (for a new project), brings up the File Selector, prompting you to select an Ace file.

- Clicking on the Stop Point hole ◯ yields the list of active and removed stop points, if any, with the associated routine and class names. This facility is part of the symbolic debugging and run-time exploration mechanism.

On stop points and symbolic debugging see chapter 9.

5.3.3 Iconifying the Project Tool window

If you "iconify" the Project Tool window, using whatever mechanism your window manager offers for that purpose, all other open tool windows will disappear from the screen, as if everything had been collapsed into the Project Tool icon, which looks like this:

When you later de-iconify the Project Tools (by double-clicking on the icon or using any other mechanism provided for that purpose by the window manager), all the earlier tools will expand again, coming back to their previous positions.

This facility makes it easier to alternate between EiffelBench and other tools; screen real estate nowadays has become a precious commodity. It is convenient to hide all of EiffelBench with a single mouse click, and bring it back later in full just as easily.

You can of course iconify any tool individually. An iconified tool will, whenever possible, indicate the name of its target development object, as with the following iconified Class Tool:

EXAMPLE

You might in some cases want to hide the Project Tool but keep other tools of the environment visible. Because of what we have just seen you will not be able to achieve this by iconifying the Project Tool. The simplest technique is to use the window resizing mechanism provided by your window manager to shrink the Project Tool until it occupies only a small area on the screen.

5.3.4 The buttons

The buttons of the right column correspond to the main compilation and execution operations. They are the following, from top to bottom:

Melt button

Run button.

Freeze button.

Special Operations button.

Freeze button.

Finalize button.

The Run button makes it possible to run an application once it has been compiled. The Special Operations button is reserved for future uses.

The Melt, Freeze and Finalize button correspond to the three compilation modes: update a system quickly after a set of changes; regenerate object code; and produce final, optimized code. Their use is explained in detail in the next chapter.

Because Freeze and Finalize may take some time to complete, it is important to have a way of canceling these operations before they get started — especially if you have clicked on the corresponding button by mistake. (Precisely to help avoid such mistakes, these two buttons are away from the more frequently used Melt button.) Whenever you press one of them, you get a request for confirmation such as the following, for Freeze:

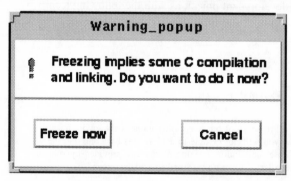

6

Compiling systems: the Melting Ice Technology

6.1 OVERVIEW: FROM COMPILERS TO CASE TOOLS

As you write the classes of a system or of a library, you will need to compile them. Compiling serves two principal purposes:

- Obviously, a system must be compiled before you can execute it.

- Even if you are still far from executing anything, however, you may already want to compile your classes. Here compiling is useful as a way to check your software and find many potential errors.

This chapter reviews the mechanisms available to compile systems, and how they relate to the rest of the environment. It will successively examine the following aspects:

- The melting ice technology: reconciling the needs of compilation and those of fast turnaround, especially in the case of large systems.

- The three compilation modes and their roles (melting, freezing, finalizing).

- How to execute a melted or frozen system, from within the environment or from the outside.

- Precompilation: compiling libraries so that they can be shared by many different developments.

- Finalization: generating optimal code and portable C packages.

- How to produce a final executable with the best possible performance.

Before studying these topics we will explore the role of compilation a little further, review the major problems that compilation raises in an object-oriented environment, and examine the concepts that lead to a proper solution.

6.1.1 Beyond programming language compilers

Of the two goals mentioned above as reasons for compiling systems, the second one (performing checks on the software), although perhaps less immediately obvious, is particularly important in the approach of this book because of the highly typed nature of the underlying language, and the many useful design rules (constraints) included in the language definition — the book *Eiffel: The Language*. Improper inter-module relations or invalid uses of inheritance, for example, will be flagged as compilation errors.

Because of the variety and scope of these rules you should not just think of compiling as an implementation step, its usual role with common programming languages. With Eiffel and the environment described in this book compilation is useful throughout the software development cycle — often as early as analysis, and continuing through high-level design as well as implementation and maintenance. In this role compilation is a system validation mechanism, performing many fundamental consistency checks.

Beyond the traditional tasks of a programming language compiler, these properties make compilation in EiffelBench cover much of the role more commonly associated with high-level CASE tools. Think of compilation, then, as your faithful assistant in getting your software correct from the start.

This help is available to you very early in the process. Because an Eiffel class may be deferred — meaning that it represents high-level abstractions, remote from implementation concerns, such as may arise at analysis or design time — you may compile a system even though many or even most of its details are missing. The earlier you start compiling your classes, the more help you will get from the environment.

6.1.2 Incrementality

This advice to start early is reinforced by another fundamental difference between EiffelBench compiling and many earlier approaches: the compilation process is (until the final stage of product delivery through finalization, which is actually optional) extremely incremental. As you understand your problem better, develop your solution, add new elements and modify previous ones, you can rely on the Melting Ice Technology to ensure that each new step only takes a compilation time proportional to the logical size of your latest increment — independently of the accumulated size of what you have developed so far. The environment thus helps you build your system layer by layer and brick by brick, keeping it at all times valid and consistent.

This chapter explains this incremental compilation process, as well as the generation of finalized code (including its C form when desired). In addition it shows how you can compile a large and stable library once and for all through the **precompilation** mechanism, which also makes it possible to distribute software components without distributing their source code.

6.1.3 An automatic process

Software systems may be complex, and during development they change continuously. Yet many compilers still require their users either to specify manually the set of modules that need to be recompiled after each change, or to maintain descriptions (Make files) of inter-module dependencies. Although clearly better than the first, this second solution still requires frequent updates to the description, and leaves open many possibilities of error.

A modern environment should rely on a totally automatic approach. Figuring out the dependencies between modules, and deducing from this analysis the smallest possible amount of recompilation that is necessary after a period of changes, is a job for computers, not humans.

The environment described in this book relies on this automatic approach. All that you will have to specify is the logically necessary information: what directories contain files for your system's classes, what class is to be used as root, and what compilation options (such as assertion monitoring) you have chosen. The rest is the business of the environment.

This automatic process is one of the most significant practical advantages of the environment. It allows users to concentrate on their own tasks — building the best possible software — and to perform as many changes as necessary, letting the supporting tools take care of the the logistics of compilation.

> In the same way that C is still used internally by the environment, Make files retain a small behind-the-scene role in the new technology: when you freeze of finalize a system, the resulting C code is equipped with a Make file, which controls C compilation and the production of an executable module. But this Make file is **generated** by the environment, not written by humans, and is normally of no direct interest to them (although you may edit it a for special purposes, such as porting a finalized C package to a platform with specific requirements). This is another example of using tools of an older technology, but with a somewhat downgraded status — not as facilities for developers any more, but as low-level mechanisms used by the environment for its own internal purposes.

6.2 THE MELTING ICE TECHNOLOGY

Apart from precompilation, EiffelBench offers not one but three compiling mechanisms: melting, freezing and finalizing. You can trigger them by clicking on one of the three buttons on the right side of the Project Tool.

6.2.1 Why three compilation modes?

Compilation should reconcile the following goals:

- C code generation: for portability, it is useful to take advantage of C in its proper role, that of a portable assembly language. C is so error-inducing and low-level as to be inadequate for use by human software developers; but its closeness to machine concepts (one of the very properties making it unsuitable for direct use), almost universal availability, and good level of standardization, make it an excellent target language for a code generator. This also enables the environment to benefit from the often extensive optimizations performed by good C compilers, and facilitates interfacing new software with the large body of existing C-based systems, tools and libraries. The final output of a compilation, then, will be a complete C package that can be ported to various platforms.

- Security and efficiency of the generated code: compiling techniques for the strongly typed Eiffel language ensure that compilers can catch many errors before it is too late, and generate more efficient code. The seventy-three "validity constraints" of the language, whose violations are caught as compilation errors, are particularly useful here, playing the role of checkable design rules.

- Quick turnaround: it should be possible to have an almost immediate transition from the time you write or (more commonly) modify software to the time when you can execute the result of what you just wrote.

In earlier environments these goals, especially the last two, were usually considered mutually exclusive. A good compiler and linker could perform extensive checking and generate good code, but this task would take a long time. Interpreters would process changes quickly, but performed few checks and usually sacrificed run-time performance.

The Melting Ice Technology, one of the principal innovations of the approach described in this book, is an effort to provide the best of the various existing techniques, while avoiding the limitations of the best traditional answer — incremental compilers.

6.2.2 The Melting Ice Principle

The idea of the melting ice is based on the observation that, for the practicing software developer, the crucial day-to-day compilation problem is not how to process an entire system but how best to process a **changed system**, of which an earlier state had previously been processed.

The change may be big or small; the system may be big or small. ("Small system" here means up to a few tens of thousands of lines.) This gives four possible cases, of which only one is really crucial:

	Small system	Large system
Small change		***
Big change		

If the system is small, as in both of the left column entries, speed of recompilation with a good compiler will be acceptable.

In the bottom-right box, the developers have spent days or weeks changing many classes in a large system, so they will not resent having to wait, perhaps until the next morning, to see the results of the recompilation. (With the technology described in this book, this case will be rare anyway, as the environment encourages you to recompile often so as to get immediate feedback from the compilation mechanism.)

The really important case — and the one that can cause most frustration — is the one marked ***: you change only a small part of a big system. Then the result should come quickly enough. More precisely:

Melting Ice Principle

The time to re-process a system after a change should be a function of the logical size of the change, not of the size of the system.

Processing such incremental changes, in time proportional to the logical size of the changes, is known in ISE Eiffel 3 as **melting**. The reason for this terminology, illustrated on the figure at the top of the facing page, is that a compiled system may be compared to a block of ice; the changes are like melted drops of water, dripping from the ice as a result of the heat generated by your work.

The Melting Ice Principle uses the notion of "logical size" of a change. This size may be different from the physical change because a small physical change in a class may have consequences in many other classes. An extreme case is a change to the Eiffel class **ANY**, of

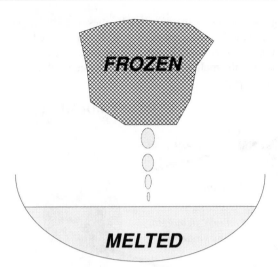

which every other developer-written class is automatically a descendant; such a change may require the compiler to inspect many other classes. But most small physical changes will also be small logical changes. In particular, the compilation will systematically detect changes that do not affect the interface of a class (for example, changes to a non-exported feature), and does not re-process clients in such cases.

Freezing is the process of putting back the melted parts into the "freezer": bringing them to the same compiled state as the parts which have not been modified.

Finalizing is the process of generating a self-contained object module that can be executed independently of EiffelBench. Another difference with the previous two modes is that finalized code is heavily optimized, making it in most cases the best choice for delivering the final version of a product, and for porting the resulting C package to other platforms.

6.2.3 Distinguishing between the three modes

The three compilation modes are complementary. The following table explains the differences:

	C code generated?	*Incremental recompilation?*
Melting	No	Yes (very fast)
Freezing	Yes	Yes (but requires C compilation of the changes, and linking)
Finalizing	Yes	No

During software development, you will alternate between melting and freezing, since both of these modes are incremental. Most of the time, you will simply melt, since melting satisfies the Melting Ice principle: the time to get a working system again is very short — proportional to the size of the changes. Note in particular that the unit of melting is the smallest possible one: each feature of a class — attribute or routine — may be melted separately. This fine level of incrementality is the key to the speed of melting.

The main difference between melting and freezing is that freezing implies re-generating C code for the changed elements, and hence relinking the system as well. In contrast, when you melt changes, you do not change any C code: it remains frozen. The environment will be able to combine the frozen part (the C code) and the melted elements. Here indeed is the full view of the picture that was previously given in part:

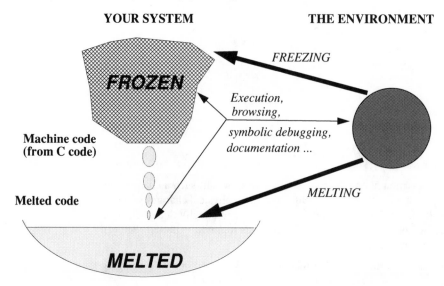

As the middle arrows indicate on the figure, you will be able, when using the environment, tto apply all its facilities for editing, browsing, documentation, controlled execution, symbolic debugging and error correcting to all the components of the system, without having to know which parts are melted and which parts are frozen. When you refer to a component of the system — for example to edit a class, produce its flat-short documentation, associate a stop point with a routine for debugging purpose, run the system, examine a run-time object — the environment will automatically know where to look for the corresponding information: the melted part or the frozen part. If one or your actions requires more elements to be melted, or more elements to be frozen, this will also be handled automatically.

As suggested by the bottom arrow, successive melting operations pour water into the bowl, corresponding to the elements that you have changed since the last freeze. Freezing, represented by the top arrow, updates the C code so that it integrates all the latest changes, emptying the bowl in the process.

Because the difference between melted and frozen code is largely invisible to users of the environment, the single term **workbench code** (an abbreviation for "code resulting from a succession of freezing and melting operations") will be used to cover both kinds. As long as you are working with the environment, you are using workbench code.

When you are happy with the results of your development, you will normally finalize the system, thereby generating **final code**. Although not strictly required, this step is in most cases appropriate since final code is more efficient than workbench code by a considerable factor; this also makes finalized code the natural choice for porting the resulting C-package to other platforms.

6.3 USING THE THREE COMPILATION MODES PROPERLY

When should you melt, freeze and finalize? The answers are simple and follow directly from the preceding overview; but they are worth a closer look, as they are the key to getting the environment to work for you in the most effective way possible.

6.3.1 Melting

Melting software elements is the bread and butter of the Eiffel developer. As you build your software, either from scratch or by modifying an existing system, you will melt regularly to benefit from the various checks that the compiler performs and, of course, to generate executable code that you can test and debug immediately.

During these repeated changes, there is no need to refreeze, since this operation (although still incremental) takes significantly more time than melting.

6.3.2 When melting is not appropriate

Only two kinds of operation require freezing:

O1 • If your software uses external (non-Eiffel) routines, such as C functions, then you must refreeze it when you add or change such external elements.

O2 • The first compilation of a new system must be a freeze unless it relies on precompiled EiffelBase.

The reason for case O1 is easy to understand: EiffelBench knows how to melt Eiffel software, but not software written in C or other languages.

Case O2 is in fact a consequence of O1: a new system will inherit from the universal class **ANY** which (through its ancestor **GENERAL**) needs some external software. If, however, you are relying on a precompiled version of **GENERAL** and other classes requiring externals , this freezing operation is not needed, since precompilation will have taken care of it once for all systems. This property allowed us in the Guided Tour to compile a system and obtain executable code from it in a matter of seconds. If, as is normally the case, your delivery includes precompiled EiffelBase, your first compilation will be equally fast. (So of course should be any later one, except if it follows an extensive set of changes.)

> For the first compilation of a system that does not use precompiled EiffelBase, the environment automatically applies rule O2: it will start a freeze even if you just click on the Melt button.

Because external features require refreezing, it is desirable, if you wish to use EiffelBench in the most effective way and take advantage of the speed of melting, to identify clearly the components which will require direct interfaces with non-Eiffel software, and to avoid modifying them too often. Spend the necessary time to develop these components properly, separately from the rest of the system. If you have to change them later, try to perform several of the necessary changes at one time. This is indeed sound methodological practice; software elements written in other languages (such as C libraries providing access to some specific facilities, or interfaces to other software systems) should be properly encapsulated once and for all in Eiffel "**wrapper**" classes. Once written, the wrappers will be used by the rest of the Eiffel software through their abstract interfaces like any other Eiffel classes, and so will only rarely need to be updated.

6.3.3 Freezing

Apart from the two cases mentioned, freezing is never strictly necessary. It is indeed possible to use melting throughout a development, never requesting a freeze after the first compilation.

As you perform additions and changes to a system and process them through repeated melt operations, you will notice that a file of name **.UPDT** in the workbench directory (*YOURDIR*/**EIFFELGEN/W_code**, where *YOURDIR* is the project directory) grows. Known as the update file, this file contains the melted code — the software equivalent of the bowl that collects the water dropping from the ice box on the figures that illustrated the Melting Ice Technology earlier in this chapter.

As the melted-to-frozen ratio grows, you may also detect a certain degradation in the time performance of the system, although this is usually not perceptible until you have a sizable amount of melted code. What counts, by the way, is how big a share of your system is melted, not how many times you melt it.

After a while, then, you may want to refreeze. There is no absolute criterion for when to do this. Some people like to start a freeze every night before leaving the office. At ISE, perhaps because we are so accustomed to the Santa Barbara climate, freezing is not very popular; for our day-to-day work we rely mostly on melting, and we freeze only every week or two, or when we need to integrate changes to external software.

Like melting, freezing is incremental: only those parts of a system that have been logically changed will be recompiled; as with melting, the determination of what needs to be recompiled is entirely performed by the environment, without any manual intervention on the developer's part.

Freezing, however, takes significantly longer than melting since in the case of a freeze C code will be re-generated for changed elements, requiring a C compilation and linking. (Melting does not generate C code and hence avoids these two steps; the only visible output of melting is an update to the **.UPDT** file.) For this reason, you are asked to confirm or cancel when you press the Freeze button ❄ of the Project Tool:

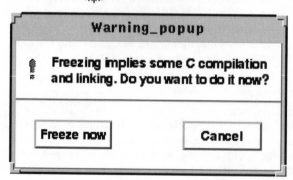

When the Eiffel part of the compilation finishes, the C compilation will be launched in the background so that you can start working with the environment again. A message in the Project Tool window tells you when this happens; C compilation messages will appear in the shell window from which you started EiffelBench. You will be able to execute the frozen system as soon as the C compilation finishes.

6.3.4 Finalizing

The main reason for finalizing a system is run-time performance of the generated system. Only with finalization will you be able to generate the high-performance executables that are such a great benefit of the Eiffel approach.

As a corollary of this property, finalized code is the best vehicle for cross-development: porting the resulting C package to various target platforms.

These two goals explain why finalization is normally useful at the end of a project, to deliver a stable and efficient production version of a product. Let us examine them in turn.

The performance benefit results from the existence of crucial optimizations that can only be performed on a system when it is in its final form, because later changes could invalidate them. Such optimizations affect both space and time:

- Typical of space optimizations is dead code removal, which strips the executable module of all the routines in the system that are not actually called, directly or indirectly, by the root's creation procedures. In a large system relying on many general-purpose classes, dead code removal can easily reduce an executable's size by one third or more.

- The gains in time, resulting in particular from the safe and systematic application of static binding to non-polymorphic calls, are even more significant, often resulting in dramatic improvements of the execution time.

As long as you continue changing, melting and freezing your system the workbench compiling mechanisms cannot perform such optimizations: if a routine is "dead" today you may resurrect it tomorrow by adding a new call to it somewhere; and if a call is non-polymorphic a single additional assignment may require dynamic binding. Compilation can only generate optimal code by working on a full, stable system. This is the task of finalization.

The second reason for finalizing is important if you are taking advantage of the environment to do cross-development: developing in Eiffel on a certain platform, and running the result on a target computer with a possibly different architecture, which has no Eiffel compiler (an unmistakable sign of its owner's backwardness) but does have a C compiler. Note that if the development and target platforms are of different architectures you will need to obtain a copy of the run-time system for the target architecture. The run-time system is also ANSI-C-based, so porting it is usually a straightforward matter.

> It is in fact possible to cross-compile a frozen system, so this second reason is not an absolute argument in favor of finalizing. In practice, however, the finalized version is usually the preferred form for porting a C package because of the performance advantage.

Finalizing is, even more than freezing, a potentially long operation for a large system; you will be asked to confirm your request whenever you press the Finalize button ⛬ of the graphical environment.

6.3.5 Command-line interface

Most of the discussion in this chapter assumes by default that you will be triggering compilations from the graphical environment, by pressing one of the compilation buttons of

the Project Tool: Melt 　, Freeze 　, Finalize 　.

A command-line interface, studied in detailed in a later chapter, is also available: command **es3**, which enables you to compile a system from outside of the graphical environment.

See chapter 10 about using **es3**. *On how to precompile libraries, see "PRECOMPILA-TION", 6.5, page 96 below.*

The form of a compilation's results does not depend on which mechanism (graphical or textual) you have used to obtain them, so that you may freely alternate between the two techniques. The only case which specifically requires one of them is the precompilation of a library, which can only be done with **es3**.

6.3.6 Compiling an entire universe

It may be useful in some cases to compile an entire universe rather than just the classes that belong to a system. This is mainly of interest as a preparation for precompiling a library.

Recall that the Ace associated with a system defines a **universe**, the set of classes in its clusters. More precisely: the Ace associates a directory with each cluster; the classes of the cluster are the contents of all files with a name of the form *name*.**e** in the directory, except for any file listed in an **exclude** clause for the cluster, and complemented by any file listed in an **include** clause. The universe is the set of all classes of all the clusters listed in the Ace.

For Ace details such as **exclude** *and* **include** *clauses, see appendix D of "Eiffel: The Language".*

In general, not all classes in the universe belong to the system, but only those which are needed by the root, directly or indirectly. (As you will remember, a class needs another if it is an heir or client of that other class.) Normally, when you compile a system, only the classes of the system proper are compiled.

To compile all the classes of the universe, specify **NONE** as the root class in the Ace. This convention is consistent with the role of **NONE** as a class that is theoretically a descendant of all classes. No useful executable is generated in this case.

6.4 EXECUTING A COMPILED SYSTEM

> ### Note: executing for best performance
>
> Although this section talks in some detail about how to execute a frozen or melted system, and how to distribute an executable version of such a system, the normal way to deliver the result of a development is in the form of a **finalized** executable module, which can be executed with no particular preparation on any compatible platform.
>
> In particular, the finalized version is the required form if you want to deliver a high-performance executable.
>
> The other execution mechanisms described below (executing a melted or frozen system) are useful to test a system during development and, if delivered to other people, as preliminary versions of a system. But they will typically execute 3 to 6 times slower than the highly optimized final version. Although this performance is in many cases still acceptable, frozen or melted versions should not be judged as representative of the speed of the system as it will eventually be delivered to its end-users.

If you have compiled a system for more than just consistency checks you will usually want to execute the result. With melting and freezing you can do so from within the environment, also it is also possible to generate an executable module and deliver it to outside parties. With finalizing you will in all cases generate such an EiffelBench-independent module.

On running a final-ized system see "Exe-cuting the result of a finalized system", 6.4.4, page 95 below.

6.4.1 Executing from within the graphical environment

A system that has been frozen or melted, but not yet finalized, can be executed from within EiffelBench.

After a melt or freeze with no compilation errors, the result is ready to run. (In the freezing case, you must wait until the background C compilation has been completed.)

To execute without having to leave the graphical environment, just click on the Run button of the Project Tool.

What you get with this Run facility is controlled execution, which is particularly precious to develop, test and debug a system. In particular, if an exception occurs during the execution of the system and would normally make it fail, the environment will catch the exception before it can cause the failure. A precise message appears in the Project Tool window and enables you, through the browsing and run-time exploration facilities of the environment, to analyze what has gone wrong. More generally, the Run facility gives you access to all the symbolic debugging facilities: you can set and remove stop points, catch exceptions, browse through the object structure. You will find the detailed description of these mechanisms in the chapter on symbolic debugging.

On symbolic debug-ging see chapter 9.

The standard input, standard output and error output of the execution use the window from which you started EiffelBench (not the Project Tool window).

You can interrupt the execution at any time by clicking on the End Run button 💣 .

When execution terminates, either normally or prematurely (through End Run), the Project Tool will display the message **Application terminated**. You can start another execution — and do so as many times as you wish — by clicking on Run again.

6.4.2 Specifying the arguments under the graphical environment

Some applications require command-line arguments, to be supplied in any session of the application by the person ("end-user") who runs the session.

The application itself will access these arguments in either of two ways, documented in chapter 3 of *Eiffel: The Language* and chapter 13 (see the discussion of class **ARGUMENTS**) of *Reusable Software: The Base Object-Oriented Component Libraries*:

• Through the argument of the creation procedure of the system's root class.

• Through features **argument** and **argument_count** of class **ARGUMENTS**.

If you run an application from within the graphical environment, as explained above, and the application requires arguments, you need a way to supply the corresponding values for any particular execution. Here is how.

If you **right-click** on the Run button 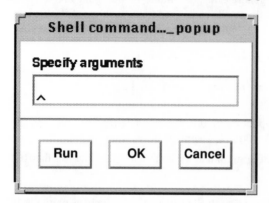 of the Project Tool (instead of left-clicking on it, which would merely run the application), you will get the following panel:

Click into the text field to make it sensitive to keyboard input and type the argument values, separated by spaces. To run the system immediately, click on **Run**; to keep the argument values for later without executing now, click on **OK**; to give up click on **Cancel**. In the last two cases the panel disappears. In the first two cases the arguments will remain in force for future runs of the system from EiffelBench, until you change them explicitly.

6.4.3 Running a frozen or melted system outside of the environment

When you have compiled an application through some combination of melting and freezing, you are not limited to executing it from the graphical environment; you can run it as a command. You can in fact deliver it to users or customers, although to give them the best possible performance you should definitely distribute them a finalized version instead.

In the rest of this discussion the phrase "workbench-generated system" denotes a system that has been compiled through some combination of melting and freezing — that is to say, not finalized.

There are four ways to execute a workbench-generated system from outside the graphical environment:

W1 • Directly from the workbench directory or a copy.

W2 • Ignoring the update file.

W3 • With the **MELT_PATH** environment variable.

W4 • With a symbolic link.

To understand these various techniques and why they are needed, two concepts are necessary: workbench directory and update file.

The workbench directory is the place containing all the files related to the workbench-related system. The path name of the workbench directory is

YOURDIR/**EIFFELGEN**/**W_code**

where *YOURDIR* is the project directory. The **W** in **W_code** stands for "Workbench mode". In this workbench directory you will find two files of particular interest: an execution file, whose name, say *systemname*, is the system name that you specified in the Ace file; and the update file.

The update file is the file called **.UPDT** in the workbench directory, already mentioned earlier in this chapter. It serves as a record of updates, that is to say of the parts of your system that have been changed and melted since the last freeze. More precisely:

- When you melt after some changes, the compiler adds a record of the melted part to the update file.

- When you freeze, C code is generated and C-compiled for these changes, so the content of the update file is not needed any more; the file is emptied, although it remains present.

To execute a workbench-generated system, you will either need to have access to the update file, or be willing to ignore any changes that may have been made since the last freeze.

The simplest technique, called W1 above, is to execute the system directly from the workbench directory. Change directory to that directory and execute

```
./systemname ... arg ...
```

This command, where *... arg ...* represents the arguments needed by your system, if any, will execute *systemname* in place. Since the update file is also present in this directory, any changes melted since the last freeze will be taken into account.

This technique also works if the execution directory, instead of being the original execution directory, is any directory that contains a copy of both the execution file (*systemname*) and the update file (*.UPDT*). Such a directory may be on any computer of compatible architecture, not necessarily the computer that served to generate the original execution file. This means you can use this approach to deliver systems to outside users, provided you include the update file and ask them to execute from the directory where they will have copied the execution file and the update file.

Of course it may be inconvenient to have to go to a particular directory, even if it is not the original workbench directory. Techniques W2, W3 and W4 will indeed work from any directory.

Assume first that you want to execute a workbench-generated system with no melted part to take into account; this may be because the last compilation was a Freeze — or, if it was in fact a Melt, that you do not want the changes made since the last Freeze to affect the current execution. Then you can just run *systemname* — the original or a copy — from any directory. (For this to be possible, the workbench directory must be part of your path, or you may call the command under its full path name, *YOURDIR*/**EIFFELGEN/W_code/***systemname*.) But you need to tell the execution not to look for any update file.

The convention to do this is simple: just add the command-line option

> **-ignore_updt**

to the arguments of the system as specified on the command line. To avoid any confusion with any other arguments that may be needed, it is usually appropriate to make this be the last argument on the command line, and ensure that the system ignores it. For example a text-processing system could be called under the form

> *systemname* **text1 font2 printer3 -ignore_updt**

where the system only uses the first three arguments, and ignores the last. This is the technique called W2 above; it also works if the command that you are executing is not the original *systemname* from the workbench directory but a copy.

It is also possible, however, even when executing from an arbitrary directory on an arbitrary computer, to take into account the changes made and melted since the last Freeze. In this case, of course, you must ensure that the execution has access to the update file. There are two ways to do this:

W3 • Set the value of the environment variable **MELT_PATH** to the path name of the directory that contains the update file (which may be the original workbench directory, or any other directory into which you have copied the update file).

W4 • In the execution directory, create a symbolic link to the update file. This is achieved by running once, from the execution directory, the shell command

> **ln −s** *YOURDIR*/**EIFFELGEN/W_code**/**.UPDT .UPDT**

(Here too, you may replace the workbench directory *YOURDIR*/**EIFFELGEN/W_code** by any directory that contains a copy of the update file.)

W3 is more convenient if you only use one Eiffel system compiled from EiffelBench. If you alternate between two or more, W4 is preferable since W3 forces you to reset **MELT_PATH** each time.

The table on the facing page summarizes the various ways of executing a workbench-generated system, and the conditions under which each one of them is applicable. The notation *... arg ...* refers to the command-line arguments needed by your system for its execution, if any.

Note that the format of the update file is platform-dependent. It is generally not possible to run on one architecture a system melted or frozen on another. For such cross-development you will need to use the portable C code generated by the environment: either the C package resulting from freezing or (much more commonly) the finalized and optimized C package, as discussed later in this chapter.

Technique	Version executed	Preparatory action	Execute from	Execution command
In-place execution (W1)	Last compiled version (Freeze or Melt)		Workbench directory (or a copy)	*./systemname ... arg ...*
Ignore update file (W2)	Last frozen version.	Include in path a directory containing *systemname* (original or copy), or give full path name for *systemname*.	Arbitrary directory	*systemname ... arg ....* **-ignore_updt**
Environment variable (W3)	Last compiled version (Freeze or Melt)	Set environment variable **MELT_PATH** to workbench directory (or to a copy)	Arbitrary directory	*systemname ... arg ...*
Symbolic link (W4)	Last compiled version (Freeze or Melt)	Make symbolic link to **.UPDT** in workbench directory (or to a copy)	Arbitrary directory	*systemname ... arg ...*

6.4.4 Executing the result of a finalized system

For a finalized system the situation is simple, since finalization always produces a ready-to-execute module.

As explained in the discussion of finalized code later in this chapter, the result of the final compilation is in a directory

Finalization is discussed in detail in "FINALIZATION", 6.7, page 107 below.

> *YOURDIR*/**EIFFELGEN**/**F_code**

One of the files in that directory is an executable binary module, which has the system's name (called *systemname* above). You can execute that module, with the appropriate command-line arguments, from an arbitrary directory. The command will simply be:

> *systemname ... arg ...*

This command may be executed from any directory of the original development computer, or of any computer of compatible architecture. The directory where the file *systemname* resides must of course be on your path.

6.5 PRECOMPILATION

Reuse is the cornerstone of the Eiffel method. Eiffel developers rely on libraries of reusable software components and, often, make their own classes reusable so as to be able to apply them to may different developments.

When building software with reusable libraries, you will not want to recompile them for every new development. Precompilation indeed enables you to compile once and for all a library or a combination of libraries. The benefits are considerable in both time and space:

- You save compilation time since the EiffelBench compilation mechanism will only concern itself with non-precompiled classes.

- Just as importantly, you save on disk space, since the space taken up by precompiled libraries is shared by all projects using these libraries. Without precompilation, every project of every developer would have to keep a compiled form of the libraries.

Precompilation also enables library developers, if they so desire, to distribute a library without distributing the source text of its classes, or with the source text of some classes only.

This section explains all the concepts of precompilation. It is divided in three parts: precompilation concepts; using precompiled libraries; precompiling libraries. The first two are of immediate interest to all developers using the environment; the last will become useful only when you have developed libraries of your own big enough to warrant being precompiled, although you may need to read it if you are in charge of installing the environment and want to precompile some libraries included, in non-precompiled form, in the delivery.

A special comment is indeed in order for installers and system administrators:

Note: precompiling libraries at installation time

Most deliveries include EiffelBase, the set of libraries of fundamental software components. In such a case the delivery always contains a precompiled version of EiffelBase, so that you will not have to worry about precompiling these libraries.

Other libraries may be included in the delivery in non-precompiled form. If some library combinations are likely to be used by many project in your installation, it is highly recommended that the installer or system administrator precompile one or more of them, preferably at installation time (although the precompilation can occur any time after that). It is also appropriate to use this opportunity to update the Ace template so that new users will naturally use precompiled libraries.

6.5.1 Precompilation concepts

The process of precompiling a library is in most respects similar to a normal compilation. But precompilation has a few distinctive properties.

When you start a normal compilation, you will only compile the classes that are needed, directly or indirectly, by the system's root. In contrast, precompilation will always compile entire clusters, whether or not they are needed by the root. (As you will recall, a cluster contains a set of classes whose texts are stored in the files of a given directory.)

Another important property is that whenever you precompile a cluster you must also precompile, in the same precompilation step, all the clusters that it needs (through client and inheritance relations).

A given project may rely on at most **one** precompiled library or (more commonly) combination of libraries. You may of course prepare as many precompiled combinations as you want, but each project must select the precise combination that it needs. Typical precompiled combinations may be:

- EiffelBase (which is used by the vast majority of applications and for that reason, as noted, is already precompiled in the usual delivery).

- EiffelBase and EiffelVision, the latter in one of the toolkit versions (such as Motif or OpenLook). Note that EiffelVision needs EiffelBase, so you cannot precompile EiffelVision just by itself.

- EiffelBase, possibly EiffelVision, and some locally developed library.

The advantages of precompilation have been mentioned above: dramatic savings in compilation time and disk space occupation. You may wonder whether there are any drawbacks. None really for the user of precompiled libraries, although we may note the following restrictions:

- To generate optimized final code, it is preferable not to use precompilation. But this property (examined in more detail below) only matters when you finalize your project, not during development.

See "Finalization and precompilation", 6.7.3, page 109.

- Obviously, in a system that uses a precompiled library, you cannot modify the precompiled classes. In some way this limitation is as much an advantage as a drawback since it enables the project leader to freeze libraries and make sure that everyone uses the same version — a good way to help promote a corporate reuse policy if there is one. (This is also of interest to instructors teaching software courses in a university.) Developers can still of course adapt classes through inheritance.

  If you do need to change a precompiled class, you will have to redo the precompilation of the library to which it belongs. This of course assumes that you have access to the source code; as noted above, it is possible to distribute a library without its source code.

Precompiled classes otherwise have the same properties as others. In particular, all the browsing facilities of EiffelBench, based on the typed drag-and-drop mechanism, are applicable in their full power to precompiled classes if the source code is available. You may of course apply all the possible compilation option, in particular assertion checking at any level, to a precompiled class as well as to any other class.

6.5.2 Using precompiled libraries

To use a precompiled library for one of your systems, you will need to include in the system's Ace file an option of the form:

---

precompiled (*"precompilation_directory"*)

Here *precompilation_directory* is the project directory that was used to precompile the library. This line appears in the Defaults paragraph at the beginning of the Ace.

The syntax of Lace is given in appendix D of "Eiffel: The Language".

The syntax of Lace includes a specific provision for Free options, which complement the universal options that should be supported by all Eiffel implementations; **precompiled** is the only Free option currently used by the environment.

When you use a precompiled library, you do not need to list its individual clusters in the **cluster** clause of the Ace file, as you would do for non-precompiled libraries. It is, however, a good idea to keep these clusters anyway; this will make it easier to switch to a non-precompiled version, in particular at finalization time.

On the facing page is an example Ace which relies on precompiled EiffelBase. It assumes that EiffelBase has been precompiled in the directory

---

$EIFFEL3/precompiled/spec/$PLATFORM/base

This is indeed the suggested directory for precompiling these libraries at installation time; the installer's manual also suggests neighboring directories for precompiling the EiffelBase-EiffelVision combination.

The example Ace describes a system with its own clusters, to which the EiffelBase clusters have been added, copied directly from file **Ace** in the given precompilation directory.

As noted above, a system can use at most one precompiled library. As a consequence, an Ace file can contain at most one **precompiled** option clause. This means that if you wish to take advantage of precompilation for two or more libraries that you often use together you should precompile all of them at once, as explained next (or ask the system administrator to do so for you).

The example Ace which follows is typical of Aces that use a precompiled library, to which they add their own system-specific clusters.

```
system

    yoursystem

root

    SOME_CLASS

default

    assertion (require);
    precompiled ("$EIFFEL3/precompiled/spec/$PLATFORM/base");

cluster

-- The specific clusters of this system:
    yourcluster : "/Napoli/fiordiligi/lastproj/dir1";
    another : "/Napoli/fiordiligi/lastproj/dir2";
    ... Other cluster specifications ...


-- EiffelBase clusters
-- (These are optional, but will serve if you go to a
-- non-precompiled version):
    access: "$EIFFEL3/library/base/structures/access";
    cursors:"$EIFFEL3/library/base/structures/cursors";
    cursor_tree: "$EIFFEL3/library/base/structures/cursor_tree";
    dispenser: "$EIFFEL3/library/base/structures/dispenser";
    iteration: "$EIFFEL3/library/base/iteration";
    kernel: "$EIFFEL3/library/base/kernel";
    list: "$EIFFEL3/library/base/structures/list";
    obsolete: "$EIFFEL3/library/base/structures/obsolete";
    set: "$EIFFEL3/library/base/structures/set";
    sort: "$EIFFEL3/library/base/structures/sort";
    storage: "$EIFFEL3/library/base/structures/storage";
    support: "$EIFFEL3/library/base/support";
    table: "$EIFFEL3/library/base/structures/table";
    traversing: "$EIFFEL3/library/base/structures/traversing";
    tree: "$EIFFEL3/library/base/structures/tree";
end
```

A restriction currently applies to the use of precompilation: the choice to use or not to use a precompiled library cannot be changed without restarting the compilation. More precisely:

Note: switching between precompilation and no-precompilation mode

If you have started a project using a precompiled library and want to go back to a non-precompiled version, or conversely, or if you want to use a different precompiled library, you must remove or rename your project's **EIFFELGEN** directory and restart compilation from scratch.

Another practical note applies if you compile from the non-graphical interface, **es3**, rather than from within the graphical environment. Command **es3** requires an operating system **ln** command before the first execution of a system using precompiled libraries. This is explained in the discussion of **es3**.

See "Using a precompiled library under es3", 10.3.4, page 168.

6.5.3 Producing precompiled libraries

Here now is how you may proceed if, instead of just using an existing precompiled library, you want to precompile a library or combination of libraries yourself.

"Library" is not a rigorously defined notion. What you will precompile is a set of clusters. As with normal compilation, the compilation will be controlled by an Ace; but here the Ace has a slightly different meaning. In all cases, an Ace lists the clusters of a system, specifies the system's root class, and gives the compilation options. What differs is the set of classes that the Ace will cause to be compiled:

- In the case of normal compilation, the set of classes to be compiled includes the root and every class which the root needs directly or indirectly. Recall that a call needs another if it is a client or heir of it.

- Precompilation, however, will always compile all classes of all clusters listed in the Ace — the entire **universe** defined by the Ace.

As seen earlier in this chapter, it is possible to compile an entire universe without doing a precompilation; the convention is to use **NONE** as root class of the system. This is particularly useful as a preparation for precompilation: you can use this facility to compile the entire set of classes that will make up the library, and use all the environment's facilities to explore and validate your library before embarking on the precompilation.

See "Compiling an entire universe", 6.3.6, page 90 above.

In both standard compilation and precompilation, of course, the list of clusters must be self-complete: if a class *C* belonging to a cluster *c1* listed in the Ace is a client or heir of a class *D* belonging to a cluster *c2*, then *c2* must also appear in the Ace. In the case of precompilation, this also implies that all the classes of *c2* will be part of the precompiled result.

Since precompilation is a potentially long operation for which the interactive graphical environment is not particularly useful, it is called outside of EiffelBench proper, using the non-graphical command **es3**. To precompile a system from outside of the graphical

*About **es3** see chapter 10.*

environment, change directory to the precompilation directory, and execute the shell command

es3 –precompile

This will perform the desired precompilation. The form given assumes that the Ace specification is in a file called **Ace** in the precompilation directory; to use a different Ace file, include the option **–ace** *filename* in the call to **es3**.

> Because precompilation will process all classes in the system's clusters, it does not matter what root class you specify in the Ace file used for precompilation. The convention is to use class **NONE** as root in such an Ace since this is the choice of class that will always — precompilation or not — compile the entire universe.

6.5.4 Moving precompiled libraries

When you precompile a library, its project directory contains everything that is needed for other systems to use it. They will refer to it through the **precompiled** entry in their Ace files, as explained earlier.

You are not required, however, to leave the precompilation pro¡ ct directory in its original location in the file system. If for any reason you need to move it elsewhere, or to make a copy and deliver it to another computer installation, you can do so without any particular precaution. Just make sure to tell the authors of projects that will rely on the libraries, so that they can set up environment variables to denote the new location.

This flexibility in moving precompiled libraries actually extends further. Assume you have an ongoing project relying on a precompiled library, whose corresponding project directory is named in the **precompiled** entry of your Ace. What if the system administrator or library maintainer moves the precompiled library to another directory?

You will in fact be able to continue using the library — the next melt or freeze adapting itself automatically to the new location — provided the directory name in the **precompiled** entry was not hardwired but used environment variables, and you update the values of those environment variables to reflect the new location. Assume for example you are using precompiled EiffelBase as suggested above, with the standard entry:

$EIFFEL3/precompiled/spec/$PLATFORM/base

Now assume that the system administrator moves the precompiled libraries (perhaps as a move of the entire installation of ISE Eiffel 3) to another directory in a new location, retaining the same local directory structure — that is to say, the precompiled library is still in the subdirectory **precompiled/spec/$PLATFORM/base**, as well it should be. Then all you have to do is to update the value of the **EIFFEL3** environment variable so that the above entry reflects the new location. (One may assume that the value of **PLATFORM** will not change.) When you trigger the next compilation, the compiler will re-evaluate all environment variables afresh, so that all will work properly.

This property applies to any **precompiled** entry that includes environment variables using the *$VARIABLE_NAME* syntax.

If you have hardwired the precompiled library's directory name into the **precompiled** entry, you have two ways to cope if the library directory is moved:

• Restart from scratch (exit EiffelBench, remove or rename the **EIFFELGEN** directory, restart EiffelBench and recompile).

• To avoid having to restart, put a symbolic link from the old location to the new.

6.6 COMPILATION ERRORS

As you compile your systems you may encounter compilation errors. Although it is preferable to avoid errors in the first place, we suggest that you treat a compilation error, in software that was prepared with great care, as a cause for joy, not sadness. Excluding the trivial case of syntax errors, a compilation error is in many cases the indication of some conceptual deficiency which — in a method, language and environment that do not enforce such static consistency constraints — would have led to abnormal results, hard-to-find bugs, unpredictable run-time crashes, or other erratic behavior. The compiler here plays the role of a computer-aided semantic verification tool for software.

Errors give rise to a message which appears in the Project Tool window. In such messages, class and routine names are clickable; this means that when you see an error message of the form

> *Some problem*, **class:** *CCC*, **feature** *fff*

you can apply the drag-and-drop mechanism to pick *CCC* and drag-and-drop it to a Class Tool, or to pick *fff* and drag-and-drop it to a Feature or Class Tool. For validity errors, as will be seen below, *Some problem* will contain error codes that are clickable too and will enable you, also through drag-and-drop, to obtain more detailed explanations.

Thanks to these facilities you can go directly to the context of an error and, in the case of a Class Tool, correct the mistake immediately and save the modified class.

> This possibility does not apply to Feature Tools since features do not have files of their own, so you cannot modify and save a feature just by itself. But you can drag-and-drop a feature to the corresponding Class Tool, edit the feature text in the class (which upon retargeting will scroll to the position of the feature and highlight its text), and save the class.

6.6.1 Syntax errors

In the case of a syntax error, a short message comes up in the Project Tool:

> **Syntax error at line** *nn* **in class** *XX*

The lines which follow the message give the context of the error in the file, as in the example that we encountered in the guided tour:

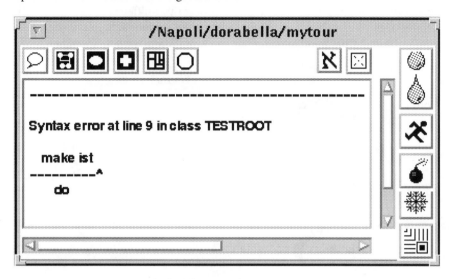

If the cause of the error is not immediately clear and you need to see more context, note that the class name *XX* (**TESTROOT** in the above example) is clickable. If you drag-and-drop it to a Class Tool (or create a new one targeted to it by control-right-clicking), the tool will be positioned in Text format at the place of the error; the offending construct will appear highlighted in reverse video. So you can go directly to the source of the problem

As noted in an earlier chapter, the reason why more elaborate error messages are not required is that Eiffel's syntax is simple; syntax errors are usually straightforward affairs such as a misspelled keyword or an extraneous symbol. By looking at *Eiffel: The Syntax*, appendix J of *Eiffel: The Language*, you will in most cases find quickly the cause of a syntax errors. If this does not suffice, please refer to the detailed language descriptions in *Eiffel: The Language*.

See "SYNTAX ERROR MES-SAGES", 2.11, page 33.

6.6.2 Validity errors

The more serious kind of error is the validity error, which results from the violation of one of the language's validity constraints.

Eiffel's consistency properties (also known as the *static semantics* of the language) are defined by seventy-three validity constraints, which express properties that syntactically correct elements must satisfy if they are to yield meaningful software. Such constraints serve to enforce the type rules (making Eiffel a statically typed language), the proper use of inheritance, information hiding principle, and other important design rules associated with the Eiffel method and language.

Each validity constraint is identified in the book *Eiffel: The Language* by a code of four letters of which the first is always V (for Validity).

Here for example is the main constraint governing repeated inheritance, of code VMRC. This is an important design rule for the orderly use of inheritance. The rule states that if you have a feature that is repeatedly inherited from a parent through two different inheritance paths, as feature **display** on the figure, and one of the two versions is redefined, then a **select** clause should indicate which one of the two versions must be used for dynamic binding.

Constraint VMRC *appears in 11.13, page 190 of "Eiffel: The Language".*

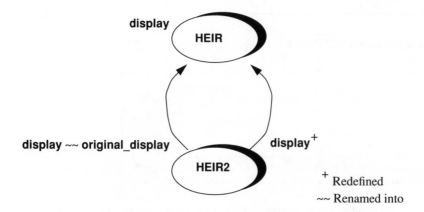

+ Redefined
~~ Renamed into

In the example, class **HEIR2**, which redefines one version of **display** inherited from **HEIR**, and renames the other into **original_display**, must list one of them in a Select clause.

Here is the formal version of this rule as it appears in *Eiffel: The language*. As many validity rules, it has been divided into separate clauses, which will be identified on error messages by numbers appended to the code, here giving **VMRC(1)** and **VMRC(2)**.

> It is valid for a class D to be a repeated descendant of a class A if and only if D satisfies the following two conditions for every feature f of A:
>
> 1 • If the Repeated Inheritance rule implies that f will be shared in D, then all the inherited versions of f are the same feature.
>
> 2 • If the Repeated Inheritance rule implies that f will be replicated in D and f is potentially ambiguous, then the Select subclause of exactly one of the Parent parts of D lists the corresponding version of f, under its final D name.

The situation illustrated on the above figure will violate the second clause of this rule if class **HEIR2** does not have a Select subclause. Here is an example of such an erroneous class, displayed in a Class Tool; in this example class **HEIR** is the class bearing that name in the Guided Tour's example.

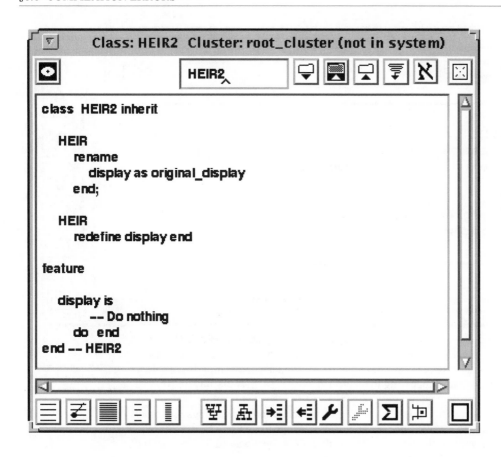

This class violates **VMRC(2)** because of the absence of a Select subclause. (A way to correct the mistake would be to add the subclause **select display** after **redefine display** in the second Parent clause, thus selecting the redefined version for dynamic binding. Alternatively, you may select the original version.)

If in the Guided Tour example you add somewhere a declaration of a feature of type **HEIR2**, making this class part of the system, and start a recompilation (normally a Melt or Freeze), the process will stop in Degree 4 for class **HEIR2** and show in the Project Tool the error message appearing at the top of the following page.

The first line of the error message gives the error code. This error code is clickable; we will see below an important consequence of this property.

The second part of the message (**Error:**) gives, on one or two lines, a short description of the error. The third part (**What to do:**) suggests a way of correcting the problem or (in some cases) several possible corrective actions.

The last part of the message, after a blank line, gives the specific information necessary to track down the error precisely: class names, feature names, where the conflicting definitions come from (here one from **HEIR** and one from the current class).

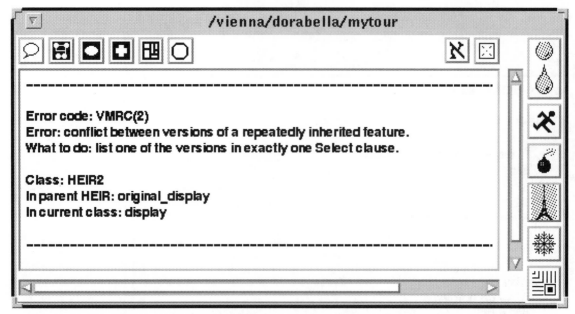

All the feature and class names given — **display, original_display, HEIR, HEIR2** — are clickable. So if you want to see a feature or class on the spot you may do so with no waste of time, simply by drag-and-dropping the chosen name. Particularly interesting is the ability to drag-and-drop a feature name appearing in an error message, such as **display** above, to a Class Tool which will show the feature (highlighted) as well as the context of its declaration. Or, in the case of a feature with a complex history of redeclarations, renamings and other transformations encountered through the inheritance process, you can use a Feature Tool to see all the **ancestor versions** of the feature. This is often the fastest way to understand and correct violations of inheritance-related rules.

On the Ancestors format of Feature Tools see "Obtaining information about the callers of a feature", 9.2.5, page 145.

Thanks to the clickability of message components, which give access to the environment's system information facilities, short messages as shown above for this example usually suffice to understand and correct the error. If, however, you do not immediately see what the error is about, you may wish to check the complete validity rule that you have violated.

This is possible thanks to the following property: the error code that appears in the first line of the short message is clickable too. It represents a development object of type Explanation. If you click on it the pebble will be of the corresponding shape: 💬.You can drag-and-drop it into an explanation hole 💬, for example the one in the Project Tool. As usual, you can also control-right-click on it

In either case you will get an Explanation Tool displaying the full text of the validity rule — for example, in the VMRC case, the complete rule as shown earlier — straight out of the latest printing of *Eiffel: The Language*. In the case of a multi-clause constraint such as VMRC, the tool shows the complete constraint, not just the violated clause, since to understand the details of a violation it may be useful to see the entire context, not just the specific clause that was violated.

6.6.3 The state of a system after an interrupted compilation

If you start a compilation, get a compilation error message, and start using the various mechanisms of the environment again — if only to explore the system and find out more about the error — the state of the system that will be available to these mechanisms is the latest consistent state, that is to say, the state that resulted from the latest successful compilation.

> A consequence is that when you first start the environment, if your first compilation leads to an error, you will not be able to use the browsing facilities of the environment. This is easily understandable, since the structures which enable these facilities to work can only be produced through compilation.

The same property applies to the case in which an EiffelBench session is interrupted by an abnormal external event — a "kill" or "quit" signal from the operating system, which is sent for example if you kill the session (using the "Break" key or otherwise) from a command shell during a compilation, or if the machine crashes while you are using the environment. In all such cases, even if the environment has been killed right in the middle of a compilation, the state resulting from the last successful compilation will have been preserved and you will be able, when you next call up the environment again, to restart from that last stable state.

6.7 FINALIZATION

Finalization, as already noted, is used to produce the most efficient executable version possible for a system, and, if needed, a C package that can be ported to various platforms

Let us look at the process in a little more detail. We begin by examining the result of a finalized system and continue with two aspects with which you will need to be familiar since they considerably affect the performance of finalized applications: use of precompiled libraries and use of assertions

6.7.1 The finalization directory

When you request the finalization of a system, either by clicking on the Finalize button of the Project Tool or by using the **–finalize** option of command **es3**, the compilation will produce a finalization directory called:

YOURDIR/**EIFFELGEN**/**F_code**

where *YOURDIR* is the project directory. The **F** in **F_code** stands for "Finalized mode".

The executable file is in the finalization directory; its name is the system name that you have chosen for the system in the Ace file. (It was referred to as *systemname* in the discussion of execution in workbench mode). As already noted, this file is a stand-alone executable which can be run anywhere on any computer of a compatible architecture.

In the finalization directory you will also find the results of the finalization in the form of a portable C package: the complete C code (**.c**, **.h** and **.x** files) and the Make file (**Makefile**) which may be use to recompile that code.

The Make file contains a reference to the file

> **$EIFFEL3/bench/spec/$PLATFORM/lib/libruntime.a**

This file is the archive containing the run-time system — the core engine that is necessary to execute a system, taking care of such fundamental tasks as memory management, exception handling, register allocation and others. To run **make** to regenerate the finalized version of the system, you need to have access to this file. If the architecture of the target computer is different from the architecture of the platform on which you generated the C package, you will need to obtain a copy of the run-time archive for the target platform, or a C version of the run-time system.

6.7.2 Porting to a different platform; the configuration file

Along with **Makefile**, you will notice in the finalization directory a file called **Makefile.SH** whose syntax is Makefile-like. This file is actually a Makefile template, which is reconfigurable for different platforms. The configuration file **config.sh**, again in the finalization directory, contains the variable substitutions that were used, during the finalization process, to generate **Makefile** from **Makefile.SH**.

The configuration file is a succession of simple definitions of values describing such properties as where the C compiler is, what version of the **grep** command should be used, whether the operating system recognizes certain signals and how it handles them, what kind of bit ordering it uses, and so on. Here is a typical extract of a configuration file:

```
                              xterm
RCSfile=''
Revision=''
Source=''
State=''
abortsig='SIGIOT'
add_log='undef'
alignbytes='8'
bin='/usr/local/bin'
bitpbyte='8'
byteorder='4321'
cc='cc'
ccflags=''
cppflags=''
ldflags=''
lkflags=''
optimize='-O'
charsize='1'
contains='grep
```

All configuration files are generated from a general-purpose one that is part of the delivery and is kept as:

> **$EIFFEL3/bench/spec/$PLATFORM/include/config.sh**

One important consequence of this mechanism is that if you are moving the C package to a new platform you can regenerate the new Makefile in a safe and systematic way by preparing a new version of the configuration adapted to the new target platform. Start with a copy of the general-purpose configuration file.

> If you do need to create a new configuration file for a different platform, you may use a utility called Metaconfig, which is in the public domain. Metaconfig performs a number of automatic tests on the target platform to determine its properties, and asks for interactive input to help find properties that it cannot determine automatically, in particular those (such as the choice of C compiler) which result from a user's choice.

6.7.3 Finalization and precompilation

A factor that developers might at first overlook may have a small bearing on the performance of finalized code: using precompiled libraries.

Although precompiled libraries are very useful, even essential, for developing a system, and it is possible to continue using them at finalization time, you should use a non-precompiled version for your final product delivery if your aim is to produce highly efficient code. The reason, roughly, is that the presence of precompiled libraries prevents the compilation process from carrying out some optimizations affecting both time performance (certain replacements of dynamically bound calls by statically bound ones) and space performance (removal of certain dead code).

Although it is impossible to give universal figures, measures that we have performed indicate a modest execution time overhead of about 8% and a somewhat higher space overhead — about 40% — for a small system finalized with precompiled libraries, as compared with the same system finalized without precompilation. The space overhead is close to the maximum possible (since the system, being small, suffers most from the presence of all of EiffelBase), and will be smaller for most realistic systems, since they will usually make more extensive use of EiffelBase. But these figures show that you do have to pay a price for continuing to rely on precompilation at finalization time.

To get maximum performance, then, you should perform the final compilation with a version of the libraries that does not rely on precompilation. To do so, use a version of the Ace that does not rely on precompilation. As noted earlier in this chapter, you will need to remove the **EIFFELGEN** directory and restart the compilation. Note that such an optimization is useful only at the very end of a development, when you are ready to deliver the final version — in all senses of the word "final" — to your customers or users.

> In light of this advice, one might question why finalization does not automatically start from a fresh, non-precompiled version of the libraries. The answer is simple: there is not always such a version! The library developer may have chosen to distribute the library in precompiled form, without including the source text. If that is the case you must use the precompiled version.

6.7.4 Assertion checking in final mode

Developers preoccupied with the performance of their final product should consider, apart from precompilation, a factor whose impact on final execution speed is actually much more drastic: assertion checking.

The importance of this factor justifies the following behavior of the environment. If the Ace file used for finalization implies some assertion checking you will get this panel:

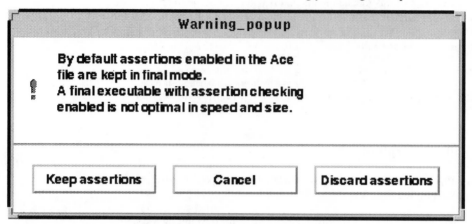

Click on **Discard assertions** if you do not want any assertion monitoring in the finalized code. This technique enables you to avoid changing your Ace, so that if you go back to melting and freezing you can use your usual Ace and have whatever assertion monitoring level you have specified for development.

> You will get the above panel even if your Ace does not include any assertion monitoring directive, since in the absence of an explicit option the default is to generate code that monitors preconditions. Only with explicit directives to disable all assertion monitoring will you not get the panel.

How serious is the impact of run-time assertion monitoring to justify such a warning? It is of course impossible to give a general answer, since the overhead depends on the actual amount of assertions that your software includes, and on the level and scope of assertion monitoring that you decide to enable. We have found, however, that enabling precondition checking on all classes of EiffelBase on a fairly typical system implies a slowdown by a factor of 2 to 3. EiffelBase classes, of course, are loaded with precondition, postcondition and invariant clauses. Even just monitoring preconditions for class **ARRAY**, for example, means that every array access or modification will check whether the index lies within the bounds. This is clearly an extremely useful facility, but it does not come for free.

Somewhat paradoxically, the overhead of assertion handling is due less to the assertions themselves than to the accompanying **exception tracing**. Exception tracing is what makes it possible, if a run-time exception causes failure of the system and abnormal termination (that is to say, does not lead to a successful Retry), to print a detailed exception trace showing the sequence of calls that led to the exception. The ability to produce an exception trace in such cases, without which monitoring assertions would not be very useful, does require, however, that the execution record trace information for every call, and implies a significant execution overhead. With all assertions discarded, the trace information is not kept; as a result there will not be any meaningful exception trace in case of abnormal termination.

An example of complete exception trace appears on page 162 as part of the discussion of debugging.

Please be sure not to misunderstand the last observation. Even with all assertions disabled, full **exception handling** is still on. Exceptional conditions such as arithmetic overflow, memory exhaustion, operating system signals or interrupts will cause exceptions which your software can handle, and from which it can recover using the full power of Eiffel's Rescue-Retry exception mechanism. All that you lose is the detailed exception trace in the case of an exception that is *not* handled properly by your software, and leads to abnormal termination. Such cases may be viewed (like assertion violations, discussed next) as bugs: situations that may arise at run time and should be handled properly but were overlooked by the design of the system.

6.7.5 Run-time assertion monitoring: the methodological perspective

Discarding run-time assertion monitoring, of course, is not a decision to be taken lightly; assertions are an essential part of the Eiffel method and you should be aware of all the arguments for and against.

First, to avoid any misunderstanding, recall that this discussion only pertains to the very last version of a system, the one that you will deliver to its end users. During development, testing, early releases and so on, you should of course enable assertion monitoring, at least at the precondition level (which is the default if you do not specify any option). This is a tremendous help for finding errors early. In particular:

- During development, you should turn on precondition monitoring for EiffelBase and other general-purpose libraries that you are using. (The theory of Design by Contract indicates that it is useless to turn on postcondition and invariant monitoring unless you are specifically looking for bugs in the libraries themselves.)

- For testing and debugging a class, turn on full assertion checking: preconditions, postconditions, class invariants and other assertion clauses.

But this does not address the question of the final version of a software product. Should you keep any assertion monitoring at all in that version? The decision is yours, individually for each system, and is based on the following pros and cons.

Here are the arguments for **discarding** all assertion checking in final mode:

D1 • If optimal performance is essential, then it is necessary to get rid of all extra baggage. Note, however, that not all applications need this full optimization and that some degradation may be acceptable if it brings some tangible benefits, such as proper error detection.

D2 • Most importantly, it is clear in the Eiffel method that any assertion violation occurring at run time can only be the result of a **bug**. As noted above, we are not talking about special conditions such as arithmetic overflow or user interrupts, which the design of your software can take into account and handle in any desired way through exception handling; final mode is no different here from workbench mode. The only cases that will lead to abnormal termination are those which result from errors in the construction or validation of the software. So the argument here is that if you have buggy software and still deliver it, it is proper that it should terminate abnormally. If you do not want this to happen, the argument continues, test and debug your software properly *before* you deliver it, using the full power of assertion checking, of detailed exception tracing, and of the high-level symbolic debugging facilities provided by the environment and described in a later chapter. But when you deliver a system it should be correct.

These arguments, especially D2, are worthy of serious consideration. But there is also a significant argument for **keeping** assertions: if you do suspect that bugs may remain, then you will need to have some information about them in case of a crash.

In the end, then, the decision is a tradeoff between two factors: how much trust you have in the correctness and robustness of your software; and how crucial it is to get the best possible performance.

Although it is impossible to give a universal rule as to keeping or discarding assertions in final mode, the following advice is always applicable. If you have any suspicion that an error, however small, might remain in software that is going into production, then:

E1 • Consider delivering two versions of the system to your users: one fully optimized, one with some degree of assertion checking. The official version is the optimized one. But if a session fails you will be able to ask the users to run it again with the assertion monitoring version, and get a precise exception trace.

E2 • Whether or not you decide to follow the previous step, always keep a workbench version of the system at your own installation. (This will be needed anyway if you continue working on future versions of the system.) Then if a user reports a failure you can try to reproduce it, and will usually be able to trace and correct the error quickly.

At ISE — where all of our products , and in particular the entire environment described in this book, are written in Eiffel, developed with EiffelBench, and compiled with the facilities described in this chapter — we have sufficient confidence in our products not to apply E1 (except in the case of experimental versions of a product that is not yet released); we do not expect tools such as EiffelBench to crash in normal usage. We do apply E2, of course, so that if an unforeseen problem occurs we can quickly reproduce and correct it.

6.7.6 Not your usual software development context

A note is in order here for developers used to other approaches, in particular C and C-based languages such as C++. Such developers are used to sneaky bugs of memory management, pointer arithmetic and the like, which come up at unpredictable times, sometimes very late in a project, and may take weeks to trace and correct.

The Eiffel picture is very different. Bugs of this kind are almost unknown; the combination of automatic garbage collection, strong typing with no loopholes (no C-like "casts"), assertions, and other safety-enhancing properties of the method, language and environment means that almost all the buts that remain, if any, are either oversights that are quickly found and corrected, or conceptual errors — wrong design or analysis decisions. Run-time assertion monitoring for a finalized application appears, in this context, as a supplementary "just-in-case" measure.

6.7.7 Generating optimal code: a summary

To avoid any uncertainty, here again are, in order of decreasing impact on optimization, the three steps that you must take if you are concerned about getting the most efficient executable system out of your compilation:

See also chapter 11, which discusses in more detail how to obtain optimal run-time performance.

• Generate finalized code, not workbench code (but of course use the workbench to develop it, and generate workbench code for all but the last, delivered version).

• In the final version, remove all assertion monitoring.

• In the final version, do not use precompiled libraries.

7

The System Tool: describing a system

7.1 OVERVIEW

An EiffelBench session works on a system — an assembly of classes, spread over a number of clusters, which will eventually generate an executable module.

The specification of where to find the clusters and how to process their classes is given by a system description also known as an **Ace** file, where the name stands for Assembly of Classes in Eiffel. Such system descriptions are written in a small Eiffel-like language called **Lace** (Language for the Assembly of Classes in Eiffel), described in Appendix D of *Eiffel: The Language*.

To create, examine and change Ace files you may use the System Tool of EiffelBench, which also provides a convenient way to examine the overall structure of a system. This chapter describes the System Tool and explains how to use it to construct a system, explore it, and specify the various options (compilation, generation) that you may require.

7.2 HOW EIFFEL SOFTWARE IS ORGANIZED

Here is a quick refresher on the overall organization of software in Eiffel. For a complete presentation of the concepts you will of course have to refer to *Eiffel: The Language*.

7.2.1 The notion of system

EiffelBench, and more generally Eiffel, allow you to work on a **system**. A system is made of one or more classes. One of the classes in the system is designated as the **root class** and one of its creation procedures as the root creation procedure. (Any Eiffel class may have one or more creation procedures; the instruction which creates an instance of the class then specifies one of the creation procedures, which will serve to initialize the newly created instance.)

A valid system is executable. To execute it means to create an instance of the root class and to apply the creation procedure to that instance. The creation procedure, which plays a role similar to that of a test driver in more traditional approaches, will normally create other objects and call further features.

7.2.2 The root and its needed classes

If you submit to the environment a set of classes, with a designated root class and root creation procedure, they do not necessarily make a satisfactory system. Additional conditions are required:

- Obviously, the classes must comply with the syntactic rules of the language and the validity constraints.

- They must satisfy a completeness property: all the classes which the root **needs**, directly or indirectly, must be present in the system. Clearly if such a class were missing it would be impossible to assemble the system.

The completeness condition is addressed by two of the validity rules in "Eiffel: The Language": VLCP and VTCT.

Here a class *A* is said to need a class *B* directly if *A* is either a client or an heir of *B*. So by taking the suppliers and parents of the root (the classes of which it is a client or heir, respectively), then their own suppliers and parents, and so on iteratively until all the resulting class set does not need any outside classes, we can find all the classes of a system.

7.2.3 The universe

How do we enable the environment and in particular the compiling mechanism to find the root and all the classes which it needs, so as to assemble a system?

The four key notions are class file, cluster, directory and universe.

First, we need a way to store each class in the file system. The solution is simple: each class must be in a separate file, called a **class file**. For clarity and simplicity, a standard convention is recommended for naming class files: store the text of a class called *NAME* in a file called *name*.**e**, where *name* is the lower-case version of *NAME*.

A note to users of ISE Eiffel 2.3 and earlier versions: in those versions the preceding suggestion — keep every class called *NAME* in a class file called *name*.e — was actually a requirement. This constraint is no longer enforced; the class file names may be arbitrary. It is of course wise to choose file names that recall the class names, and what was previously the required rule remains the suggested policy, especially on platforms which do not impose stringent limitations on the length of file names.

Grouping mechanisms, coming from different backgrounds, are available for both classes and files:

- The Eiffel method suggests grouping classes into **clusters**. A cluster is a set of closely related classes.

- The operating system groups files in **directories** with a hierarchical structure; a directory is a set of files, of which some are plain files (such as class files) and others are directories with again the same structure.

EiffelBench takes the natural consequence and, in the same way that it associates a class file with each class, associates a directory with each cluster. Conversely, any directory defines a cluster: the set of all classes whose texts are contained in the directory's class files. (By default the class files of a directory will be all those whose names end with **.e**, although Lace, as seen below, makes it possible to extend this convention if desired.)

Now take a set of directories. It defines a set of classes called a **universe**, containing all classes of any of the clusters associated with the given directories. In other words, the classes of the universe are the contents of all the class files (by default, all the **.e** files) in these directories.

An Eiffel system, then, will be built out of a universe. You must provide EiffelBench with three elements of information:

- The name of the system's root class.

- The name of the creation procedure.

- A set of directories, each defining a cluster, and together defining a universe.

This system description is valid only if the root, and every class on which it depends directly or indirectly, are part of the universe. It will enable EiffelBench to assemble and compile the system, starting from the root and looking repetitively for needed classes until any class needed by a class of the system is already itself in the system.

7.2.4 Lace

A system description containing the above elements is called an Ace; the EiffelBench's System Tool is devoted to the construction and manipulation of Aces. Lace is the notation used to write Aces.

Lace is Eiffel-like and easy to understand. There is usually no need to write an Ace from scratch; the normal way to work is to start from an Ace template, provided by the environment, and fill in any addition or modification required by your system. The guided tour showed a typical Ace; you will see a variant of it in a System Tool below.

Every Ace must include the three elements of information listed above. In addition, you may use Lace to give various directives to EiffelBench. Examples include:

See appendix D of "Eiffel: The Language" for the complete list of Lace clauses and options.

- For any cluster, exceptions to the *name***.e** naming rule: files with a *name***.e** name which must be excluded from the class files (**exclude** directive of Lace), and files with non-conforming names which must be included in the class files of the cluster (**include** directive).

- Compilation options specifying the level of run-time assertion checking (**assertion** option) and debugging level (**debug** option).

- Use of precompiled libraries (**precompiled** directive).

- What classes should be made available, in a generated C package, for calls from non-Eiffel software (**visible** clause).

7.3 CREATING THE ACE FOR A NEW PROJECT

The System Tool allows you to create and modify the Ace for your system. As soon as the system has been compiled, the System Tool also gives you access to important information about it.

When you create a project, you must provide it with an Ace to start the first compilation.

You may do so by clicking on the system hole ▓ of the Project Tool. Alternatively, if you request any compilation operation (by pressing the Melt, Freeze or Finalize button, although the last is unlikely for a new project) and you have not specified an Ace yet, you will be asked to do so.

In all cases the following panel appears:

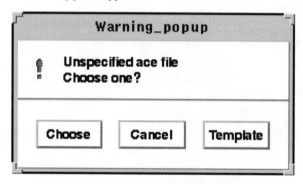

Click on one of the three buttons of the panel:

S1 • Press **Template** if you do not have a ready Ace file, and want to work from the Ace template provided as part of the installation. Your system administrator may have adapted this template so as to include the most appropriate options for your installation, in particular precompiled libraries. The template, in case you ever want to examine it, is the file called **Ace.default** in the directory **$EIFFEL3/bench/help/defaults**.It appears later in this chapter, filled with the options corresponding to the Guided Tour system.

See "ADAPTING THE DEFAULT ACE", A.5, page 236.

S2 • Click on **OK** if you have an Ace file ready (not necessarily in final form, however: you will be given the opportunity to edit it). The File Selector, studied in an earlier chapter, will pop up and enable you to select the desired Ace file.

On the operation of the File Selector see "THE FILE SELEC-TOR", 4.7, page 70.

S3 • Click on **Cancel** if you changed your mind and want to cancel the requested operation.

In cases S1 and S2, the System Tool will come up, showing the text of the selected file, which you can edit if necessary. In case S1, in particular, the template is not directly usable as it is; you must fill in the name of your system, the root class, the root creation procedure if any, and the root cluster.

If you do make changes, save them by clicking on the Save button (▽ after a modification, ▓ after a Save) of the System Tool. In case S1, where you started from the template, this will by default create a file called **Ace** in the project directory; if you prefer a different file, use the Save As button ⌨ instead of Save; this will bring up the File Selector so that you can use the file name that you wish.

Once you have saved the Ace file, its content becomes the Ace associated with the project. If you later click on the system hole of the Project Tool, in the same EiffelBench session or in a later session using the same project, the System Tool will come up, showing the current contents of the Ace file.

Note: changing the Ace file selection

Once you have selected an Ace file for a project, you may not change that selection. You may change the *contents* of the Ace file, of course (for example to add clusters, change options or correct errors), but you may not use a different file.

If, when creating a project, you select the wrong Ace file from the File Selector, or (using the template) save the Ace into the wrong file, you should restart in the following way:

• Exit from EiffelBench.

• In the project directory, remove the entire **EIFFELGEN** directory (or move it to some other location).

• Start EiffelBench again and make the correct Ace file selection.

7.4 SYSTEM TOOL OPERATIONS

The System Tool makes it possible to edit the Ace file for your system. It also provides a global view of your system, cluster by cluster, serving as a starting point for browsing operations.

7.4.1 Tool window layout

The organization of the System Tool's window is shown on the figure of the following page.

As in all tools, the Quit button ⦂⦂ at the top right serves to terminate the System Tool. You can bring it back later by clicking again on the system hole ▦ of the Project Tool.

In the row of buttons at the top right, you will find the tool-independent buttons which were reviewed in a previous chapter: Open ⌨, Save ⌨ ▦, Save As ⌨, Search ⩮ and Font 𝕏 .

Also as in other tools, the Shell button at the bottom-right ☐ enables you to start an editor session or some other command on the Ace file.

At the bottom left, you find the only two tool-specific buttons, controlling the format under which the system specification is displayed:

≡   Text format (the default, appearing as always at the bottom-left).

▤   Clusters format.

7.4.2 Text format

The Text format shows the Lace system description. You may edit it to change the properties of the system, for example to add or remove a cluster, and to change compilation options. Make sure you save the Ace after such a change if you want it to be taken into account.

Here is a System Tool showing the Text format for an Ace obtained from the template by just filling in the compulsory information (system name, root class, creation procedure):

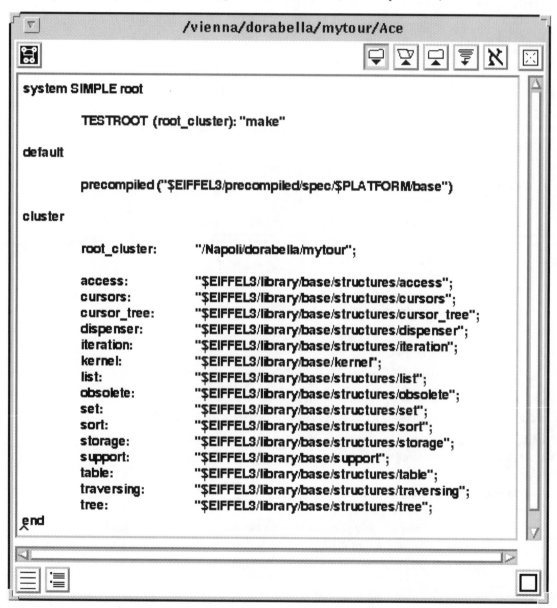

```
/vienna/dorabella/mytour/Ace

system SIMPLE root

        TESTROOT (root_cluster): "make"

default

        precompiled ("$EIFFEL3/precompiled/spec/$PLATFORM/base")

cluster

        root_cluster:        "/Napoli/dorabella/mytour";

        access:              "$EIFFEL3/library/base/structures/access";
        cursors:             "$EIFFEL3/library/base/structures/cursors";
        cursor_tree:         "$EIFFEL3/library/base/structures/cursor_tree";
        dispenser:           "$EIFFEL3/library/base/structures/dispenser";
        iteration:           "$EIFFEL3/library/base/structures/iteration";
        kernel:              "$EIFFEL3/library/base/kernel";
        list:                "$EIFFEL3/library/base/structures/list";
        obsolete:            "$EIFFEL3/library/base/structures/obsolete";
        set:                 "$EIFFEL3/library/base/structures/set";
        sort:                "$EIFFEL3/library/base/structures/sort";
        storage:             "$EIFFEL3/library/base/structures/storage";
        support:             "$EIFFEL3/library/base/support";
        table:               "$EIFFEL3/library/base/structures/table";
        traversing:          "$EIFFEL3/library/base/structures/traversing";
        tree:                "$EIFFEL3/library/base/structures/tree";
end
```

The root class name (here **TESTROOT**) and other class names that may appear in the Ace are clickable. To start a Class Tool on a certain class, control-right-click on its name. You can also drag-and-drop a class name into a Class Tool.

This example also illustrates the basics of Lace. **TESTROOT** is the name of the root class; **make** is the name of the root creation procedure; the **cluster** clause serves to list the various clusters and their directories.

The system must have a name, here **SIMPLE**; by default the executable files generated for that system will have the corresponding name (in lower case), in the subdirectory **EIFFELGEN/W_code** of the project directory in workbench mode, and **EIFFELGEN/F_code** in final mode.

Each cluster must be given a name (such as **kernel** or **root_cluster** in the example) which is followed by a colon and the name of the associated directory, in double quotes. The directory names may use the values of environment variables, such as **$EIFFEL3** and **$PLATFORM**. The cluster specifications must be separated by semicolons.

The Ace does not explicitly specify any compilation option. As a result, assertion monitoring will be enabled for all classes at the default level: monitor preconditions only.

The example deserves another comment. If you remember the Guided Tour, you will notice that the above Ace can indeed be used to compile the Guided Tour system, although the earlier Ace was simpler. There are two differences, both significant:

The original Ace for the Guided Tour was shown on page 13.

- The directory for **root_cluster** in the Guided Tour Ace was given simply as **"."**, meaning the current directory. This is fine if (as suggested) you start the Guided Tour project directly from the corresponding directory. But if you want to be able to start a project session from any directory, you need a full path name (as **/Napoli/Dorabella/ mytour** here), since **"."** would denote the directory from which the session is started.

- The **cluster** clause of the Guided Tour Ace only listed the root cluster, and omitted the clusters of the EiffelBase libraries. They are indeed not required since in both cases the system relies on precompiled EiffelBase (see the **precompiled** clause). It is preferable to include them, however, if at the end of the project you want to generate a finalized version that does not rely on precompilation — a step recommended in the previous chapter for maximum performance. For that reason the template Ace includes all the clusters of Base even though it also specifies the use of precompiled Base.

7.4.3 Clusters format

The other format for a System Tool is the Clusters format, given by the second button from the left in the format row: ⠿.

Under this format, the system description appears as a list of clusters with, for each cluster, the list of all classes that it contains. The figure on the next page shows the beginning of the System Tool in Clusters format for the Guided Tour system.

The names given for the clusters are those which appear in the Ace.

All the class names are clickable, allowing you to start a new Class Tool on any class (by control-right-clicking) or to retarget an existing Class Tool (by drag-and-dropping the class name to the tool)

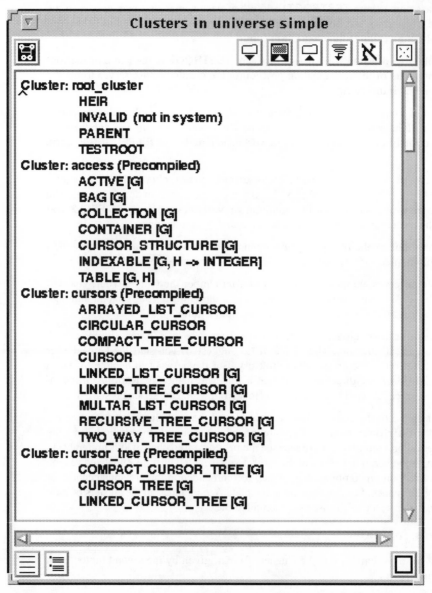

For generic classes (except if "not in system", as explained next) the format shows the list of formal generic parameters. If one of the parameters is constrained, the constraining type is also shown; this is the case with **HASH_TABLE** on the figure.

As with all formats for any tool, you may save the Clusters format of a system description into a file. If you use the Save button, the resulting file will be called *name*.**clusters** where *name* is the name of the Ace file; use Save As if you prefer a different file name.

The System Tool is not editable in Clusters format: in other words, you may not make any change. To change the system description, go back to Text format.

If you request the Clusters format on a system that has never been compiled — for example during the very first session for a new project — this will produce a blank window since in the absence of any compilation information the environment does not know anything about the clusters of the system. In this state only the Text format is meaningful, enabling you to view and modify the Ace text. The Clusters format becomes available after the first compilation.

7.4.4 "Not in system" classes

In the System Tool displayed under Clusters format, some entries may bear the mention **not in system**, signaling classes that are in the universe but not in the system.

In the above example this is the case with class **INVALID** in the root cluster. As you may remember, this class served to illustrate the handling of validity errors in the Guided Tour. Here it has been removed from the system; in other words, neither the root class **TESTROOT** nor any class reachable directly or indirectly from the root contains any reference to it. (To use the more precise terminology introduced earlier, the root does not need it, either directly or indirectly.) The class file containing its text still exists, however, in the root cluster directory, and is not removed from the universe by an **exclude** clause in the Ace. So the class is part of the universe but not of the system.

The example involving class **INVALID** *was in "A VALIDITY ERROR", 2.12, page 34.*

You can still see the text of such a class by targeting a class tool to it, for example by drag-and-drop, but you will not be able to submit it to any other operation. In particular you will not be able to display the class under the other formats presented in the next chapter, such as Ancestors or Flat, since those formats require information that is only available for a compiled class. For the same reason, the class and feature names that appear in the Text format applied to a "Not in system" class are not clickable.

If you want to apply the full scope of the environment's mechanisms to such a class, you must insert it into the system. (In the case of **INVALID** you must of course correct the validity error first, so that the class will not deserve its name any more.) A simple way is to re-melt your system after adding somewhere a reference to the class, for example a function declaration of the form

```
auxiliary: INVALID is do end;
```

8

Class Tools:
browsing through software

8.1 OVERVIEW

The class is the most important notion in the Eiffel method and language, so it is not surprising that developers using the environment spend much of their time using Class Tools.

Class Tools serve to create and modify classes; they also are also essential for browsing — exploring the various components of a system to find out quickly about their properties and their relations.

Browsing relies on all tools of the environment, especially the System, Class and Feature tools, but Class Tools provide the most important functionalities. This is made possible in particular by the wide range of formats available in a Class Tool, which give access to all the information about the context of a class — features of various kinds, ancestors, descendants, clients, suppliers. The formats of Feature Tools, studied in the next chapter, provide important complementary mechanisms.

This chapter describes in detail the facilities offered by Class Tools and their application to browsing.

8.2 CLASS TOOL OPERATIONS

You may create as many class tools as you wish during a session of the environment.

8.2.1 Tool window organization

The following figure shows a typical Class Tool, targeted to class **GENERAL** — the highest-level class, of which every Eiffel class is a descendant.

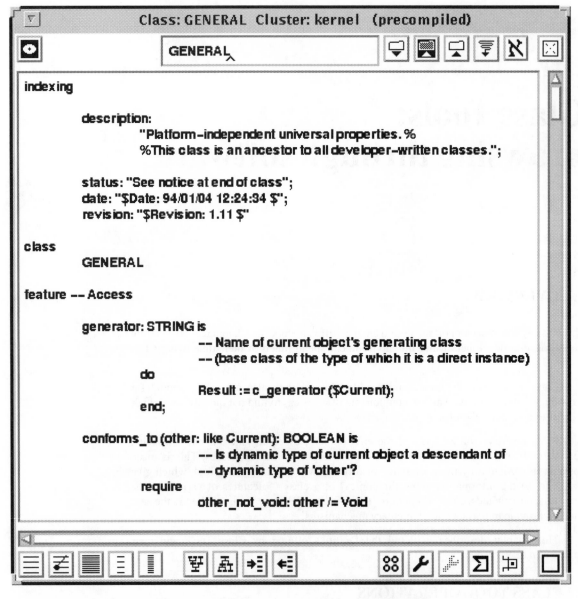

The tool window organization is the by now familiar one. The buttons on the top row were reviewed in the discussion of tool-independent buttons. At the top left appears the class hole ⬡, into which you may drop class pebbles or (as will be seen below) feature pebbles. At the top right is the Quit button ⊡, which you can use to terminate the Class Tool. At the bottom-right is the Shell Command button, □, which makes it possible to call an arbitrary command on the class file — by default the **vi** editor.

See "GENERAL TOOL ORGANIZATION", 4.4, page 62.

Since the above tool is targeted, its top-left Class hole includes the tiny dot that represents the underlying class. So if you need to drag-and-drop that class you can pick it in this hole. This will be convenient if the display, unlike here, is positioned far from the beginning of the class, at a place where the class name does not appear.

8.2.2 Retargeting to a class or a feature

You may retarget a Class Tool to another class, using the drag-and-drop mechanism.

You may also drag-and-drop a feature to a Class Tool. This will retarget the tool to the routine's class and show the routine text highlighted in it, as in the following example where procedure **copy** from class **GENERAL** has been dragged to a Class Tool.

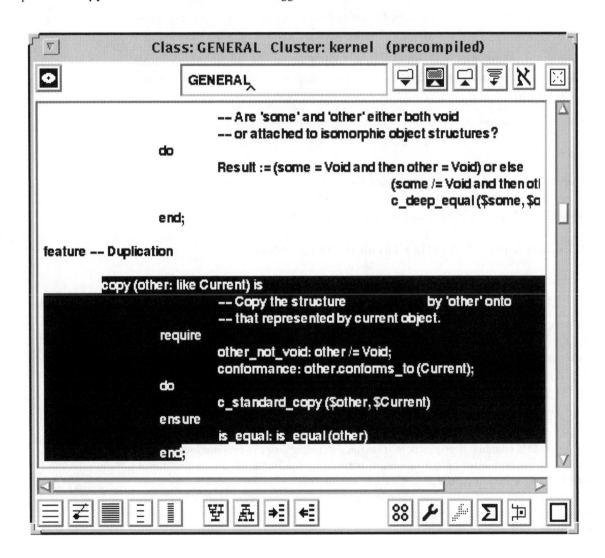

The name of the feature that is dropped into the Class Tool may have been picked anywhere: in another Class Tool displayed under a different format (for example the Feature format seen below) or in a Feature Tool.

This ability to drop a feature in a Class Tool is particularly useful when you spot a feature somewhere and want to see its declaration but also the context of that declaration — the enclosing class. The text shown in the Class Tool extract will not necessarily be the beginning of the class text; it starts a few lines before the feature declaration.

Here is a typical application. You are exploring a class text in a Class Tool and see a feature call of the form **x.f (...)**. You are not quite sure what **f** does. To find out:

- Make sure that the Class Tool is in Clickable format (a format which, as explained below, makes just about everything clickable, including a feature appearing in a call).

- Click on **f** and drag-and-drop it to an existing Class Tool; you can use the original Class Tool for that purpose but it is preferable to use another one so as to keep the original context active.

- The new Class Tool shows the text of **C** (the class serving as base type for **x**), at the place of the declaration of **f**, giving you immediately the desired declaration as well as its context.

In this example we are using two Class Tools: one to explore a class of interest, the other two explore various properties of the features of the class. As you will probably find out for yourself, this technique is useful in many different cases.

8.2.3 Class Tool retargeting through name input

To retarget a Class Tool you may also use another convenient mechanism: just typing in the name of the desired class.

In any Class Tool, the field in the middle of the top row, just below the upper border, is called the class name field. It indicates the name of the tool's current target; here it is for the last example:

This field is editable. If you click in it (to make it responsive to keyboard input), enter the name of another class of the universe, overwriting the name of the current target (**GENERAL** in the example), and press the Enter key, the tool will be retargeted to the chosen class. You may use lower case as well as upper case for typing the letters of the class name. While editing the text you can use Backspace to erase letters of the original name, or double-click to replace the entire name at once.

Double-clicking is a mechanism of the underlying toolkit, not of EiffelBench. As noted, EiffelBench proper does not use double-clicking.

You can also use this facility to create a new class from within EiffelBench. Assume that you enter the name **my_class**, and there is no such class in the system or the universe. The following panel will come up:

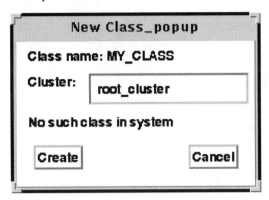

If this was an error, click on **Cancel**. But if you want to use the opportunity to create a new class in the current cluster, click on **Create**. EiffelBench will create a new class file in the given cluster, of name **my_new_class.e**, and retarget the class tool to the newly created file, which contains just an empty (but syntactically correct) class skeleton:

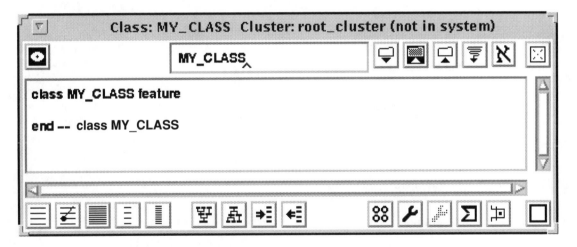

If you started from a previously targeted Class Tool, the **Cluster** field of the New Class panel (the first of the two preceding figures) shows the name of the cluster containing the original target. In this example the retargeted Class Tool was initially targeted to class **TESTROOT** from the Guided Tour example; so the **Cluster** field showed the name of its cluster: **root_cluster**. That field is also editable; so before you click on **Create** you may type the name of another cluster in the universe. This allows you to create a new class in any cluster, not just in the cluster of the original target class.

The cluster must exist, however; you may not use a Class Tool to create a new cluster. To add a cluster to your system, edit the Ace using the System Tool, and melt.

If you started from a Class Tool that was not initially targeted (obtained for example by clicking on the Class hole of the Project Tool) the **Cluster** field will initially show **<cluster name>**, which you should replace by the name of one of the clusters of the system.

If the name that you enter in the **Cluster** field is not the name of an existing cluster, clicking on **Create** will have no effect; correct the entry and click again on **Create**, or click on **Cancel** to cancel the retargeting. If you need to see a list of the available cluster names, bring up the System Tool in either format.

8.2.4 The format button row

The formats available in the Class Tool are reviewed in the next section. Here, for ease of reference, is the complete list, each with its default file suffix (whose use is explained later).

Text (the default, appearing as always at the bottom-left). Suffix: **e**.

Clickable form. Suffix: **clickable**.

Flat form. Suffix: **flat**.

Short form. Suffix: short.

Flat-short form. Suffix: **flatshort**.

Ancestors. Suffix: **ancestors**.

Descendants. Suffix: **descendants**.

Clients. Suffix: **clients**.

Suppliers. Suffix: **suppliers**.

Attributes. Suffix: **attributes**.

Routines. Suffix: **routines**.

Deferred features. Suffix: **deferred**.

Once routines. Suffix: **once**.

External routines. Suffix: **externals**.

8.3 CLASS FORMATS

The formats available for a Class Tool belong to three categories, corresponding to the three separate button groups that appear in the format row at the bottom of each Class Tool ⊟ ▤ ▤ ▮ ▯ ▯ ▯ ▯ ▯ ▯ ▯ Σ ▯ :

- Representations of the class text.
- Information about related classes.
- Information about the features.

The Text format is applicable to all classes except those for which the class file is not available. Two reasons might make the class file unavailable: the class may be part of a precompiled library which has been distributed without the source code; or the class file may have been made unreadable to you, voluntarily or not. (As an example of the voluntary case, professors have been known to make the source text of classes unreadable to students to encourage them to use classes on the basis of more abstract specifications, such as the flat-short form studied below.)

Students have also been known to make class texts unreadable to professors, for reasons about which one can only conjecture.

Formats other than Text are only available for a class that is part of the system — that is to say, has been compiled.

Note: computation time for Flat and Flat-short formats

In most cases, producing a class format is a fast operation. The Flat and Flat-short formats, however, take significantly longer to compute. On a class with more than a few ancestors you may expect a waiting time of 30 seconds or more when requesting either of these formats.

8.3.1 Saving and editing

Under all formats, you can save the contents of the tool window into a file using the Save or Save As button.

Use Save As ⊡ to save into a file or your choice, determined with the help of the File Selector.

The File Selector was presented in "THE FILE SELECTOR", 4.7, page 70.

If you use the Save button (▽ or ▣), the generated file will have a name of the form *prefix.suffix*, where *prefix* is the name of the class file (usually of the form *prefix*.**e**) deprived of its last two characters, and *suffix* characterizes the format; the list of suffixes was given earlier. So in the Guided Tour directory or a copy, where **TESTROOT** is stored in a file of name **testroot.e** (following the standard convention whereby the class file for a class *NAME* has the name *name*.**e**, that is to say *prefix* is the lower-case version of *NAME*), saving the Ancestors format for that class will yield a file called **testroot.ancestors**.

Only in Text format are the contents of the tool editable (changeable). All other formats are read-only.

8.3.2 Basic representations of the class text

The Text format $\equiv$ shows the text of the target class exactly as it appears in the class file.

The Flat format $\equiv$ gives the flat form of the target class. The flat form, an important concept of the Eiffel method, gives a reconstructed version of a class, equivalent to what would have been written in the absence of inheritance. All features inherited from ancestors, however distant, are included at the same level as the immediate features (those introduced in the class itself), taking into account any renaming and redeclaration that may have occurred; the invariant is reconstructed as the concatenation of the ancestors' invariants and of the class's own; routine preconditions and postconditions are given in full, integrating the result of any *require else* and *ensure then* clauses.

The Clickable format $\rlap{\rule[0.5ex]{1em}{0.5pt}}\rlap{\rule[0.25ex]{1em}{0.5pt}}\neq$ is similar to the Text format but makes many more elements of the class clickable. In particular, a feature (attribute or routine) is clickable not only in its declaration (as in Text format) but wherever it appears in a call as target, feature or argument of the call. So for example if **x** is an attribute, **r** a procedure and **a** an attribute or function without arguments, all three of them are clickable in the call **x.f (a)**.

To appreciate the difference between Clickable and Text formats consider the following extract from the Guided Tour's **TESTROOT** class, displayed in a Class Tool:

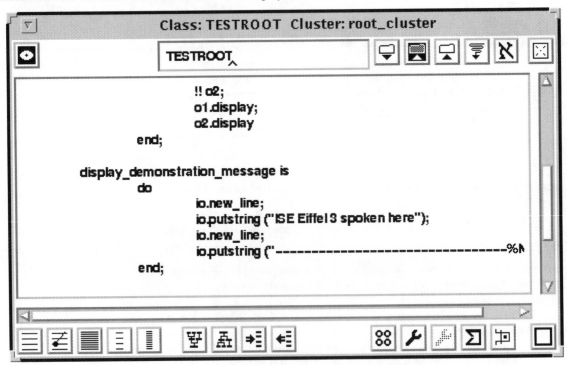

This display is the same in Text and Clickable format. In Text format, the only clickable element in the extract shown is **display_demonstration_message** in its declaration. But in

Clickable format you may perform a drag-and-drop operation on any of the feature names that appear in the text of the routine: **io, new_line, putstring**. In the text of the preceding routine (**make**), whose last few lines appear in the first part of the window, you can similarly click on the names of procedure **display** as well as those of **o1** and **o2**, both of which are attributes of the class. Only local entities of a routine are non-clickable.

The Clickable format is extremely useful when you want to find out about the properties of a feature at a place where it is called, or used as the target of a call. Assume for example that you see one of the above calls to **new_line** and want to know more about this feature. Without even searching for the declaration of **io** (which actually comes from a proper ancestor of the current class) you can simply click on **new_line** in one of the calls:

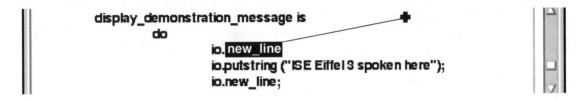

If you then drop the cross into an existing Class Tool, or, if none is available, into the Project Tool so as to create a new Class Tool, the result will show the class **STD_FILES**, corresponding to the type of **io**, positioned at the declaration of **new_line** which it shows highlighted:

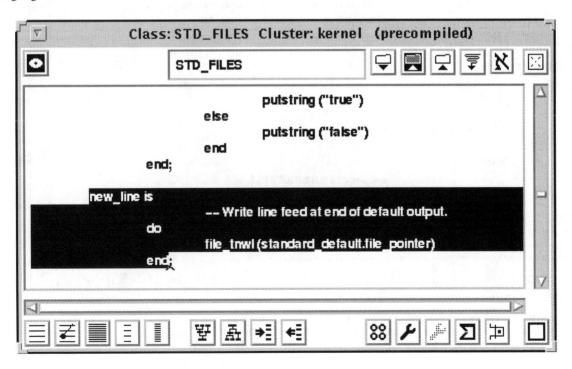

8.3.3 Short, flat and flat-short forms

The Short format Ξ gives an abstract form of the target class, useful for implementation-independent documentation. It is obtained from the class text by removing all implementation information: non-exported or selectively exported features, and routine bodies (***once***, ***do*** and ***external*** clauses). For each exported feature, the short form retains the feature name, the signature (arguments and result if any, their types), the header comment, and the assertions. It also retains the class invariant and the indexing clause.

The Flat-short format $\equiv$ is the short form of the flat form. Here is the beginning (Indexing clause omitted) of the Flat-short format for class **LINKED_LIST** from EiffelBase:

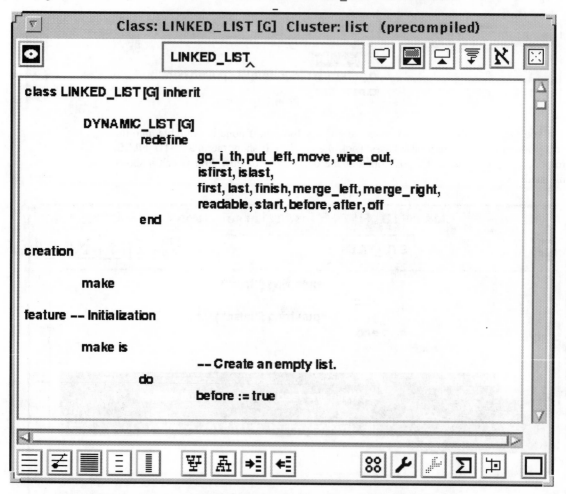

Like the Short format and unlike the Text and Flat formats, the flat-short form is abstract (not encumbered by any implementation information); but like the Flat format and unlike the Text and Short formats it is inheritance-complete, integrating information from all ancestors, not just the class itself. These properties make the Flat-short form the ideal client-oriented documentation for a class. The basic library reference — *Reusable Software: The Base Object-Oriented Component Libraries* — entirely gives its class specifications in the form of Flat-short forms, produced by the environment.

As with other formats, the feature and class names that appear in the Flat and Flat-short forms are clickable.

8.3.4 Information about related classes

The Ancestors format 𝕎 shows the ancestor classes of the target: the inheritance structure that led to the target class. Here is the result of applying this format to class **CHAIN** from EiffelBase. Only the top half is shown; the indentation indicates the various levels of ancestry.

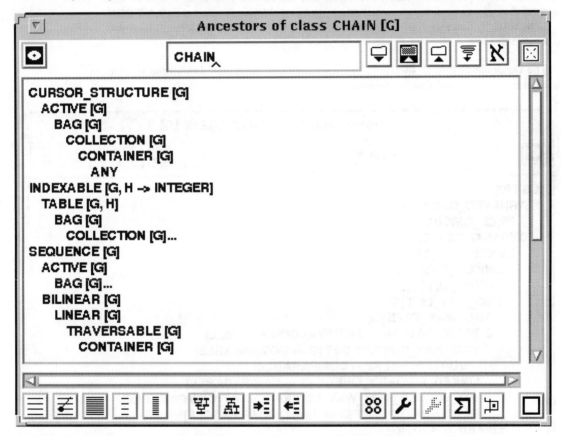

All the class names that appear in the Ancestors display are clickable. This means that you can use the Ancestors format to traverse the ancestor hierarchy of a class quickly and find out about its inherited features. To make such in-depth browsing particularly comfortable it is helpful to use a technique already mentioned: keeping two or more Class Tools open, one to display the Ancestors format as above, the others to obtain further information about specific classes (dragged-and-dropped from the first tool) and their features.

Formal generic parameters are shown, as well as generic constraints when present. The formal generic parameters are not clickable since they do not represent any actual development object, but the generic constraints are; for example in the constraint for class **INDEXABLE** you may click on the generic constraint **INTEGER**.

When, as a result of repeated inheritance, a class appears in more than one inheritance branch, its ancestry is shown only for the first occurrence; for later occurrences it is replaced by an ellipsis "...". This is the case above with **COLLECTION** and **BAG**. This convention is useful to simplify the display of ancestor structures for classes, such as those in the Data Structure library of EiffelBase, which make a rich use of repeated inheritance.

Every developer-written class is a descendant of the class **ANY**, which itself inherits from **PLATFORM** (platform-dependent features) and **GENERAL** (universal features). The display of the ancestor structure normally stops at class **ANY**, not showing the **PLATFORM** and **GENERAL**. If, however, you apply the Ancestors format to class **ANY** itself, then you will see its ancestors.

The Descendants format ![icon] shows the descendants of the target class in the system. The structure is similar to that of the Ancestors format:

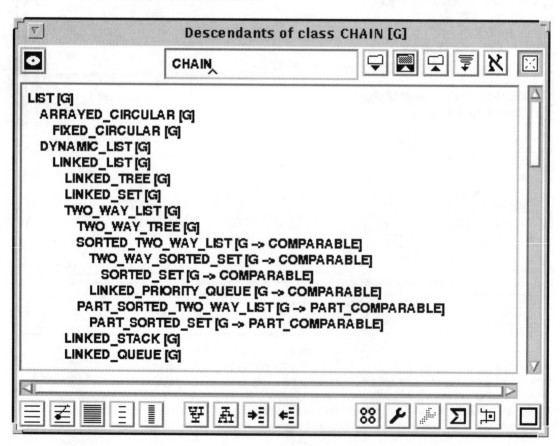

If you choose class **ANY** as the target and request the Descendants format, you will see the entire class hierarchy of the system. Class **NONE**, which theoretically is a descendant of all classes, is never shown. (Actually this class is a convenient fiction, which serves to make the type system a complete lattice but does not physically exist in the environment.)

The Clients format ➡▤ shows the clients of the target class— the classes that use its features through its interface. The Suppliers format ⬅▤ shows the suppliers of the target class — the classes of which it is a client. Here is the Suppliers format for class **LINKED_LIST**:

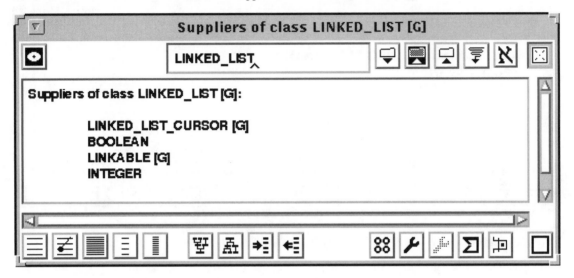

All the class names that appear in these formats are clickable.

8.3.5 Information about features of the class

With the next group of formats you can obtain information about the features of class, grouped by categories:

- Attributes.

- Routines.

- Deferred features.

- Once routines.

- External routines.

The Attributes format ⚏ shows the list of attributes of the target class. The attributes are grouped according to the ancestors in which they were introduced and, within each ancestor section, ordered alphabetically. Here is the result for class **LINKED_LIST**:

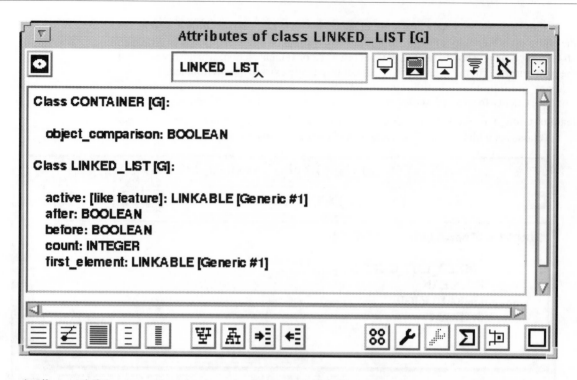

Attribute and class names appearing in such a display are clickable.

The Routines format 🔧 shows all the routines of the target class, ordered as above according to the ancestor in which they were introduced. For each routine, the format gives the complete signature (list of arguments and their types, result and type for a function).

An argument or result type which is a formal generic parameter appears in a form such as

---

Generic #1

---

which indicates the first generic parameter. The actual name used in the class for that parameter (typically **G** for the first, **H** for the second) would be ambiguous here, as it may change across the inheritance hierarchy.

The screen at the top of the facing page shows the beginning of the Routines format display for class **LINKED_LIST**.

All routine names are clickable, so that you can select a routine and see its text right away. If you drag-and-drop such a routine name (for example **empty**, appearing on the last line of the figure) to a class tool, you will see the original routine declaration, highlighted, and the rest of the class (**FINITE** in the example) where it was declared. This is particularly useful to understand the context that led to a particular feature that the class under study, **LINKED_LIST** in this example, has inherited from one of its ancestors.

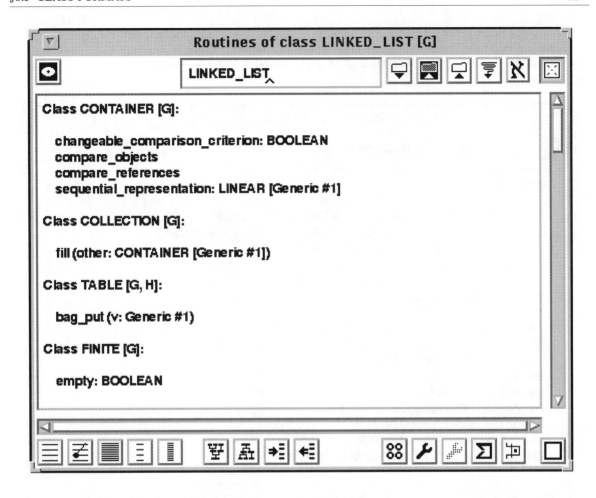

All class names are clickable too; for example in the above tool you can drag-and-drop **BOOLEAN** (in the declaration of **empty**), or **CONTAINER** (appearing on the top line as the name of one of the ancestors of **LINKED_LIST**).

All these properties also apply to the last three format buttons: Deferred, Once and External. Each gives the same information as Routines, but for certain routines only.

The Deferred format ⬚ selects the deferred features of the target class — those which have no implementation, and make the class itself deferred. The form of the output is the same as for the Routines format.

The Once format Σ selects Once routines. The body of a Once routine is executed only on the first call; later calls have no effect and, for a function, return the value computed by the first. The form of the display is the same as for the preceding formats.

Finally, the Externals format ⊞, also using the same display form, selects the external routines of the target class: those which are implemented in another language. Here is the beginning of the output for class **UNIX_FILE** which, understandably, relies on a significant number of external routines:

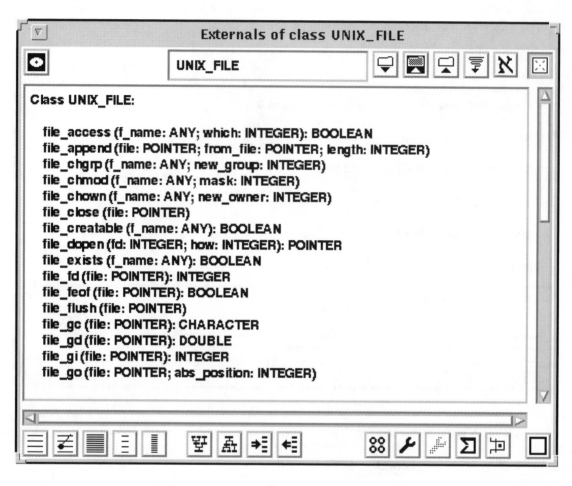

Class UNIX_FILE:

    file_access (f_name: ANY; which: INTEGER): BOOLEAN
    file_append (file: POINTER; from_file: POINTER; length: INTEGER)
    file_chgrp (f_name: ANY; new_group: INTEGER)
    file_chmod (f_name: ANY; mask: INTEGER)
    file_chown (f_name: ANY; new_owner: INTEGER)
    file_close (file: POINTER)
    file_creatable (f_name: ANY): BOOLEAN
    file_dopen (fd: INTEGER; how: INTEGER): POINTER
    file_exists (f_name: ANY): BOOLEAN
    file_fd (file: POINTER): INTEGER
    file_feof (file: POINTER): BOOLEAN
    file_flush (file: POINTER)
    file_gc (file: POINTER): CHARACTER
    file_gd (file: POINTER): DOUBLE
    file_gi (file: POINTER): INTEGER
    file_go (file: POINTER; abs_position: INTEGER)

9

Feature Tools, Execution Object Tools, and symbolic debugging

9.1 OVERVIEW

In the set of tools constituting the EiffelBench environment, Feature and Execution Object Tools are useful not just for what their names imply — working on features, in particular routines, and on execution objects — but also because they offer browsing mechanisms that complement those provided by System and Class Tools and, even more importantly, they help provide the environment's mechanisms for symbolic interactive debugging. (Debugging also relies on the Project Tool, but the main development abstractions involved are the concepts of feature and execution object.)

This chapter reviews the following concepts in turn:

• Feature Tools and their browsing facilities.

• Stop Points, an abstraction closely related to features and important for the run-time debugging mechanism.

• Execution Object Tools: examining the contents of objects at run time.

• Symbolic debugging: how to combine the previous facilities to control execution, insert stop points, explore object structures, catch exceptions before they occur — and, more generally finding out what is happening at run time.

The last comment suggests that the scope of the execution monitoring mechanisms described in this chapter is broader than just debugging. Of course if you have an unexplained run-time error they will help you find it; but such bugs tend not to be that common in Eiffel thanks to the powerful array of facilities, from static typing to assertions, from constrained genericity to garbage collection, which can be used to eliminate bugs before they have had time to strike. Beyond helping to catch any bugs that may have survived these obstacles, the tools described below give you a way to see for yourself what happens during the execution of your system, by running its routines step by step and exploring the object structures that they manipulate.

9.2 BROWSING WITH FEATURE TOOLS

Let us first see how Feature Tools extend the browsing mechanisms of Class and System Tools, as seen in the previous chapters. These facilities will be particularly useful to trace the successive versions of a feature, and to find out from where it is called.

Feature Tools apply to both kinds of feature, attributes and routines, although they are most helpful for routines.

9.2.1 Tool window layout

Here is a typical Feature Tool in the default Text format, targeted to a feature of the EiffelBase class **ARRAYED_LIST**: procedure **put**, which replaces the value of the item at the current cursor position.

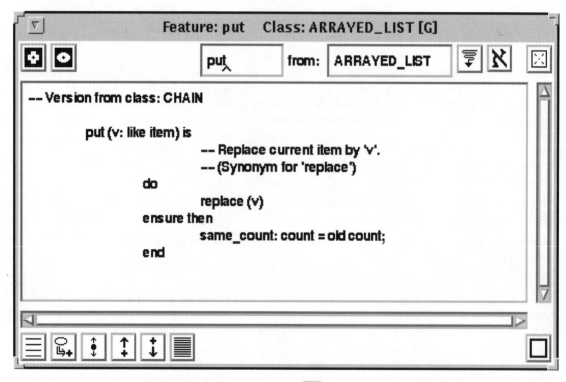

The tool hole at the top left shows the feature icon ![feature icon]. When you are dragging a feature, the pebble has the matching ![pebble] shape. Next to the Feature hole there is also a Class hole ![class hole] representing the class to which the feature belongs. As we will shortly see, this provides for two kinds of retargeting mechanism: you can go to a different feature, but you can also go to a different class.

> We may consider that a Feature Tool, in contrast with other kinds of tool, has not one target but two: the primary target is the feature being operated on, and the secondary target is the class to which this feature belongs.

Since the above tool is targeted, both the Feature and Class holes include the tiny dot that represents the underlying development object. This means that if you need to drag-and-drop the feature or its class you can pick it in one of these holes.

The buttons at the top right are the usual ones: Search ≣, Font **Ҟ**, Quit ⸬. There is no Open, Save or Save As since features have no associated files, in contrast with classes which have class files. To modify a feature, modify it in a Class Tool targeted to its class, and click on Save to save the result. (Remember that to obtain this class tool you may drag-and-drop a feature to a Class Tool, which will show the class at the place of the feature declaration, and highlight that declaration.)

At the bottom right you find the Shell Command button ☐, which enables you to apply any shell command to the feature, through the class file of its class.

See "APPLYING OPERATING SYSTEM COMMANDS TO DEVELOPMENT OBJECTS", 4.5, page 65.

9.2.2 Feature Tool formats and commands

The other icons which appear in the bottom row are specific to features (although you will recognize some of them since they have their counterparts in Class Tools). Here, for ease of reference, is the complete list:

≡ Text format (the default, appearing as always at the bottom-left).

⧉ Callers format.

↕ Ancestor Versions format.

↨ Descendant Versions format.

↕ Implementers format.

▤ Flat format.

9.2.3 Retargeting a Feature Tool

A Feature Tool can be retargeted in more ways than tools of any other kind. This flexibility comes from the presence, noted above, of two targets — a primary one, the feature, and a secondary one, the class — reflected in the tool by the presence of two holes and two text fields. Assume a tool previously targeted to a feature f of a class C. You may use any one of several retargeting mechanisms:

R1 • Pick a feature g, belonging to a class D, in any tool, and drag-and-drop it to the Feature hole (or anywhere in the tool window). This retargets the tool to g; D, its class, becomes the secondary target. This is useful for example if you see a feature name in a Class Tool, in any of the available formats, and want to find out more about the corresponding feature. You need not know in advance to what class D the feature belongs; the resulting display will tell you what D is.

R2 • Pick a class D in any tool, and drag-and-drop it to the Class hole (or anywhere in the tool window). The tool retargets itself to the version of f in D, if any.

R3 • Type the name of a feature g in the feature text field and press Enter. The tool retargets itself to the feature, if any, having that name in the current class, C in our example.

R4 • Type the name of a class D in the class text field and press Enter. The tool retargets itself to the feature of name f (the current primary target) in class D, if any.

R5 • Combining R3 and R4, type both a new feature name g and a new class name D, then press Enter. The tool retargets itself to the feature of name g in class D, if any.

In cases R3, R4 and R5 you will usually have to click first in the corresponding text field to make it responsive to keyboard input.

If you start from a void (non-targeted) Feature Tool, where the holes appear as ⬤ and ✚, only R1 and R5 are applicable.

With R3, R4 and R5, if you enter the name of a class that does not exist in the system, you get a panel of the form

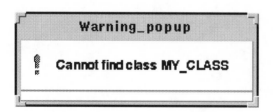

Also with R3 and R5, if the class exists but has no feature of the requested name, you get a panel of the form

```
╔══════════════════════════════════════════════════╗
║               Warning_popup                        ║
╟────────────────────────────────────────────────────╢
║                                                    ║
║  ▌  Cannot find feature my_feature for class LINKED_LIST  ║
║                                                    ║
╚══════════════════════════════════════════════════╝
```

Both of these error panels are of the "pseudo-Gotcha" type: you do not need to dismiss them explicitly; they will go away at your first significant next action, for example when you press Enter after retyping your entry to correct it, or perform a drag-and-drop.

The notion of pseudo-Gotcha was introduced on page 51.

Another error message seems similar to the second of the above two but corresponds to a slightly different semantics. Assume you have a tool targeted as before to feature **put** of class **ARRAYED_LIST**. Using R2 you drag some class which does not have a version of that feature, for example **TESTROOT** from the Guided Tour system. You get a message such as the following (in the Project Tool window):

**No version of feature put
for class TESTROOT**

9.2.4 Textual retargeting vs. abstract retargeting

The difference between the last two error messages reflects the important semantic distinction between **textual** retargeting, achieved through keyboard input, and **abstract** retargeting, achieved through drag-and-drop and using development objects treated as abstractions. More precisely:

- When you type in the feature name (with techniques R3 to R5) you are requesting a certain **feature name**.

- When you drag a class into a Feature Tool (R2) you are requesting the version of a certain **feature** in a certain class. That class must be an ancestor or descendant of the original, and have a version of the requested feature, which may have been redeclared, renamed or both. The feature and the class are treated as abstract development objects; each exists independently of its name, and indeed the same feature may, thanks to Eiffel's renaming facility, have different names in different classes.

To understand this difference better let us study it on an example that causes two successful retargeting operations — unlike the preceding attempts, both of which were erroneous.

We start again from the above Feature Tool targeted to procedure **put** of class **ARRAYED_LIST**. If you drag class **ARRAY** (one of the ancestors of **ARRAYED_LIST**) to the Feature Tool you get the version of the feature for this class:

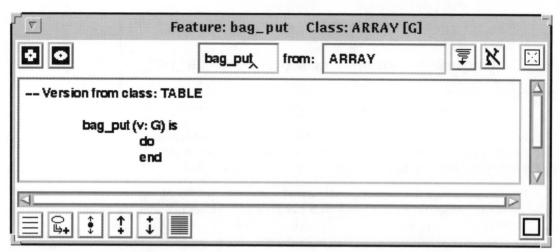

What you see now is a feature with a different name: **bag_put**. The reason lies in the history of **ARRAYED_LIST**'s feature **put**; that feature indeed comes from **ARRAY**, but is called **bag_put** there. The feature as it appears in **ARRAY** comes in turn from feature **put** of class **COLLECTION**, one of the highest-level classes in the general taxonomy of data structures that underlies EiffelBase. This feature was last redeclared in **ARRAY**'s ancestor **TABLE**, which in addition renamed it **bag_put** to avoid a name clash. (The Feature Tool formats studied below, such as Ancestor Versions, make it possible to dig up such feature histories quickly.)

The fundamental taxonomy of data structures is described in the book "Reusable Software: The Base Object-Oriented Component Libraries".

The drag-and-drop operation, which requests the version of the feature for the selected class, retargets the Feature Tool to feature **bag_put** of **ARRAY**. The display indicates that this version actually comes from **TABLE**. This is an example of abstract retargeting: the result is the **ARRAY** version of the **put** feature of **ARRAYED_LIST**.

Now let us start from the original again (**put** for **ARRAYED_LIST**) and simply type the name **ARRAY** in the class field at the top. We get something different this time:

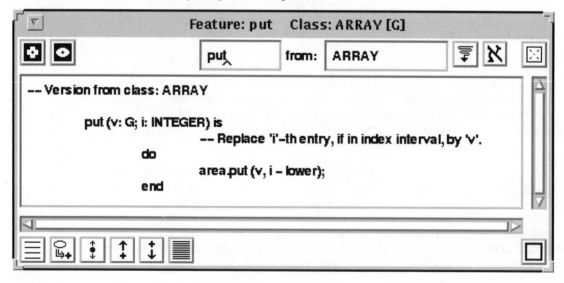

Here we have explicitly requested the feature by its name, **put**. It so happens (as will not be surprising to anyone that knows the principles of feature naming used in the Eiffel library design method and discussed in detail in *Reusable Software*...) that besides its ineffectual **bag_put** feature, coming from **TABLE**, class **ARRAY** also has a feature called **put** — a very useful one, since it is the basic procedure for replacing the value of an array entry. This is an example of textual retargeting: the result is simply the feature called **put** in class **ARRAY**, and need not bear any connection to what this feature name means for class **ARRAYED_LIST**.

9.2.5 Obtaining information about the callers of a feature

Let us now look at the various feature formats.

The Callers format ⬚ enables you to find all places from which the target feature is called. (The icon uses the standard graphical conventions: an oval for the calling class, a double arrow for the client relation, a cross for the feature.)

The output is a list of line pairs, where the first line of each pair is the name of a class and the second line, indented, is the name of a routine of that class that calls the given feature. Both the class name and the routine name are clickable.

Here is the beginning of the result for the last feature encountered above: **put** from class **ARRAY**.

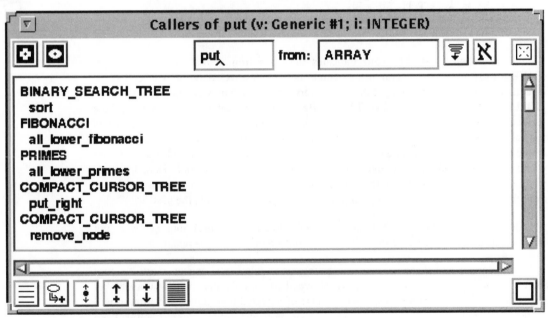

9.2.6 Finding out about the history of a feature

The next three formats on the format row — Implementers, Ancestor Versions and Descendant Versions — are particularly useful to follow what happens to features in the inheritance games: redefinition, undefinition, effecting, renaming, join.

The Implementers format 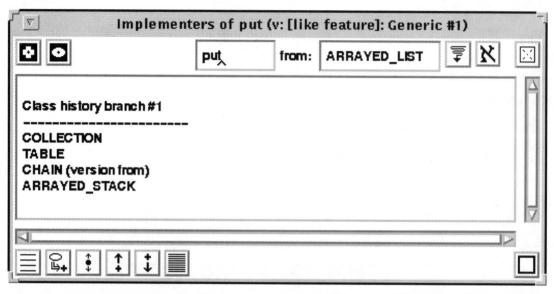 gives the basic history information: the list of classes where the feature is declared or redeclared. Here is its result for feature **put** from **ARRAYED_LIST**:

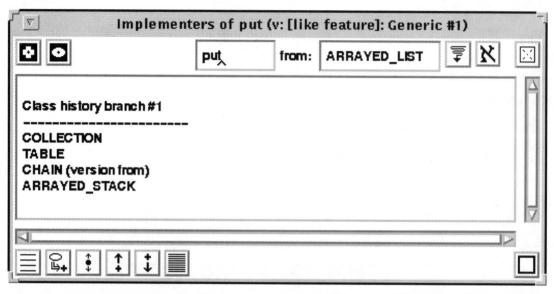

The line labeled **version from** indicates the class from which the current class, **ARRAYED_LIST**, draws its version of the feature; here the last redeclaration was in **CHAIN**. Above the **version from** line you see the earlier versions: the feature was initially introduced in **COLLECTION**, then redeclared in **TABLE**. Below the **version from** line you see the descendants that redeclare the feature; here there is only one. This display is precious when you want to see quickly all the successive incarnations through which a feature goes — for example because you are not quite sure which one is being called in a particular case. To see any one of these versions, drag-and-drop it to a Feature or Class Tool. Here too it is convenient to work with two tools: the above one for applying various formats to a feature; and another to obtain details about anything that catches your attention in the first.

This format only takes redeclaration (redefinition or effecting) into account, not renaming. The next two formats will enable you to find where a feature is renamed.

In this format and the next two, the history is divided into one or more "history branches". For the example feature shown above there is only one history branch, but features that have a more complex history because of repeated inheritance and joining will have more. (Joining is what happens when one or more deferred features coming from various ancestors have the same name as an effective feature, so that they can all be merged into one feature.)

Here is the beginning of the Ancestor Versions format ↑ as applied to the same feature:

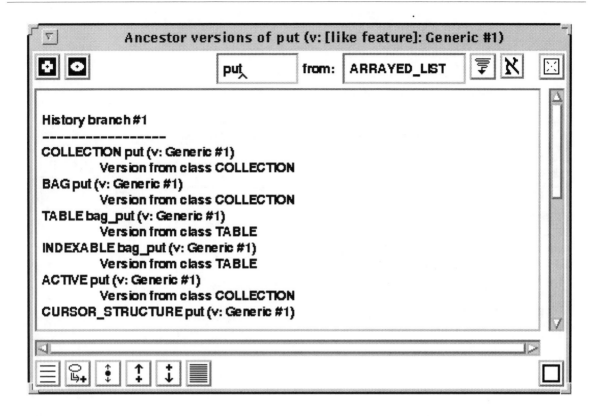

This format shows the complete history of the feature, that is to say, for each one of the ancestors of **ARRAYED_LIST** where a version of the feature exists:

- The name of the class.

- The name of the feature (which may be different from the final name because of renaming, as for example in **TABLE**).

- The signature.

- Where the version comes from (for example the version in **INDEXABLE** comes from **TABLE**).

The example shows that this particular procedure comes from quite high in the inheritance hierarchy, and that when it reaches **ARRAYED_LIST** it has already had a distinguished career in the parent organization.

As usual, all class and feature names in this format are clickable. So if you want to see how the feature was redeclared in **COLLECTION**, just drag-and-drop the occurrence of **put** appearing on the first line into a Feature Tool; or right-click on it twice to retarget the current tool to it, then select Text format ≡. You may also drag-and-drop the feature name, or class

COLLECTION itself, into a class tool; in the first case the Class Tool will position itself at the location of the feature, which it will show highlighted.

The Descendant Versions format ‡ uses the same conventions, with the same clickability properties, to display information about the descendants:

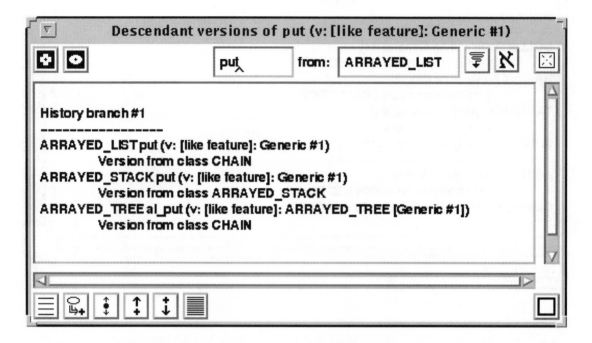

Here procedure **put** appears in **ARRAYED_LIST** and in the two proper descendants (both of them classes of EiffelBase) that this class has in our system. One of these descendants, **ARRAYED_STACK**, redefines the feature; another, **ARRAYED_TREE**, keeps the feature's version, coming from **CHAIN**, but renames it **al_put**.

9.3 STOP POINTS

A developer abstraction closely connected to features plays an important role in the debugging mechanism: Stop Point.

A stop point is simply a mark associated with a certain routine, indicating that execution (in workbench mode) must stop on that routine.

The interface for putting and removing stop points is particularly simple. Only one Stop Point hole (actually a buttonhole) is provided, at the top of the Project Tool window:

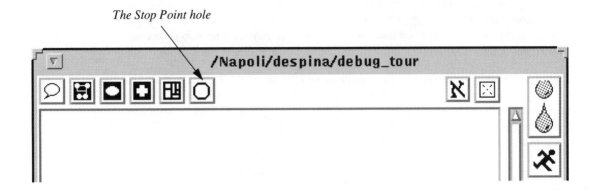

The Stop Point hole

The octagonal shape of the icon ◯ recalls the shape of STOP road signs.

You can drag-and-drop a routine (through its pebble ✚, which fits in the sign) to the Stop Point hole. As usual, you can pick up the routine in any context where its name appears — Class Tool, Feature Tool, Project Tool — or through the tiny dot that represents it in the primary tool hole of a Feature Tool currently targeted to it.

Dropping the routine into the Stop Point hole associates a stop point with it. If you want to remove the stop point, just drag-and-drop the routine again to the Stop Point hole. Each time you drop, the Project Tool window will show the list of active stop points and the list of those which were removed. For example, after inserting and removing a few stop points for the "Debug Tour" example studied later in this chapter, you will see the following display in the Project Tool:

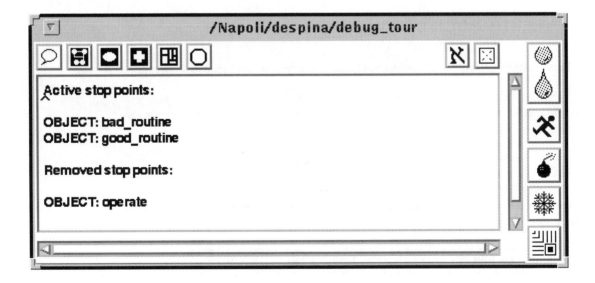

If at any time (other than just after dropping a routine into the Stop Point hole) you want to see the above display to find out what stop points are active and which ones have been removed, just click on the Stop Point hole, used here as a buttonhole. If no stop points were introduced, this has no effect.

Each line of the display indicates a class name and the name of a routine in that class. The class name is clickable; so is the routine name. So if you want to remove an active stop point, or reactivate a previously active stop point, you do not need to go back to the context where you originally spotted the routine name; just obtain the display illustrated above (by clicking on the Stop Point hole if necessary) and grab the routine of interest.

For reasons that are easy to understand, you can only associate a stop point with an effective routine. Dropping into the Stop Point hole an attribute or a deferred routine (all of which are features, represented by the same cross pebble ✚ as routines) has no effect.

If a routine has an associated stop point, execution under the workbench, triggered, as you will remember, by clicking on the Run button , will stop at the routine's entrance whenever there is a call to the routine. A message in the Project Tool will give you all the details; since classes, features and execution objects referenced in the message are all clickable, you can explore the static and dynamic structure of the system at the point where the execution stopped. You can also, of course, add and remove stop points at that stage. To restart execution, click on Run again. To stop execution at any time, click on End Run 💣 .

The mechanisms for executing a system from the workbench were studied in "Executing from within the graphical environment", 6.4.1, page 91.

Later in this chapter we will see a complete debugging example using stop points. To appreciate this notion and the example fully, it is useful to turn first to the study of Execution Object Tools.

The debugging example is in "USING THE DEBUGGING MECHANISM", 9.5, page 155.

9.4 EXECUTION OBJECT TOOLS

An Execution Object Tool represents an object captured during the execution of a system.

Execution Object Tools enable you to explore your object structures at run time and hence to find out what your system actually does. Let us see how they look and what you can do with them.

We will use a small example involving linked lists and the corresponding "linkable" objects. You may find a small system corresponding to this example, ready to be compiled, in the directory **$EIFFEL3/examples/bench/object_tour**. As usual, before compiling and executing this example, copy it into one of your directories *YOURDIR1* through the shell command

```
cp $EIFFEL3/examples/bench/object_tour/*    YOURDIR1
```

The example creates a small linked list (instance of the EiffelBase class **LINKED_LIST**) through the following procedure, whose text is taken here from a Feature Tool:

```
make_a_list is
                -- Create 'my_list' with three known values.
        do
                !! my_list.make;
                my_list.put_right (3.5);
                my_list.put_right (0.0);
                my_list.put_right (-6.5)
        end
```

The procedure creates a list and inserts three real numbers. Feature **my_list**, an attribute of the enclosing class, is declared as **LINKED_LIST [REAL]**.

Using the Run and Stop Point mechanisms described earlier, we start the execution of a system including this procedure's class, and stop it right after has called the procedure. We want to know what is in the list; perhaps we are not sure what happens when **put_right** is applied repeatedly to a list that was initially empty: in what order were the elements inserted? (Of course the answer can be found by looking at the flat-short form of class **LINKED_LIST** and, more generally, by reading the discussion of the class in the library book, *Reusable Software*... But here we actually want to see what happens during execution.)

What we will find is an object structure of the following form:

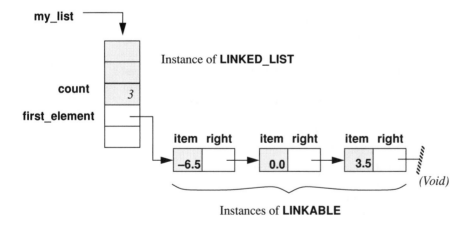

Instances of **LINKABLE**

As the figure shows, the list proper is an object of type **LINKED_LIST** whereas the actual list elements are of type **LINKABLE**.

Let us create an Execution Object Tool and (through the simple mechanisms explained below) target it to the object attached to **my_list**. Here is the result:

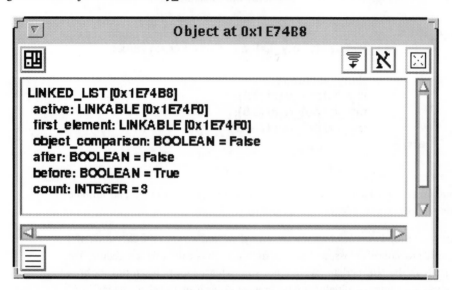

Execution Object Tools are the simplest of those studied in this book: there is only one format available, Text, and only three buttons, the general-purpose Search, Font and Quit. As usual, the top-left hole is the target hole; when the tool, as here, is targeted, you may use that hole to grab the underlying object (represented by the tiny dot in the hole) and drag-and-drop it somewhere.

As the first line indicates, the target object is an instance of class **LINKED_LIST**. This class name is of course clickable, so that if you want to see some of its properties you can on the spot obtain a Class Tool targeted to it. The next few lines show the various fields of the object, each corresponding to one of the attributes of the class and given with its type (which is of course clickable).

There are two kinds of field: those of basic expanded types, for example **after**, of type **BOOLEAN**, and **count** (the number of elements in the list), of type **INTEGER**; and those of reference types, for example **active** and **first_element**, both of type **LINKABLE** (actually **LINKABLE [REAL]** since the class is generic). In the first case, the corresponding line directly shows the value, for example **3** or **False**. In the second case, the line also shows the value but that value is an internal object reference, uniquely identifying the attached object.

Although at first sight these internal values might seem useless (except for detecting whether two references are attached to the same object), in reality they are precious: as you have probably guessed, they are clickable, since they represent meaningful and important abstractions — execution objects. This yields the basic mechanism for exploring run-time object structures: drag an object reference into an Execution Object Tool, the same or another.

The object identification numbers that you will see if you run this example may of course be different from those appearing on the above figure and in the rest of this presentation

Let us use this facility to explore the linked list. Attribute **first_element**, as illustrated on the earlier figure, is attached to the first list element. Start by dragging the corresponding reference:

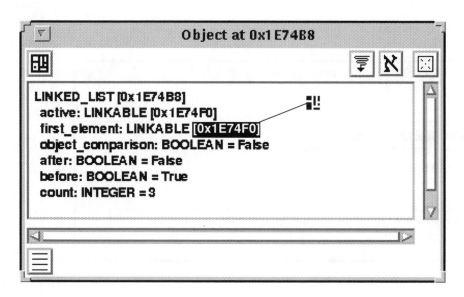

Drop the Execution Object pebble 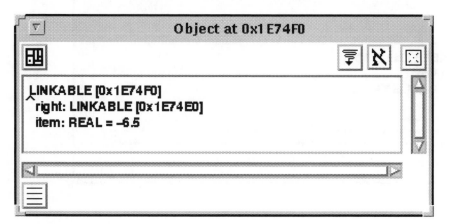 into an Execution Object Tool (the same one if you do not need to see the **LINKED_LIST** object any more, a different one if you wish to keep it visible). This displays a view of a **LINKABLE** object:

This object is the first element of the list, with an **item** value of –6.5 and a **right** reference attached to another linkable object.

To see this other object, click twice on the reference in the **right** field; as you certainly remember, this is equivalent to drag-and-dropping the reference into the current tool, hence retargeting it to the selected Execution Object.

On the two-click facil-
ity and how it fits in
the drag-and-drop
mechanism, see
"Quick Retargeting",
4.3.3, page 60.

The effect is to display the second list element:

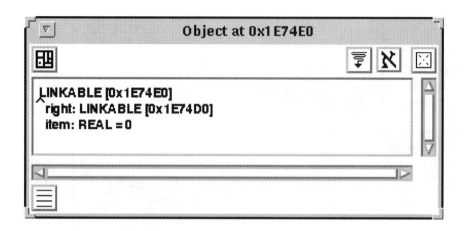

Repeat the operation, following the second element's own **right** reference to see the last element in the list:

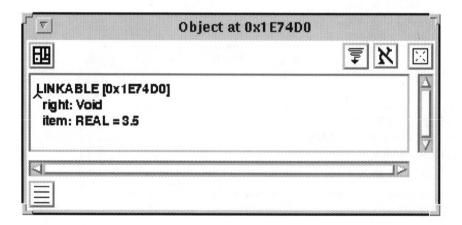

Here the **right** reference is void, so there are no more list elements to be explored. We have seen the list elements, which the procedure **put_right** has indeed inserted in the order shown on the earlier figure.

9.5 USING THE DEBUGGING MECHANISM

We now have almost all the elements enabling us to get all the benefits of the debugging and execution monitoring mechanism.

To illustrate the various possibilities it is useful to rely on a simple example, which is included in the delivery. The needed classes and Ace for the example are in the directory

$EIFFEL3/examples/bench/debug_tour

You may run the example yourself. As with the guided tour of chapter 2, you should first copy it to one of your own directories. You will notice in later figures that for this demonstration the example directory has been copied into **/Napoli/despina/debug_tour**.

9.5.1 The classes

The example directory contains just two classes: **EXAMPLE** and **OBJECT**. Class **EXAMPLE** serves as the root. Here is a Class Tool showing its text:

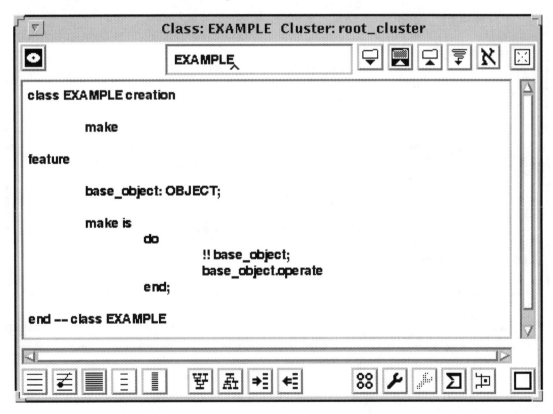

The creation procedure **make** creates an object **base_object** and applies procedure **operate** to it. Here is class **OBJECT**, which serves as the type of **base_object**:

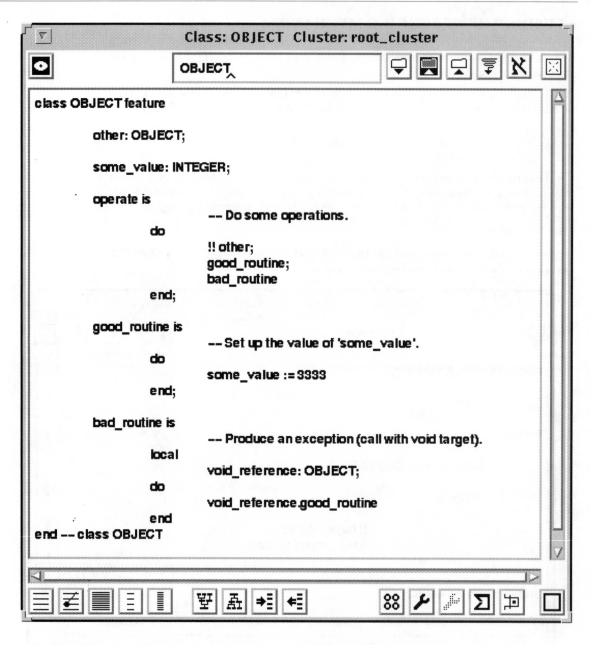

```
Class: OBJECT  Cluster: root_cluster

OBJECT

class OBJECT feature

        other: OBJECT;

        some_value: INTEGER;

        operate is
                        -- Do some operations.
                do
                        !! other;
                        good_routine;
                        bad_routine
                end;

        good_routine is
                        -- Set up the value of 'some_value'.
                do
                        some_value := 3333
                end;

        bad_routine is
                        -- Produce an exception (call with void target).
                local
                        void_reference: OBJECT;
                do
                        void_reference.good_routine
                end
end -- class OBJECT
```

This class has two attributes: **other**, also of type **OBJECT**, and **some_value**, an integer. The procedure **operate** creates an object an attaches **other** to it; then it calls **good_routine** and **bad_routine**. The first of these procedures assigns a specific value, 3333, to **some_value**; this will enable us to distinguish the current instance from the object attached to **other**, for which **some_value** is still 0, the default value at creation.

The procedure **bad_routine** executes on purpose an instruction that will cause an exception: it calls a feature, **good_routine** (any other applicable feature would have served our purpose equally) on a void reference. Any other exception, such as an assertion violation, or an attempt to allocate a string of one billion characters, causing a "no more memory" exception, would have been just as appropriate to illustrate how EiffelBench will catch exceptions before they occur.

9.5.2 Setting up stop points

Before triggering the exception the system will perform some legitimate operations. Let us plant a few stop points so that we will be able to explore the run-time state of the system at various stages of its execution.

We may for example put stop points on procedure **make** from **EXAMPLE**, and on **bad_routine** and **good_routine** from **OBJECT**. We saw above how to do this: find a place where the routine names appear (for example in the above Class Tools, successively targeted to the two classes), and drag-and-drop them, one after the other, to the Stop Point hole ◯ of the Project Tool. After each drop the Project Tool window displays the list of active stop points; here is the final display:

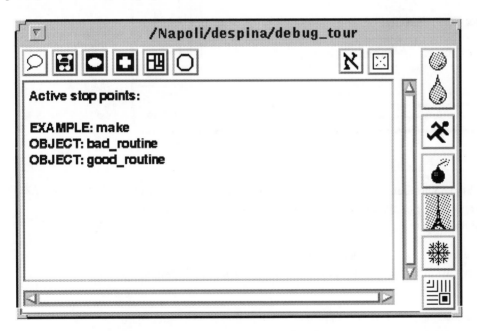

For each applicable class, the Project Tool window shows the set of routines on which you have put stop points. As noted, the class and routine names are clickable; to remove a stop point, drag the corresponding routine again into the Stop Point hole.

9.5.3 Executing

We are ready now to execute the application.

Simply click on the Run button ![run button icon]. Execution begins and stops right away; the Project Tool window shows why:

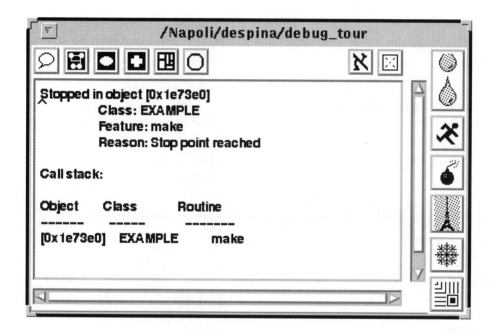

The reason was: Stop point reached. The stop point was in feature **make**, the creation procedure, applied to an instance of class **EXAMPLE**. The message gives an identification number, **0x1e73e0**, for that object.

As in the earlier example, the object identification numbers that you will see when running this example may be different from the numbers that appear in the illustrations of this chapter.

The display also shows the call stack, not very interesting at this stage — procedure **make** was called on instance **0x1e73e0** of class **EXAMPLE**.

To proceed, click again on Run. This time execution hits the stop point of procedure **operate** of class **OBJECT**:

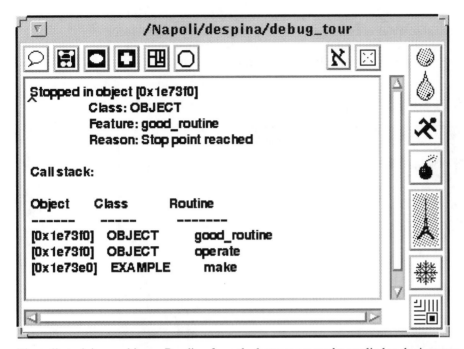

The call stack is now bigger. Reading from the bottom up: **make** applied to the instance of identifier **0x1e73e0** of **OBJECT** called **operate** on instance **0x1e73f0** of **EXAMPLE**, which called **good_routine** on the same object. If you look at the text of class **EXAMPLE** given earlier you will note that this instance is the object attached to the attribute **base_object**, and created in the first instruction of the **make** procedure.

The text of class **EXAMPLE** *was on page 155. You can of course obtain it again by drag-and-drop.*

If you want to see that object, just drag its identifier (which will be tracked by an Execution Object pebble ▓!!) and drop it into the Execution Object hole ▓. An Execution Object Tool comes up, showing the contents of the object:

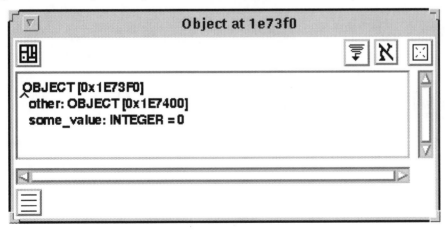

Attribute **some_value** is an integer, which the creation operation has initialized, for the current object, to zero; attribute **other** is a reference to a newly created object (**0x1E7400**), also of type **OBJECT**. You can see this from the text of class **OBJECT**; if that text is not immediately available, just grab the name of the class as it appears in the window and target a Class Tool to it.

Click on Run 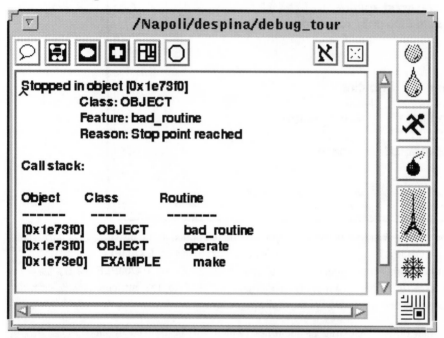 again. Execution stops on **bad_routine** because of the stop point:

Drag-and-drop the object on which execution stopped (**0x1e73f0**) to the previously opened Execution Object Tool (remember that you can drop anywhere in the window, not just on the top-left hole). You will see that **good_routine** did its job:

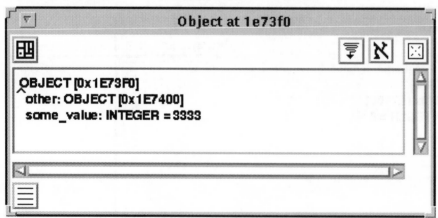

The execution of **good_routine** has set the **some_value** field to 3333. In contrast, that field still has value 0 in the object attached to **other**; to see this, right-click twice on **other**'s object number (**0x1E7400** here) to retarget the tool to that object:

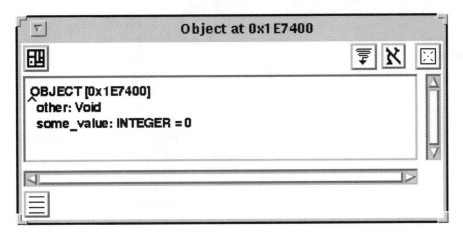

9.5.4 Catching an exception before it occurs

Now let us see what happens in case of an exception.

As a refresher let us look at the text of **bad_routine** by right-clicking twice on its name, which appears in the last Project Tool display (see the next-to-last figure). The resulting Feature Tool shows what the routine is trying to do:

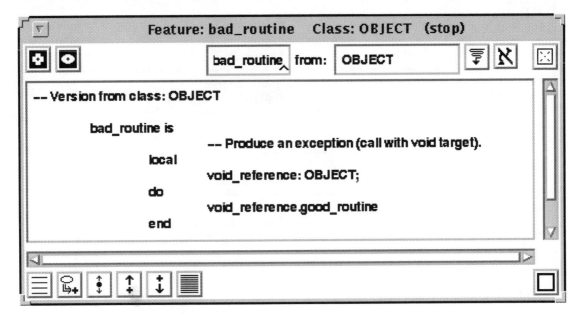

As you can see, the body of **bad_routine** attempts to call a feature, the procedure **good_routine**, on a target, the local entity **void_reference,** whose value at the time of the call will be void as its name suggests. (Any local entity of reference type is initialized to **Void** on routine entry; normally, of course, the routine must assign it a non-void value before using it as the target of a call.)

Such an attempt to call a feature on a void target is a typical example of a run-time incident that will cause an exception. Since there was a stop point on **bad_routine** its execution has not started yet. But as soon as you restart execution the "Feature applied to void reference" exception will result.

It is possible to catch and process such an exception, in the routine where it arose (the **recipient** of the exception) or one of its direct or indirect callers up the call chain, through a Rescue clause, which may take a corrective action and try again through a Retry instruction. But here there is no Rescue clause anywhere; so if we were executing the system from a window outside EiffelBench, the exception would cause execution to terminate abnormally, leaving an exception trace in the original shell window:

On the Rescue-Retry exception handling mechanism see "Object-Oriented Software Construction" and "Eiffel: The Language".

```
┌─────────────────────────────────────────────────────────────────────┐
│ ▼                              xterm                                  │
├───────────────────────────────────────────────────────────────────  │
│ Debug Tour - cd EIFFELGEN/W_code                                      │
│ Debug Tour - ls                                                       │
│ .UPDT   simple@                                                       │
│ Debug Tour - simple                                                   │
│                                                                       │
│ simple: system execution failed.                                      │
│ Following is the set of recorded exceptions:                          │
│                                                                       │
│ ---------------------------------------------------------------       │
│ Class / Object     Routine          Nature of exception      Effect   │
│ ---------------------------------------------------------------       │
│ OBJECT             bad_routine      good_routine:                     │
│ <001E73F0>                          Applied to void reference.  Fail  │
│ ---------------------------------------------------------------       │
│ OBJECT             bad_routine                                        │
│ <001E73F0>                          Routine failure.           Fail  │
│ ---------------------------------------------------------------       │
│ OBJECT             operate                                            │
│ <001E73F0>                          Routine failure.           Fail  │
│ ---------------------------------------------------------------       │
│ EXAMPLE            make                                               │
│ <001E73E0>                          Routine failure.           Fail  │
│ ---------------------------------------------------------------       │
│ EXAMPLE            root's creation                                    │
│ <001E73E0>                          Routine failure.           Exit  │
│ ---------------------------------------------------------------       │
│ Debug Tour - █                                                        │
└─────────────────────────────────────────────────────────────────────┘
```

Thanks to the debugging facilities of EiffelBench, however, we can catch the exception **before** it occurs. Click on Run 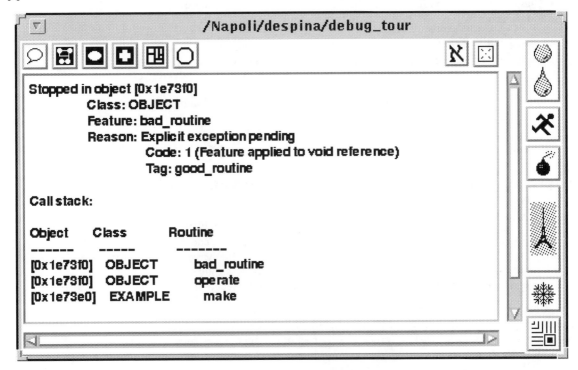 once more; execution stops, but this time not because of a stop point:

```
/Napoli/despina/debug_tour

Stopped in object [0x1e73f0]
        Class: OBJECT
        Feature: bad_routine
        Reason: Explicit exception pending
                Code: 1 (Feature applied to void reference)
                Tag: good_routine

Call stack:

Object      Class       Routine
-------     -----       --------
[0x1e73f0]  OBJECT      bad_routine
[0x1e73f0]  OBJECT      operate
[0x1e73e0]  EXAMPLE      make
```

The **Reason** field now indicates: **Explicit exception pending**. It is followed by a **Code**, which gives the nature of the exception, here **Feature applied to void reference**; in other cases it might indicate some other type of exception such as "Precondition violated", "No more memory" or "Operating system signal". The **Tag** field gives context information, here the name of the routine, here **good_routine**, which was called on a void reference. The **Tag** information is adapted to each kind of exception; for an assertion violation, for example, it would give the tag of the violated assertion clause.

The call stack that follows indicates that the offending call was in procedure **bad_routine** and shows the sequence of calls that led to this situation with, for each call, the target object.

It this were a real bug — not one consciously planted to experiment with the debugging mechanism — you could at this stage use all the facilities of the environment to find out what is wrong.You could start Class Tools, Feature Tools, Execution Object Tools and the System Tool on the appropriate components of the system, using all the available formats to find out quickly all the necessary information about the context of the error. In particular:

- Execution Object Tools allow you to explore quickly and effectively the run-time object structure of your system just before the exception occurs, looking for strange values.

- Class Tools allow you to examine the classes that may have caused the problem and find out about their ancestors, clients and other acquaintances.

- Feature Tools, through the mechanisms described at the beginning of this chapter, allow you to see the history of a suspicious feature and check what exact version each call will trigger.

Together, these tools provide all the mechanisms that you will need to determine what the problem is.

Coming back to the example: if you click one last time on Run ⚒ the execution will indeed trigger the exception and stop, producing on the original window the exception trace shown earlier. The Project Tool will display **Application terminated**, as it also would in case of normal termination.

Of course you remain within EiffelBench; so you can perform all applicable operations, such as browsing through the system, changing it and recompiling it. You may also run it again as many times as you wish — either because you have not found the source of the error yet, or, in the more likely case that you have (Eiffel run-time errors, as noted, tend to be easy to detect and to fix) to check your correction and proceed with the execution.

Combined with the other execution and exploration mechanisms, this ability to catch exceptions just before they occur and to go straight to the source of the problem turns the act of debugging, often a painstaking process with traditional approaches, into a relatively effortless task.

9.5.5 From debugging to run-time exploration

Beyond their application to debugging, the tools and mechanisms that we have examined in this chapter enables software developers to get better control and understanding of their software.

Even if you are not specifically looking for a bug, it is always useful to take a peek at the execution of your system, examine the objects that it creates and their various fields, follow references to explore the overall object structure in depth (as we briefly did, earlier in this chapter, with a list structure), run important routines one by one, try the effect of different input data, and in general attempt to grasp the dynamic interpretation of the static system description provided by the text of your software.

The Melting Ice Technology provides a precious complement by processing experimental changes quickly, so that you can right away see their run-time effect on the execution and on the objects.

Together, these facilities provides software developers with a major benefit: the ability to get a concrete and detailed understanding of the run-time picture.

10

Using the non-graphical interface

10.1 OVERVIEW

Because the graphical facilities of the environment are so conducive to effective software development, most of this book focuses on using the graphical version of the workbench.

It is possible, however, to execute some of the most important operations outside of any graphical environment. This may be useful in three cases:

- Obviously, you will need this possibility if you do not have access to graphical facilities, for example if you are using ISE Eiffel 3 from a non-graphical terminal.

- Even if hardware and software support for graphics is not a problem, you may occasionally need to exercise some mechanisms from the command line, or call them from other programs. As a typical example, suppose you need to produce the flat-short forms of all the classes in a library, or just of those whose names begin with the letter **A**. You may want to write a shell script (a program in the operating system's command language) that processes all of them in turn; this is more convenient than repeating for each class a sequence of EiffelBench visual manipulations such as drag-and-dropping the class into a Class Tool, pressing the Flatshort button, and saving the result into a file. Another advantage of using a shell script is that after a series of changes you may re-process the classes in exactly the same way.

- One specific operation, precompiling a library, requires a command that can only be executed from the command line.

See "Producing precompiled libraries", 6.5.3, page 100.

The facilities described in this chapter give access to some of the most important environment facilities in a non-graphical fashion. In particular, you can use the **es3** command to compile, freeze or melt a system, and produce such information about a class as its flat and flat-short forms. An interactive version, the **–loop** option, makes it possible to start **es3** just once and then repeatedly request any of the available operations.

10.2 A REMINDER: EXECUTING FROM OUTSIDE EIFFELBENCH

One topic related to the rest of this chapter was discussed earlier: how to run a system from outside of the environment. As you will recall:

See "EXECUTING A COMPILED SYS-TEM", 6.4, page 90.

- You may use the executable module resulting from finalization as a normal executable module; it can be run under the operating system like any other command.

- In the case of a workbench version (an executable form resulting from a sequence of melting and freezing operations) you have several possibilities: executing directly from the generation directory; executing elsewhere provided you also have access to the update file, **.UPDT**, through either a copy or a symbolic link to the original; using the **ignore_updt** command-line option; setting the value of the **MELT_PATH** environment variable to the path name of the generation directory.

10.3 COMPILING AND BROWSING

The command for executing EiffelBench operations from outside the graphical environment is called **es3**. To use it you must have your path properly set up, as explained in chapter 1.

See "SETTING UP YOUR ENVIRON-MENT", 1.3, page 2.

10.3.1 Using **es3**

The command is used in the following form:

> **es3** *option* ... [*class_name*] [*feature_name*]

Each *option* consists of a minus sign **–**, immediately followed by a keyword indicating the desired operation, for example **–freeze** or **–flatshort**, followed in some cases by a space and a name, as in the option **–ace** *file_name*.

The *class_name*, if present, must be the name of a class of the system to which **es3** is applied. This system is identified by its Ace file; by default this is the file called **Ace** in the directory where you call **es3**, but you can select any other one through the **–ace** *file_name* option. The project directory is similarly by default the one from which you called **es3**, but you can select another one through the **–project** *directory_name* option. The *feature_name*, if present, must be the final name of a feature of the class called *class_name*.

The table on the facing page lists the available options, the arguments they require, and their effect, with the following conventions:

- Words in *italics* indicate names that you must provide.

- The second column indicate whether you must provide just a *class_name*, both a *class_name* and a *feature_name*, or neither.

- In the third column, indicating the operations' effect, to "print" means to produce the requested information on the default output of the **es3** command.

10.3.2 The options

OPTION	ARGUMENTS	EFFECT
–ace *file_name*		Use as Ace the file of name *file_name*. (Default: file **Ace** in current directory.)
–ancestors	*class_name*	Print ancestors of this class.
–aversions	*class_name, feature_name*	Print all versions of this feature in ancestors of this class.
–callers	*class_name, feature_name*	Print all routines that call this feature.
–clients	*class_name*	Print clients of this class.
–descendants	*class_name*	Print des cendants of this class.
–dversions	*class_name, feature_name*	Print all versions of this feature in descendants of this class.
–finalize		Produce finalized version of system (optimized ANSI C code and executable module).
–flat	*class_name*	Print flat form of this class.
–flatshort	*class_name*	Print flat-short form of this class.
–freeze		Freeze system.
–help		Print short help message listing options of **es3**.
–implementers	*class_name, feature_name*	Print all classes that declare or redeclare this feature.
–keep		Keep assertions in final mode (useful with **–finalize** only).
–loop		Enter interactive mode where you may repeatedly request **es3** operations without having to restart **es3**.
–precompile		Precompile system, treating it as a library.
–project *directory_name*		Use as project directory the directory called *directory_name*. (Default: current directory.)

10.3.3 Using the options

If you use two or more options they may appear in any order. The command may take at most one of each of the options **–ace** and **–project**, and at most one of the other options, called the operation options.

If no operation option is present, the command will cause a freezing if the system has never been compiled, and a melting otherwise. This is the reason why there is no "melt" option: the normal way to melt an already compiled system (the most common operation) is to call **es3** with no argument. The operation options include compilation options (**freeze** and **precompile**) and browsing options (all the others except **loop**).

The browsing options will only work if the system has already been compiled and the given *class_name* is part of it. If not, you will get the message

> *class_name* **is not in the system**

In case of a compilation error, **es3** under any one of the compilation options produces the same message as the graphical compiler would, then outputs the following message:

> **Press <return> to resume compilation**

This gives you an opportunity to correct the error by editing the appropriate class. When you have performed the correction, press the Return (or Enter) key as the message suggests, and compilation will resume exactly as it would if you had been using a Class Tool to correct the error under EiffelBench, and then had clicked again on the Melt or Freeze button.

10.3.4 Using a precompiled library under es3

If you are using a precompiled library with **es3**, you will need to execute an operating system command after the first compilation before you can execute your system. (When you compile a system under the graphical environment this command is also executed, but the compilation mechanism takes care of it automatically. Only when you use **es3** do you need to execute explicitly.)

Compile your system normally; its Ace will contain a **precompiled** entry listing the directory of the precompiled library. When the first compilation is complete, execute the following command from the generation directory — the subdirectory **EIFFELGEN/W_code** of your project directory:

> **ln –s** *precompilation_directory*/**EIFFELGEN/W_code/driver** *systemname*

where *precompilation_directory* is the project directory of the precompiled library, and *systemname* is the lower-case version of the name of your system as it appears in the Ace specification. The **ln** command ("link") is an operating system command that connects the executable version of your system to the "driver" produced as a result of precompilation.

You only need to execute this command once for a given project. In fact it can be performed (from another window) shortly after compilation has started — as soon as the compilation mechanism has created the generation directory.

10.3.5 Producing a finalized system with es3

To produce a finalized system, you may use the command **es3 –finalize**. The effect is the same as when you press the Finalize button ⣿ in the graphical environment, except for two differences.

On finalizing from the graphical environment see "Finalizing", 6.3.4, page 89. The impact of assertion checking on the performance of a finalized system was discussed in "Assertion checking in final mode", 6.7.4, page 110

First, all assertion checking will by default be turned off in the resulting finalized system. The reason is the performance issue discussed earlier. In the graphical environment, an interactive panel asks you whether you want to keep or discard assertions. Command **es3**, however, was designed to be callable automatically from shell scripts or programs, and for that reason never asks for interactive user input. To retain the assertion checking options specified in the Ace file, use the option **–keep** in connection with **–finalize** (the order of the two options is arbitrary).

Second, at the end of the Eiffel part of the compilation you are presented with the message

```
System recompiled.
You must now run "finish_freezing" in
      ./EIFFELGEN/F_code
```

To execute the C compilation and linking part of the finalization, change directory to **./EIFFELGEN/F_code** as indicated and execute the requested command. It is of course easy to write a shell script that will do all that is asked without human intervention:

```
es3 –finalize
cd ./EIFFELGEN/F_code
finish_freezing
cd ../..
```

The reason why **es3** does not execute this script by default is that some developers may wish to insert an intermediate operation, such as modification of the Make file, before starting the C compilation and linking through **finish_freezing**. Also, under some circumstances it is desirable to start **finish_freezing** as a background process, whereas in others you may want to execute **es3** and **finish_freezing** in sequence as a single process. You can write a shell script that fits your exact needs.

10.3.6 The interactive mode: –loop

If you need to use **es3** to executive a number of successive operations on a system — for example to compile it, make changes, compile again, obtain a flat-short form, make a new change and recompile after seeing the flat form, list the ancestor versions of a feature and so on — you do not need to restart **es3** each time. This possibility is useful for an obvious reason of convenience, and also for efficiency, since you will avoid the delay that may result from having to load the **es3** executable for each new operation.

To use the interactive mode just start the command once as

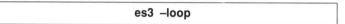

```
es3 –loop
```

This option enables you to execute successive operations without leaving **es3**. The immediate result is this display:

```
==== ISE Eiffel 3 - Interactive Batch Version ====

        ancestors: print the ancestors of a class.
        aversions: print the ancestor versions of a feature.
        callers: print the callers of a feature.
        clients: print the clients of a class.
        descendants: print the descendants of a class.
        dversions: print the descendant versions of a feature.
        finalize: finalize the system (discard assertions by default).
        flat: print the flat form of a class.
        flatshort: print the flat-short form of a class.
        freeze: freeze the system.
        help: print list of commands.
        implementers: print the classes implementing a feature.
        melt: melt changes.
        quit: terminate session.
        suppliers: print the suppliers of a class.

Command =>
```

From then on you can repeatedly request any one of the various indicated operations. To execute a command, type the operation name followed by the appropriate arguments if any, as given by the preceding table; then press Enter. To leave **es3** use the **quit** operation (or just **q**)

Here there is no default operation; this explains the presence of a "melt" operation, which was not needed as an option of **es3** since it is the default operation for that command.

You cannot select a different project from within **es3 –loop**; also, you cannot select a different Ace file from within the command, although you may of course change the contents of the Ace (for example by using an editor in an other window). If you are using an Ace file other than the file of name **Ace** in the current directory, or a project other than defined by the current directory, or both, you will need to use the **–ace** or **–project** options together with **–loop**.

11

Obtaining the best possible performance

11.1 OVERVIEW

The remarkable gains in software quality and productivity made possible by the Eiffel approach need not be achieved at the expense of efficiency. It is possible with ISE Eiffel 3 to produce systems that compare quite favorably, in their use of time and space, with software produced with older and more primitive techniques such as Fortran, C or C++ — and may in fact beat them handily.

For large applications, time-critical, space-critical or both, you may have to exercise some care to avoid paying an undue price for the most advanced facilities of Eiffel. This chapter describes a few techniques which can solve performance problems, or help avoid running into them in the first place. It also, by the way, discusses two areas that tend to frighten newcomers but should usually *not* be a concern thanks to the sophisticated compilation and run-time technology of ISE Eiffel 3: dynamic binding, and garbage collection — neither of which normally causes any significant performance degradation.

The main focus of the discussion is on *run-time* performance, although some hints will be given first on improving *compilation* speed if it is found to raise problems.

A methodological note. Although high-level performance considerations should play a role throughout the design of production quality software, we suggest concentrating first on making the software correct and ensuring that it uses the best possible algorithms and data structure implementations. Optimizations of the kind described below are meant to be applied *a posteriori* to a system that is running correctly and has been found to raise performance problems even though it uses adequate algorithms and data structures. In most cases, they will only affect a small subset of the system.

> **Note: array operations**
>
> The most common source of performance problems in Eiffel is array operations. If you system makes significant use of arrays and performance is a major concern, be sure to read the description of **direct array access** in this chapter before you release the system.

Direct array access is described in "EFFI-CIENT ARRAY OPERATIONS", 11.4, page 175 below.

11.2 COMPILATION PERFORMANCE

Two important observations may help reduce the time and space cost of compilation.

11.2.1 Compilation speed

The compilation of an Eiffel system requires a large number of disk input-output operations. If you experience slow compilation steps, check whether EiffelBench is not spending its time transferring data across the network.

It is highly desirable, especially for a large system, to make sure that the project directory (more specifically, the **EIFFELGEN** subdirectory where the compiler generates all the internal data for your project) be physically located on a **local disk** rather than on a disk accessible only through the network. A specific symptom is easy to recognize:

Note: after-melting delay

When you melt after a changes under the graphical environment, the message **Melting changes** will appear in the original shell window (after the **Degree** *n* compilation steps). After this message, the environment should take at most a few seconds to display **System recompiled** in the Project Tool and return control to you.

If the interval between these two messages is longer than a few seconds, you are most likely suffering from network delays. To correct this situation, use a project directory stored on a disk on the local machine rather than on a remote host.

It is important here to avoid any confusion: this advice applies only to the project directory, more specifically its **EIFFELGEN** subdirectory. It does **not** apply to the source text of your classes or to precompiled libraries, both of which can be located at arbitrary places:

- The source text of your system's classes is parsed only once; so you may store it anywhere in the network without any significant performance overhead. Different clusters may be stored at different places.

- Precompiled libraries are often stored at some central location, for example on a network server, so that they can be shared between different developers. This common practice does not cause any performance problem since there is no large transfer of information for precompiled classes.

It is only for the **EIFFELGEN** directory, which stores the internal information generated by the compilation mechanism for your specific project, that with a limited-bandwidth network you may need to check whether the accesses are local or remote.

11.2.2 Disk space used by a large system

When you develop a system under EiffelBench, freezing and melting will generate several internal files for each class, in particular the result of compiling the class into C, and the corresponding object code.

In the absence of precompilation, these files will be generated for every project using a given class. If many users have projects relying on the same classes, this may lead to undue disk usage.

The solution is simple: precompile the commonly used class combinations, using the precompilation mechanism described in an earlier chapter. Then there will be only one copy of the internal files; each project will only use disk space for its specific classes.

See "PRECOMPILA-TION", 6.5, page 96.

If you are only using the fundamental libraries, EiffelBase, you do not need to take any special action: EiffelBase is delivered in precompiled form. If you are using EiffelVision as well, make sure your system administrator precompiles the Base-Vision combination.

11.3 HOW TO ASSESS SPEED OF EIFFEL-GENERATED CODE

The rest of this chapter concentrates on run-time performance.

It is important, when evaluating the speed of code generated by the ISE Eiffel 3 compiler, to make sure that the evaluation is performed under the best possible conditions: final mode compilation, no assertion checking. Let us briefly review these two points, and also examine two factors which are usually *not* serious performance issues.

11.3.1 Using final mode

The remainder of this discussion will assume that the systems under review have been compiled in final mode.

On finalization see "FINALIZATION", 6.7, page 107.

Final mode is the only compilation mode that makes advanced optimizations possible, since such optimizations require a complete and stable system. Code compiled under final mode is typically several times faster than frozen or melted workbench code.

In many cases, a non-finalized system, partially frozen and partially melted, will still show a quite acceptable performance. As an example, the ISE Eiffel 3 environment, including the compiler, is written in Eiffel and processes itself; during the development of the environment we mostly used, within ISE, versions of the compiler that were not finalized, so as to be able to perform changes quickly. The response time was still more than acceptable and did not penalize the development.

But when it comes to delivering a stable product, meeting stringent performance demands or performing speed evaluations, the only reference is final mode.

11.3.2 Assertions

To obtain the best possible performance, you should disable all Debug instructions and assertion checking.

The chapter on compilation discussed this question in detail and examined the tradeoffs involved. It also noted that the major penalty does not come from assertions per se but from the need to keep a call stack for detailed exception tracing.

See "Assertion checking in final mode", 6.7.4, page 110, and the subsequent section.

Assertions should of course be enabled, at least at the *require* level, during development. When you are ready to deliver a system, however, no assertion violations should remain; if your application is time-critical and you have a high degree of confidence in its correctness, you should remove assertion checking. If either of these properties is not satisfied, then you most likely should leave assertion checking on.

11.3.3 A non-problem area: polymorphism and dynamic binding

One performance aspect which newcomers to Eiffel often fear, but which turns out usually *not* to be a problem, is the cost of dynamic binding.

Dynamic binding is efficiently implemented in ISE Eiffel 3. (In fact we believe it is not possible to find a faster implementation.)

In addition, the finalization process applies static binding to non-polymorphic calls, without any manual intervention from the software developer.

These sophisticated techniques are among the most advanced elements in the ISE EIffel 3 compiling technology. They make the cost of dynamic binding small or inexistent as compared to the techniques, such as multiple conditional instructions, that other approaches would require to achieve the same goals.

> This compilation technology also provides a considerable performance advantage over the C++ approach, which forces programmers to decide case-by-case which routines may be dynamically bound ("virtual") and which ones will always be statically bound. Because an erroneous static binding decision is so dangerous, C++ programmers are tempted to declare many routines as virtual, thereby preventing compilers from applying legitimate static binding and obtaining the considerable performance optimization that ISE Eiffel 3 safely achieves thanks to this technique.

Use the full extent of object-oriented technology, relying on your experience as a software engineer and your sense of what is performance-wise reasonable and what is not. Polymorphism and dynamic binding are there to help, not to penalize.

11.3.4 The case of garbage collection

For most applications, the overhead of garbage collection will be hardly visible. In fact many developers, and most users of the systems they develop, are not aware that there is a garbage collector running. This is a benefit of the efficient techniques used by ISE Eiffel 3 to handle garbage collection and, more generally, memory management.

If necessary, you can disable garbage collection at execution time thanks to procedures of the EiffelBase class **MEMORY**.

On class **MEMORY** *see chapters 13 and 23 of the book "Reusable software: the Base Object-Oriented Component Libraries".*

Garbage collection may, however, cause some difficulties in the case of applications with extremely demanding real-time requirements. In such cases, you may have to fine-tune the mechanism so that it fits your system's response time demands. Here too features of class **MEMORY** provide the basis for a solution tailored to the needs of your application.

More generally it is important, when considering the performance effect of garbage collection, to use a global perspective. Garbage collection is not the costly overhead that the concept still evokes for most people, but a performance-enhancing mechanism. To see this it suffices to consider the alternatives: using manual C-style *free* operations, which, together with *malloc*, are much less efficient than automatic memory management; or leaving dead objects unreclaimed, which causes increased swapping activity and waste of space.

11.4 EFFICIENT ARRAY OPERATIONS

The single most significant source of inefficiencies in Eiffel software, as noted at the beginning of this chapter, arises from the use of arrays in applications that manipulate large arrays, or perform a large number of operations on small arrays.

The reason is the power and flexibility of Eiffel arrays, which are treated as normal objects:

- They are indexed from an arbitrary lower bound.

- They may at any time be resized to arbitrary bounds.

- They are subject to garbage collection.

- They support run-time bounds checking through the preconditions of features of class *ARRAY*: the function *item* for accessing elements, its synonym **infix** "@", and the procedure *put* for modifying elements.

These properties may imply a penalty if you are using arrays in a more traditional fashion, especially in scientific computation where it is common to encounter loops that perform relatively simple operations on all or many elements of an array; typically, the array will never need to be resized during the loop, although you may still want to resize it at some other stages of the computation.

In such a case a technique known as **direct array access** is available to remove the overhead of the more advanced array properties, and yield a performance that is as good as that of array manipulations in Fortran or C. As noted at the beginning of this chapter, this technique should only be applied to those elements of a software system that have turned out to raise actual performance problems.

Direct array access applies in particular to loops manipulating an array *arr* under the general form

```
from
    some_initialization;
    index := some_initial_value
until
    index = some_final_value
loop
    ... Various operations, which may include:
        arr.put (some_value, index)
        access to arr.item (some_value)
            (No resizing.)
end
```

An array such as the object attached to *arr* is an instance of the EiffelBase kernel library class *ARRAY*. It includes an attribute *area*, coming from an ancestor of *ARRAY*, and representing a reference to an object of type *SPECIAL* which contains the actual array items.

To improve the performance of such a scheme, the direct array access technique uses a direct reference to the *SPECIAL* object throughout the loop body.

Before the loop, include an assignment of the form

> *arr_direct* := *arr.area*

where *arr_direct* is declared of type *SPECIAL* [*T*], type *T* being the same as used for the declaration of *arr* as *ARRAY* [*T*].

Then, within the loop, replace all *put* and *item* operations on *arr* by the same operations on *arr_direct*. This is a valid replacement since the corresponding features are also available in class *SPECIAL*, where they work directly, and hence much faster, on the actual array contents.

Direct array access as shown above will not work correctly if the loop body contains any operations that might resize the array (such as procedures *force* and *resize* of class *ARRAY*). Perform any such operations, if required, outside of the loop. You also will not be able to benefit from bounds checking, since *put* and *item* in class *SPECIAL* have no preconditions. (For gaining the utmost performance, you should probably, as noted above, disable assertion checking anyway.)

Note that an instance of *SPECIAL* is always indexed from zero. If the lower bound of *arr* is not zero, you would in principle have to subtract it from *index* throughout the loop body. But there is a better and simpler technique.

Let *low* and *high* be the bounds of *arr*. If *low* is 1 (as it most commonly is in Eiffel), create the array not with bounds 1 and *high* as you normally would, but with bounds 0 and *high* (keeping the original value of *high*). Now perform all array operations, in particular calls to *put* and *get*, as if the lower bound were 1. You waste the space for the item of index 0, but that is a trifle. The advantage is that you can simply replace operations on *arr* by identical operations on *arr_direct* within the loop, without any index translation. This technique remains applicable if the value *low* is a positive integer other than 1 but still reasonably small.

Direct array access has been shown to yield considerable performance improvements in applications whose performance is array-bound. If you experience performance problems and your system performs significant array manipulations, you should probably use it.

11.5 OTHER HINTS

One more optimization tip is worth noting: using local entities rather than attributes when appropriate.

Local entities are accessed faster than class attributes. In some cases you do require attributes, of course, but if you have a choice use a local entity.

The main reason to be careful about introducing attributes, especially in classes that appear high in the inheritance hierarchy, is in fact space rather than time performance: every instance of the class and its descendants will carry a field corresponding to the attribute. This observation, however, essentially affects non-boolean attributes. Boolean attributes are packed and so cause minimal overhead.

12

Building GUI applications:
an introduction to EiffelBuild

12.1 OVERVIEW

The preceding chapters have focused on advanced tools for building object-oriented applications quickly and effectively.

More and more software developments must address a complementary need: providing users of the resulting systems with friendly Graphical User Interfaces (GUI), without imposing undue extra effort on the systems' developers.

This chapter describes a set of principles for building such systems in a convenient interactive fashion, and presents the environment component that implements these principles: the EiffelBuild graphical application builder.

This is a rich enough subject, and the underlying ideas (the **Context-Event-Command-State** model of GUI application development) are novel enough, to warrant a book of their own. This chapter, then, can only serve four simple purposes: showing that the principles and techniques introduced in the preceding chapters can bring great benefits to much wider a domain than just the basic development environment, to which we saw it applied so far; giving you a feel for what EiffelBuild offers; providing enough concrete information to enable you to guess some of the rest and start using the tools for your own advantage; and perhaps making you want to read the future book on object-oriented GUI development when it becomes available.

Do not expect a full description, then. This chapter will take you through a Guided Tour of EiffelBuild — similar in spirit to the tour of EiffelBench at the beginning of this book — to introduce the basic concepts, get you started on the practical use of EiffelBuild, and tempt you to learn more.

As with the earlier Guided Tour, the presentation uses an example that you are invited, if you have access to the environment, to practice for yourself as you read about it.

12.2 GUI APPLICATION BUILDING: THE CONCEPTS

Let us first examine the goals of a graphical application builder and get a glimpse of the underlying mathematical model.

12.2.1 More than a pretty interface

The facilities described in this chapter benefit from the experience brought by a category of tools that have appeared in recent years: graphical interface builders, which enable software developers to use convenient visual techniques to design and test the graphical interfaces which the systems they build will present to their users.

The system that we are about to explore offers all the capabilities that you may expect from a modern interface builder, made even more powerful and convenient by the environment and interface techniques of this book. But its real aim is more ambitious: to provide a framework for constructing entire applications.

This more extensive scope corresponds to what users really expect from any system that you build: not just windows and menus, but useful functionalities — the system's **semantics** — into which windows and menus simply provide a convenient entrance. As with a house, we want a beautiful façade, but a façade is useless without what must lie behind it.

What is required, then, is not just an interface builder but a full-fledged **application builder**, based on the premise that developers and their users need more than a pretty interface.

The development abstractions underlying the objects that you will manipulate with EiffelBuild cover not just the interaction of your system with its eventual users, but also its semantics. Among the abstractions describing what the system does, rather than how it presents itself to its users, are such notions as **Command**, **State**, **Behavior**, **Transition** and **Application**. Presented later in this introduction, these abstractions cover what is needed to put together a complete application — the interface and the rest.

12.2.2 Seamlessness

The combined coverage of interface and semantics is part of a general characteristic of the Eiffel approach and of the environment described in this book: seamlessness. This concept means a constant effort to emphasize the commonality between different aspects of software construction, from analysis and design to implementation and maintenance, from method to language and environment, from the interface to the semantics, from text to graphics.

The goal is to avoid the "impedance mismatches" that traditional approaches introduce between various steps and activities of software development, and instead to ensure consistency between them. The principle of semantic consistency studied in an earlier chapter is a direct consequence of this central requirement.

The principle of semantic consistency was discussed in "SEMANTIC CONSISTENCY", 3.4, page 46.

The unity between the different phases and tools is ensured by the method and the language: object-oriented software construction presides over all tasks, and Eiffel constructs and concepts provide the common thread.

This focus on consistency implies in particular that EiffelBuild is naturally interfaced with the rest of the environment, especially with EiffelBench, which brings to the EiffelBuild developer the Melting Ice compilation technology and other mechanisms studied in the rest of this book.

12.2.3 No need for simulation

Thanks to its seamless approach to application building, the method and tools described in this chapter are able to integrate system semantics closely with the interface.

It is interesting to compare this approach to semantics with what is usually available in interface builders. Most interface builders offer "hooks" for plugging in calls to C or C++ functions, also known as callbacks. To develop the code behind the hooks developers still need to rely on primitive techniques (in particular low-level languages and slow tools such as compilers and linkers) unconnected to the "screen painting" tools of the interface builder.

With the EiffelBuild approach, commands and other objects covering the semantics are full-fledged development objects, just like windows or menus; developers can create, access, reuse, manipulate and modify them interactively from within the environment.

These properties also imply another difference, surprising at first, between the EiffelBuild approach and interface builders: the absence of a simulation or test mode.

In an interface builder, a simulation mode enables developers to exercise the interface before building the application. But this is only useful in a context where adding semantic actions forces you to go outside of the environment, or if compilation is a long and tedious affair (or if both of these properties hold, as is often the case). With EiffelBuild you can define the semantics within the environment, and you can use the power of EiffelBench's Melting Ice Technology to compile your system in seconds and start exercising it right away. Why then play with a mockup when you can test the real thing?

Of course if you want to concentrate on the interface first, the initial version of the semantics may be pure scaffolding: commands that do nothing or almost nothing, serving as placeholders for classes to be completed later. Here the approach also provides a great advantage in allowing smooth, incremental development; you can progressively transform the original scaffolding classes into versions that support the desired final semantics. This seamless form of development is much preferable to having to switch abruptly from simulation mode to real mode — that is to say, start all over again.

12.2.4 The graphical and the textual

A consequence of the seamlessness principle is the reconciliation of textual and graphical modes of software construction.

Many aspects of EiffelBuild make it a member of the general class of products known as **visual programming** tools, supporting the development of applications through visual interaction techniques rather than by typing program texts. But EiffelBuild does not apply the sometimes dogmatic anti-text attitude underlying many visual programming tools. There is nothing wrong with text; the cliché that "a picture is worth a thousand words" fails miserably as soon as one needs to describe advanced semantic properties. A look at the various devices proposed over the years to represent loops graphically is sufficient *a contrario* proof of the power and elegance of some of the constructs of a good programming language.

The environment described in this book is meant for ambitious software developers who — although like everyone else they will appreciate an easy, intuitive graphical interface, and will resent tedious tasks and repetition — are not scared by the need to write software elements when that is the best way to express a novel and useful design.

Graphics and text, then, are complementary rather than exclusive. Each has its own strengths. Text is irreplaceable for describing new software elements with non-trivial semantics, algorithms or data structures. Interactive graphics is ideal in three cases:

- Specifying the graphical part of a system (the interface).

- Specifying overall system structures (the equivalent of function block diagrams found in traditional engineering disciplines).

- Most importantly, supporting reuse. As noted above, you will usually require some use of text to build elements implementing complex semantics; but once such elements have been written, validated, proved to be of good quality, and included in a library of reusable software components, it is possible and advantageous to provide graphical mechanisms for accessing them and including them in new applications.

EiffelBuild applies these ideas. It is definitely a graphical environment, where most of the interaction uses direct manipulation and the other principles discussed in chapter 3. But it does not shun text, and when you come across the need for a command that is not yet available you will naturally be led to fill in a few feature declarations or redeclarations in a class text whose template has been generated by EiffelBuild. This is exactly the role of a development environment: handling predictable tasks; taking care of repetitive actions; providing access to reusable components; and facilitating the creative part of the software construction process, which only software developers can carry out.

Recognizing that developers may want to alternate between textual and graphical interaction, EiffelBuild takes great care to support this mixed process and to ensure that the results are the same regardless of the interaction mode that produced them. In particular:

- The Eiffel text generated by EiffelBuild as a result of graphical interaction is readable — similar in style to what a competent developer would have produced manually — and can be modified through text editors.

- The environment includes advanced (although silent) mechanisms for reconciling changes that you can make at various times to a given system, using textual means in some cases and graphical techniques in others.

12.2.5 The model: Context-Event-Command-State

EiffelBuild relies on a mathematical model whose name was introduced above: Context-Event-Command-State. (This discussion will attempt to avoid using the acronym.)

A full presentation of this model can be found in the second edition of the book *Object-Oriented Software Construction* (Prentice Hall, 1994). Let us limit ourselves here to the basic ideas. If you do not immediately get a concrete feel for some of the concepts, the example discussed in the rest of this chapter, which uses all of them, should help you understand them better.

One of the major themes of this book is that, as any application system is defined in the object-oriented approach by its data abstractions, so is any object-oriented development environment defined by its **development abstractions**; to use the environment is to manipulate development objects, which are instances of these abstractions. The EiffelBuild model, then, is defined by a set of development abstractions for building GUI systems.

See "Object-orientation for the software and its developers", 3.2.2, page 42.

In the earlier chapters of this book we saw the EiffelBench development abstractions: Class, System, Feature, Execution Object, Stop Point. Let us now examine the EiffelBuild development abstractions: Context, Event, Command, State, Behavior, Transition and

Application. Each will be described in terms of its instances, the corresponding development objects (for example the explanation of the Context development abstraction describes a typical context — a typical instance of that abstraction).

A **context** is a graphical object that will be part of the system under development, offering some interaction possibilities to the users of that system. Examples of context include buttons, windows and menus. A context is characterized by a boolean function, yielding true if the mouse cursor is inside the context's graphical area and false otherwise.

> It is also possible to define non-graphical contexts as long as they have an associated boolean function. For example there could be a "file" context for which the boolean function is true if and only if the file is open. For this discussion, however, we will limit ourselves to graphical contexts.

An **event** is a user-triggered action that can occur at run time. Typical events are Activate (press a mouse key) and Text Modify (in an editable context where users can enter characters). Many events, such as Text Modify, are meaningful for certain contexts only; this property will be reflected in EiffelBuild, where you will obtain the visual representation of events inside the Context Tool describing each context.

A **command** is an object describing the execution of some operation by the system. Commands provide the basic mechanism for achieving the goal described above of covering system semantics as well as the interface. A command object is an instance of a command class, a descendant of the EiffelVision class **COMMAND**; every such effective descendant must provide a procedure **execute** which describes the intended effect. This procedure, which can include arbitrary instructions and calls to other features, provides the link with the rest of the system. A command may also inherit from **UNDOABLE** (an heir of **COMMAND**), in which case it will also provide a feature **undo**, supporting a convenient undo-redo mechanism similar to what EiffelBuild itself (which is built out of the techniques described here) provides to its own users, as described later in this chapter.

The undo-redo mechanism of EiffelBuild is described in "THE HISTORY MECHANISM", 12.6, page 200 below.

A **state** defines the possibilities that are open to users at a given stage of a session. For example you may be presented at a certain stage with a number of windows and other tools, offering you the choice between various actions. Later on in the session, as a result of your earlier choices of action, the possibilities and effects may be different, meaning that you have entered a different state. So a state is characterized by a three-component association between contexts, events, and commands. More precisely, the ingredients are:

- A set of recognized context-event pairs — for example, in a simple state for a text editing system, the three pairs <**OK_BUTTON**, **click_event**>, <**CANCEL_BUTTON**, **click_event**> and <**CLOSE_BOX**, **click_event**>.

- For each of the recognized context-event pairs, a command (for example commands **SAVE**, **CANCEL** and **CLOSE** for the three preceding pairs).

In the formal model, *STATE* is described by a function of signature $CONTEXT \times EVENT \xrightarrow{f} COMMAND$, used in curried form: $CONTEXT \xrightarrow{f} EVENT \xrightarrow{f} COMMAND$.

A **behavior** is an association between events and commands; in other words it is the $EVENT \xrightarrow{f} COMMAND$ part of a state — the part describing the state's behavior for a particular context.

The arrow denotes finite functions and the cross cartesian product. See "Introduction to the Theory of Programming Languages", Prentice Hall, 1991, which also explains the notion of currying a function.

A **transition** is a value attached to a command. The definition of a command includes the definition of a set of possible transition values, or **labels**. When a session of the system executes an instance of the command, it will set the value of the transition to one of the possible transition labels. For example a file opening command might have the transition labels **opened**, **failed** and **canceled**, corresponding to three possible outcomes of the command. Any particular execution of the command will set the transition value to one of these labels.

An **application** consists of a set of states connected by a transition diagram. For each state, each command that is part of that state (as a member of the range of the corresponding mathematical function), and each transition label that the command may trigger, the transition diagram specifies the new state that the session will enter when the given command, executed in the given state, terminates with the given label.

12.2.6 Reuse and extension, tools and catalogs

One of the outstanding contributions of the object-oriented method is the solution it brings to the problems of software reusability and extendibility — and to the problem of reconciling these two goals. We need to be able to build systems from reusable components, and to adapt both the systems and the components to new requirements without undue effort.

EiffelBuild supports this essential requirement in its own corner of object-oriented technology. One of the main techniques through which it achieves this aim is to provide, for each fundamental data abstraction as studied above, both **catalogs** and **tools** of the corresponding type. You will for example find command and context catalogs, as well as command and context tools.

The catalog concept serves reuse: to build an application you will draw from the existing catalogs of predefined development objects. You will also be able to add your own reusable elements (in the *producer's view* of reuse, complementing the *consumer's view*).

The consumer's and producer's views of reuse are discussed in "Object-Oriented Software Construction".

The tool concept serves extension: using a tool (also known in some cases as an editor) you can define your own development objects, either from scratch or more commonly by extension and addition to preexisting ones.

These ideas are another example of the theme of semantic consistency that runs through this book: making sure that the environment directly supports the goals of the method.

12.2.7 Direct manipulation and conventional wisdom

One more note is in order to conclude this glimpse of the principles underlying EiffelBuild. The design method that EiffelBuild promotes tends to depart from conventional views on system design, which hold that one should strive to keep the user interface and the rest of the systems separate.

Some of the reasoning between this traditionally recommended approach is of course sound: it is desirable to allow developers to change the interface without affecting the rest of the application (what has been called the semantics above); and it is sometimes necessary to provide more than one interface to a single semantics. EiffelBuild of course supports these ideas, which are part of the general effort towards abstraction and information hiding that underlie the object-oriented approach and are enforced particularly strongly in Eiffel.

> Note, however, that the object-oriented method really talks about *module* interfaces, which it advocates keeping conceptually separate from module implementations; the *user* interfaces in interactive systems are a different matter. Even if the former advice has some bearing on the latter problem, we should not confuse the two areas.

The desire to separate the user interface from the semantics may sometimes have gone too far, at the risk of contradicting such other important principles as direct manipulation. As stated in its earlier presentation, the direct manipulation principle encourages building systems that foster the illusion that the visual objects representing semantic objects *are* these objects. For example a user of a library management system built along these lines may be able to drag-and-drop the representation of a book to the representation of the books-in-stock catalog, and by this simple action record the returning of the book by its latest borrower. Similarly, when you use EiffelBench to grab a class representation (the class name, or the tiny dot representing the class in a hole) for drag-and-drop, everything proceeds as if you had actually grabbed the class itself.

When the user interface enforces such a direct connection between semantic objects and visual objects, it is natural that the software should attempt to do the same. Such approaches as the Smalltalk MVC model (Model-View-Controller) may introduce unnecessary intermediate levels between the two worlds — the graphical and the semantic.

> It is of course possible to implement MVC using the environment of this book and specifically EiffelBuild. But we must question whether this is the best approach.

It falls beyond the scope of this discussion to describe the design techniques that are best suited to define flexible interactive system architectures, enforcing direct manipulation while retaining the ability to change the interface independently of the semantics and to provide different interfaces for the same semantics. Let us simply note some useful ideas:

- Using the client relation, we can provide displayable semantic objects with "visual handles" that enable them to request display and other graphical operations.

- The client relation can also be set the other way around: a visual object has a reference to the associated semantic object.

- We can make the classes describing semantic objects inherit graphical properties. (Since semantic classes will already have their own non-graphical parents, this technique requires an environment supporting multiple inheritance, which may help explain why it was not considered in Smalltalk environments.)

- We can define new classes that inherit from both semantic and graphical classes. (This too will require multiple inheritance.)

Arguments may be found for each one of these various solutions, and the topic undoubtedly deserves a deeper discussion. But this overview will at least, I hope, have brought to your attention the need to reexamine conventional ideas about the architecture of interactive systems — in particular the laudable but simplistic maxim that "one should separate the user interface from the implementation".

12.3 THE EXAMPLE SYSTEM

The system that we will build for this Guided Tour of EiffelBuild is a small text editing system, offering the following facilities:

- Opening a file for editing (**Open** command).

- Editing the file.

- Save the current state of the editing into the file (**Save** command).

- View another file (**View** command).

- Once done with viewing, resume editing of the original file (**Back** command).

The **View** command will be very similar to the **Open** command, enabling us to see how to use EiffelBuild to create a new command class by inheritance from another. The presence of the **Back** command will make it appropriate to have more than one state in the application.

The interface of the system will look like this (or more precisely this figure is a black-and-white approximation of what the interface will look like on a color display):

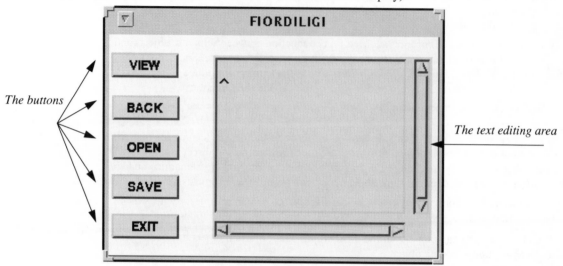

This interface has one main window (called **FIORDILIGI**), containing a scrolling area, which will show the text being edited, and five command buttons.

12.4 SETTING UP AND STARTING EIFFELBUILD

To start EiffelBuild you must have your path, environment variables, libraries and graphical properties correctly set up.

12.4.1 Setting up the environment

The two environment variables of EiffelBench, **EIFFEL3** and **PLATFORM**, are also used by EiffelBuild — and no others are needed. Make sure that they are properly set up. Also, you must have a license that covers EiffelBuild, and your path must contain the directory containing the EiffelBuild executable; its location is

$EIFFEL3/build/spec/$PLATFORM/bin

You must also make sure that you have the proper settings for the window system. This may be achieved through the following operating system command:

xrdb −load $EIFFEL3/build/app-defaults/_defaults-file_

where **$EIFFEL3** is the installation directory, and *defaults-file* is the file that corresponds to your window system in the directory **$EIFFEL3/build/app-defaults** (if you are not sure which defaults file to choose check with your system administrator; it is important that you get the proper file if EiffelBuild is to work properly).

As with EiffelBench, you will use a project directory. Assume that the name of this directory is of the form *YOURDIR/build_dir*, that is to say, that the parent directory is called *YOURDIR*. We need the name of that parent directory, since EiffelBuild will create its own directory ; so the best way to start the session is to call EiffelBuild from *YOURDIR*. The subdirectory *build_dir* should not exist yet; EiffelBuild will create and initialize it for you.

> If, as is likely, you are using EiffelBuild in connection with EiffelBench, it is probably a good idea to use as Build project directory a subdirectory of the Bench project directory. In this case *YOURDIR* is simply the EiffelBench project directory.

The example EiffelBuild session that served to prepare the figures of this chapter used the project directory **/Napoli/Fiordiligi/build** (that is to say, *YOURDIR* is **/Napoli/Fiordiligi** and *build_dir* is **build**).

12.4.2 Libraries

EiffelBuild-generated applications will need the EiffelVision graphical libraries. For best results, and in particular speedy compilation using the Melting Ice Technology, it is recommended that you use EiffelVision in precompiled form.

On precompiled libraries see "PRE-COMPILATION", 6.5, page 96.

12.4.3 Starting EiffelBuild

To start EiffelBuild change directory to *YOURDIR* and execute the command

```
ebuild &
```

The following control panel (Base Tool) comes up.:

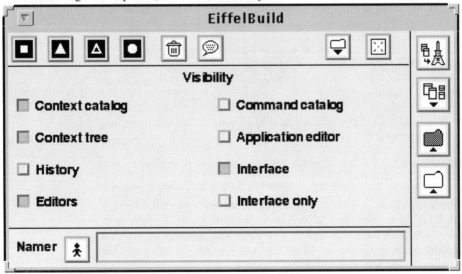

To avoid confusion with the tools of EiffelBench, the EiffelBuild tools all appear in this chapter with lightly shaded background as in the preceding figure.

See "GENERAL TOOL ORGANIZA- TION", 4.4, page 62.

The general organization of this tool and the other tools of Eiffel Build is the same as for EiffelBench tools: holes at the top left, Focus Area at the middle top, buttons at the top and on the right border.

As with EiffelBench, you can use the Focus Area facility to get familiar with the different buttons and holes: move the mouse cursor, without clicking, over the various parts, and see the display in the middle top section, just below the window border.

The Base Tool lists the various categories of tools and catalogs that you may need during a session. Since you may have to create many such graphical objects, it is important to avoid cluttering the screen. The checkable boxes appearing next to the various components enable you to make these components visible or invisible. For example the Context Catalog will be visible as soon as you have selected a project; to hide it, click on the corresponding box (the little square appearing to the left of **Context catalog** on the figure of the preceding page); to bring it back later, click again on that box.

As with EiffelBench, closing the Base Tool window closes all EiffelBuild windows; this provides a convenient way to switch temporarily to some other activity that also requires screen space.

12.4.4 Opening a project

To get started with this Guided Tour you need to open a project.

Click on the Open button ⬜. The File Selector comes up; use it, as you have learned to do with EiffelBench, to select the full project name, *YOURDIR/build_dir* (you will have to type the last part of that name, *build_dir*, into the **Selection** field since as noted above that directory must not exist yet).

The File Selector was described in "THE FILE SELECTOR", 4.7, page 70.

The top part of the window briefly shows the message **Creating new project...** You will indeed be able to see that EiffelBuild has created *build_dir* and three subdirectories — **Backup**, **Classes** and **Storage** — which will serve to store the project, in both an internal retrieval form and Eiffel source form.

In later sessions, the message when you retrieve an existing project rather than creating a new one will be **Retrieving project ...**

At any time during the session you can store the current state through the Save button 🏛 of the Base Tool. This should not be confused the Generate button 🏛⚒, which produces the resulting Eiffel text (in the **Classes** subdirectory of **build_dir**) and is useful when you have sufficiently advanced in the development to compile and execute the resulting system. The Save button stores an image of the entire application, which you can retrieve in a later project by entering the name of the application's project directory into the File Selector when you start a new session and click on the Open button.

12.4.5 The basic windows

EiffelBuild now creates two more basic windows

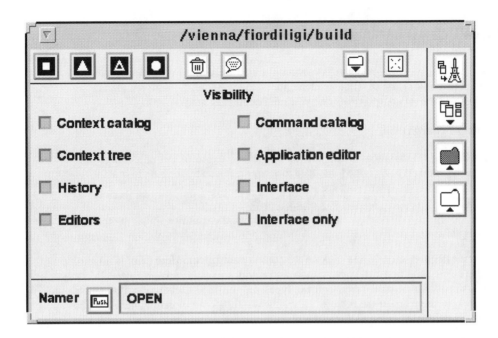

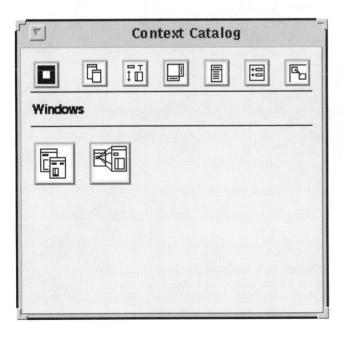

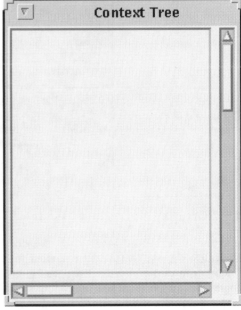

The Context Tool window will enable you to select the contexts making up your application and, more generally, to build the interface. The Context Tree will faithfully record the structure of the interface as you add components to it.

12.5 DRAWING THE INTERFACE

Let us now draw the interface of our text editing system: the window containing the five buttons and the text editing area. All these elements — the window, the buttons, the editing area — will be instances of context types that you can find in the Context catalog.

12.5.1 Context categories

The Context Catalog (the window at the bottom-left on the figure of the preceding page) offers many such context types, divided into categories represented by the icon row at the top right of the window: . Once again you can use the Focus Area mechanism to become familiar with the context categories simply by moving the cursor over these icons.

To select a category you will just click on the corresponding icon. Here there is no need to go anywhere since the first category, Windows, provides exactly what we need. More precisely, we want the first of the two context types offered in this category: Permanent window, the first of the icons at the bottom. (The other is Temporary window; here too and anywhere else you can use the Focus Area to find out.)

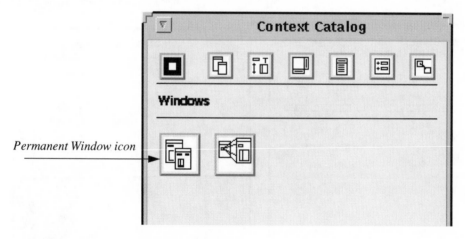

Permanent Window icon

12.5.2 Creating a permanent window

To create a permanent window use the drag-and-drop mechanism. The mechanism is identical to the one that we have studied for EiffelBench: right-click on the Permanent Window icon shown above, release the button, bring the cursor (which takes the Context pebble shape: a solid square ∎) anywhere in the Context Tree window (the one that appears at the bottom-right of the figure on the preceding page), and right-click again.

Drag-and-drop is described in "THE TYPED DRAG-AND-DROP MECHA-NISM", 4.3, page 59.

This creates a permanent window , which comes up on the screen:

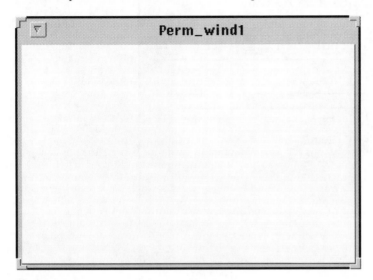

This window will be the topmost component of the interface for users of the system under development; all the other contexts will appear in it. You may resize it to the desired dimensions using the resizing mechanism of your window system. Note that the Context Tree has registered the existence of a new context:

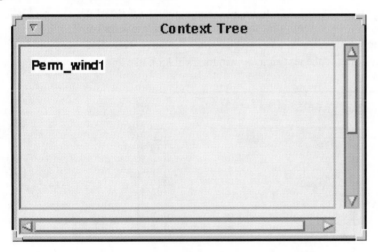

12.5.3 Adding, moving and resizing contexts

Now we can add the other contexts. First, the text area; its type belongs to the Scroll category, the third one in the Context Catalog. Click on the **Scroll** icon in the Context catalog (again, the Focus Area will tell you when you are at the right place); the Context Catalog displays the Scroll context types:

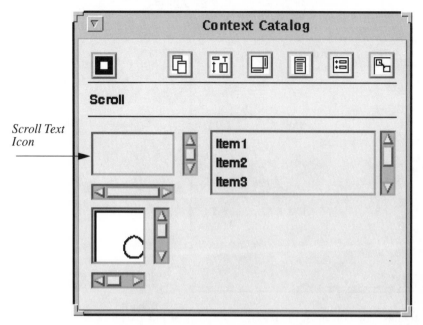

Scroll Text Icon

The context we need for the text area is the first one in the Scroll list; as the Focus Area will tell you, it is called simply Text. Drag-and-drop it to its intended position into the permanent window. If it does not land in the exact intended position, you may move it using the left button (kept pressed; this convention comes from the underlying toolkit). Also, if it does not have the proper size, resize it by dragging its top-left corner using the leftmost mouse button, kept pressed; you know that you are ready to resize when the cursor takes this shape: ↖ . After you have properly adjusted the text area the window will look like this:

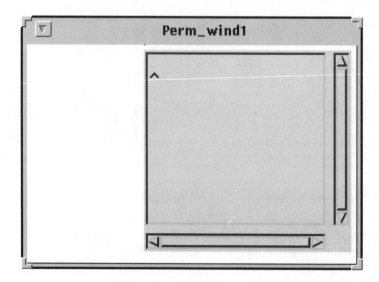

12.5.4 Adding and modifying a button

We must now add the buttons. They belong to the second category of context categories (the first after Windows): Primitives. Here is the set of context types in that category, obtained by pressing the corresponding icon in the Context Catalog:

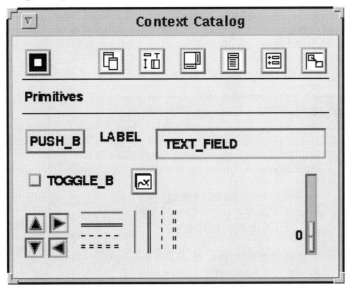

The "primitives" include label, text field, toggle button, arrow buttons of four possible orientations, separators, scale, "pict color" button. Here the context type of interest for our immediate purposes is again the first: **PUSH_B** at the top-left. Drag-and-drop this context type to the permanent window. Again, if you do not quite shoot straight, you can subsequently move the button. Here is the desired result:

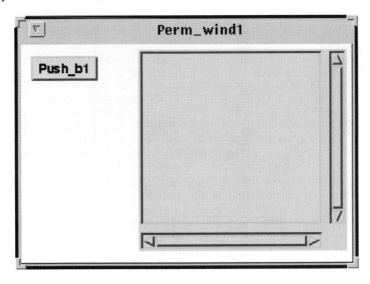

12.5.5 Editing contexts

Before including the other buttons (which, as you may have guessed, will not be added individually but simply duplicated from the first one) let us improve the appearance of what we have built so far.

To edit the push button temporarily known as **push_b1** drag-and-drop it to a Context Tool. (Remember to use the rightmost mouse button for drag-and-drop; the leftmost button would simply move the context.) The place to drop the context pebble is the Context hole at the top of the Base Tool:

The Context hole

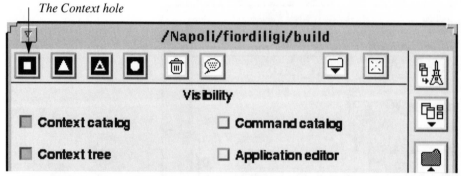

The pebble for the push button is of the context type, ■. When you drop it into the Context hole it brings up a Context Tool, whose top portion looks like this:

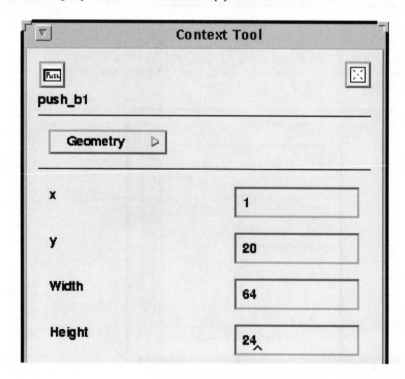

This tool makes it possible to edit various properties of a context. The properties are grouped into categories, also called formats. The formats appear in the menu whose first entry, shown above, reads **Geometry**. Bring up the menu (normally by pressing the leftmost mouse button on Geometry and keeping it down); you see the other formats: Attributes, Resizing policy, Color, Font, Behaviors.

Select the **Attributes** format. The display changes:

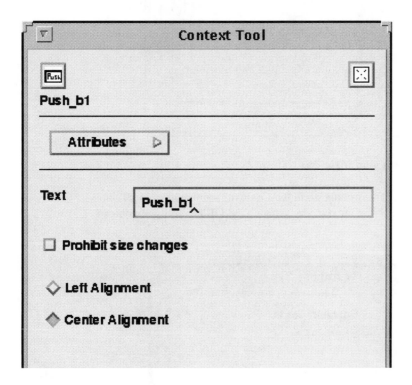

First, click on the box next to **Prohibit size changes**; this implies that if you change the name of the button its size will remain the same. The default policy is to adapt the button size to the length of the name; here since we are going to obtain the other buttons by replication it is desirable for visual consistency that they all have a fixed size. Next, replace the EiffelBuild-generated name of the context, **Push_b1**, by a name fitting the application: **VIEW** (since this is going to be the button for the **View** command of our system).

To change the name just type the new name in the **Text** text field, overwriting the old one; as usual you may first have to click to make the field responsive to keyboard input, and you may backspace over the original characters or double-click to replace the entire entry. Press Enter (or Return); this updates the display in the interface window:

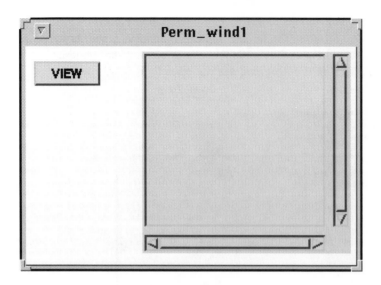

12.5.6 The Context Tree and semantic consistency

You may have followed what was going on in the Context Tree window. At all times that window will reflect the state of the interface by showing the full hierarchy of contexts. Here is what it now looks like:

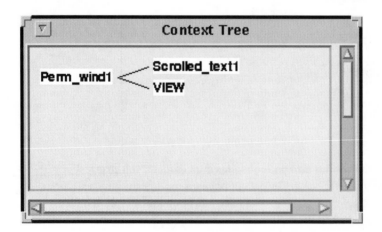

If at any time you want to know what a name appearing in the Context Tree represents in the interface, just click on it using the **middle button** of the mouse. As long as you maintain the button down, a solid line will connect the selected Context Tree element to the associated visual object in the interface. For example if you middle-click on **Scrolled_text1** above you will see that this name represents the text area:

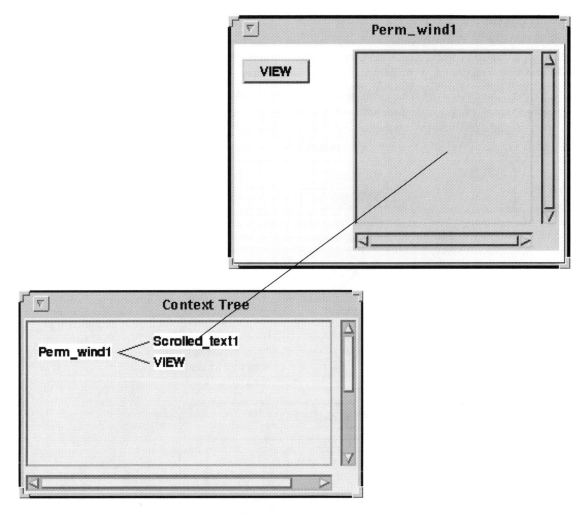

This technique does not just apply to the Context Tree; you can use it whenever you see a representation of some interface object in a tool of the environment other than the interface window. If you have any doubt as to what interface object the representation denotes, just middle-click on it as above and you will see the link to the interface object.

In the discussion of environment and interface principles, we studied a fundamental rule: semantic consistency, which states that a visual object, regardless of the format in which it appears, must always stand for the underlying development object and provide users with all the valid operations on that object. We saw this principle applied to EiffelBench. It holds here too: the representation of a context as a node in the Context Tree or other tool, for example **Scrolled_text1** for the Text Area, is fully equivalent to the button itself as it appears in the interface window (**Perm_wind1**). So for example if you want to drag-and-drop the button to a Context Tool you can indifferently pick it through its final graphical representation in the interface or through its symbolic representation in the Context Tree.

See "SEMANTIC CONSISTENCY", 3.4, page 46.

12.5.7 Duplicating objects

We need four more buttons. We could of course obtain them like the first, by instantiating from the corresponding context type in the Context Catalog, but since their basic properties are all the same it is more convenient to duplicate them from the first.

A simple technique is available for that purpose. Move the mouse cursor to the bottom-right corner of the first button; the cursor will start looking like this: ⬂ . Holding down both the SHIFT key and the leftmost mouse button, move the cursor towards the bottom right. As you do so new rectangles of the same size as the button start appearing:

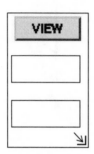

Since the total number of needed buttons is five you should go far enough to have four duplicate rectangles (if you go too far just move the cursor back) and release the mouse button. The result is five identical buttons:

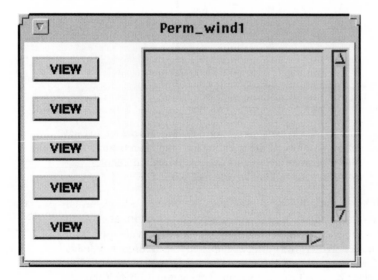

Four of these buttons should be renamed. We have seen a way to do this, through the **Attributes** format of the Context Tool. It is also possible, and faster in this case, to use the Namer hole and the associated field appearing at the bottom of the Base tool:

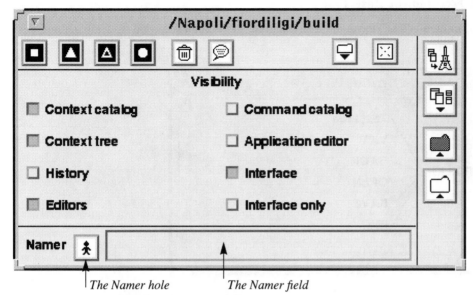

The Namer hole   *The Namer field*

If you drag-and-drop an object to the Namer hole, its name appears in the Namer field. This is by default a name generated by EiffelBuild, such as **Perm_wind1** or **Push_b1**. You can change it by typing the desired name in the Namer field; when you press Enter the new name will replace the original one.

Use this mechanism to rename the four new buttons **BACK**, **OPEN**, **SAVE** and **EDIT**. While you are at it, rename the scroll text **Text Area** and the permanent window **FIORDILIGI** (to drag-and-drop it into the Namer hole, pick it from any part of the window where no other context appears). This gives the desired layout of our interface:

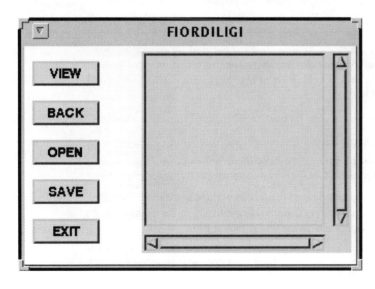

12.5.8 The Context Tree and the Base Tool

It is interesting to consider the Context Tree again. It now reflects all the contexts added to the interface:

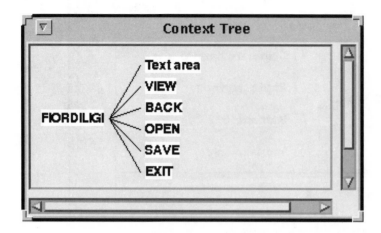

It is possible, by the way, to gather objects into groups; in such a case the hierarchy displayed in the Context Tree will have a depth of two or more, not just one as here. We will not need to use this possibility for the present example.

For any of the name changes done earlier you could have dragged the object to the Namer hole starting from the Context Tree rather than from the interface window.

If you temporarily want to get rid of some windows (for example the Context Tree), use the boxes on the Base Tool window next to **Context Catalog**, **Context Tree** and so on. When a box is checked, the corresponding window will be shown; when the box is unchecked, the window will be hidden. As mentioned at the beginning of this discussion, this facility makes it possible to avoid cluttering the screen. To check an unchecked box, or conversely, just click on it.

The layout of the Base Tool is shown, among other places, in the figure of page page 187.

If a window is open but you cannot see it because it is obscured by others windows belonging to EiffelBuild or to other systems that compete for the space on your screen, uncheck the corresponding box and check it again — that is to say, click twice. The second click will put it above any other window.

12.5.9 Adding color

If you have a color terminal (or your users will have color terminals) you will probably want to use color. All objects created so far in this session have their default colors. Let us add a little fantasy; there is nothing like discreet but well-chosen color to make an interface smile.

To change the foreground or background color of an object, use the Context Tool. One of the formats (obtained through the top menu) is **Colors**. If you display it for a context such as the **VIEW** button you will see the display appearing on the facing page.

Actually what you will see on a color screen is of course prettier — the little squares at the bottom will show the various color available, from light blue to deep Bordeaux.

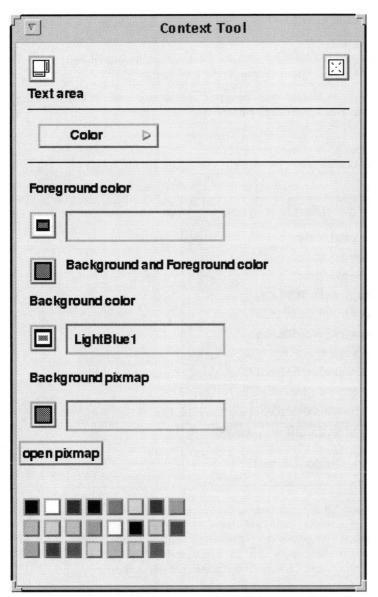

It would be surprising if you had not guessed how to change a color: drag-and-drop the selected square to either the **Background** or **Foreground** field. You can also type the color name; for possible values, see the file **$EIFFEL3/build/help/defaults/color_names**.

Whether you drag or type, the effect is just about the only mechanism that this book, being printed in black and white, cannot quite show. How unfortunate! The example as prepared for this chapter, displaying the most delicate combination of pastel tones, from angelic blue to fluid salmon, would have caused any (already pale) masterpiece by Boucher, Chardin or Watteau to pale in comparison, and made the artists paler yet with jealousy.

12.6 THE HISTORY MECHANISM

You may have noticed the garbage can hole in the Base Tool 🗑. If so you have probably guessed its use: you can drag-and-drop any object into it to get rid of the object.

A more general and interesting mechanism for correcting erroneous decisions, and more generally for trying out various avenues of development, is the history facility.

12.6.1 The history window

To see the history mechanism at work click on the **History** box in the Base Tool. The History window comes up:

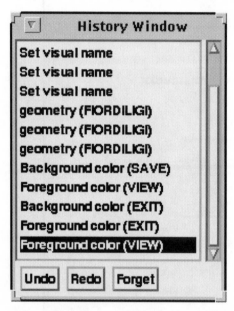

Big Brother was watching you! All the commands that you executed in the current session have been recorded: changing context names (**Set visual name**), moving or resizing windows (**geometry**), experimenting with colors for the system's buttons (**Background color**, **Foreground color**). Of course the display that you get may be a little different depending on the order in which you executed the various operations requested above.

12.6.2 Undoing and redoing

To cancel the last commands, click one or more times on **Undo**. At each stage the highlighting bar, positioned above on the latest command (here **Foreground color** applied to button **VIEW**), moves up one step to highlight the most recent command not yet undone. Each time, the session goes back to what it was one step earlier. A great way to relive earlier stages of your life. (Unfortunately, or fortunately in some cases, this applies to the EiffelBuild part of your activities only. ISE Eiffel 3 makes many claims, but will not bring back your youth, although we do think it will make you feel young and enthusiastic.)

Of course you do not really want to undo all this great and useful work of the recent session. Once you have undone a few times, click on **Redo** as many times. The commands replay themselves.

12.6.3 Unrolling and replaying an entire session or session slice

It is also possible to undo or redo many steps at once. Just go to any command listed in the window (use the scrollbar to move up if necessary) and click on that command. The whole set of commands executed since that one unrolls itself in a single sequence, as if you had clicked on **Undo** repeatedly. Now scroll back to the latest command and click on it; the session replays itself. At each step, of course, the highlighting bar moves to show the command being replied. This goes quite fast.

The history window records the entire current session, with no size limit. You can also restart from scratch — give yourself a new life — by clicking on **Forget**. The history is not preserved if you exit EiffelBench.

12.6.4 Undo-redo for your own systems

You will certainly be interested to know a little more about the technique used to support this history mechanism. There is nothing mysterious about it: it is a direct implementation of the notion of command object, which is described in detail in the book *Object-Oriented Software Construction* and will play a key role later in this chapter to enable us to define the semantics of our application.

This notion of command is also one of the principal development abstractions of EiffelBuild, as studied next, and is supported by a number of classes, such as **COMMAND** and **UNDOABLE** in the Command cluster of the underlying EiffelVision library.

As an important consequence, all the mechanisms to support arbitrary level undo-redo are available for you to include in your own applications, so that your users will be able to benefit from the same facilities. More details are given later in this chapter.

See "Making a command undoable", 12.7.10, page 215 below.

Needless to say, having such a general undo-redo mechanism is a great advantage for just about any interactive application that you can write.

12.7 SPECIFYING BEHAVIORS AND COMMANDS

We have obtained the interface of our system. Now we must make it do something useful — build the system's semantics. As noted at the beginning of this chapter, we need to build systems, not just their interfaces.

The basis of the semantics will be defined by **behaviors**, which associate commands with events for given contexts.

12.7.1 The Behaviors format

Let us start with the behavior of the **OPEN** button.

Retarget a Context Tool to that button by dragging the button into the tool hole of the existing Context Tool (the one that served earlier to set the attributes of the **VIEW** button) or, if you dismissed that tool earlier, by drag-and-dropping the **OPEN** button into the Context hole of the Base Tool to start a new Context Tool.

Through the menu of the Context Tool, select the Behaviors format. It appears as follows after a little while. (A short delay is normal the first time you bring up any format of the Context Tool; later requests for the same format will be served immediately.)

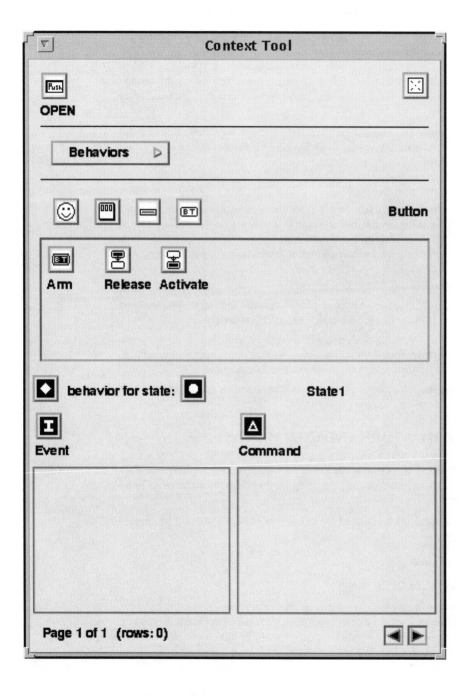

The middle part of the window (after the row of buttons
that ends with the word **Button**, and including the rectangle immediately below) is the Events part. The bottom part (two rectangular columns) will serve to record the behaviors.

As indicated in the line towards the middle of the window, on the right, the behavior that we will build is for state 1 — the default state. Later we will see how to introduce more states, and to give more evocative names to states.

12.7.2 The notion of behavior

A behavior is the semantics attached to a certain **context**. It is an association of **commands** to **events**. The behavior attached to a context such as the **OPEN** button will define what (what command) must be executed for any possible situation (any event) occurring in the given graphical object (the given context).

Since each context has a type — once again, the typing principle of ISE Eiffel 3 is at work— we do not need to consider all possible kinds of event, of which there may be several hundred in a sophisticated window system. This is why behaviors are attached to contexts: the above Context Tool targeted to **OPEN** gives us the list of possible event types for such contexts, of the Push Button type. Only three event types are displayed: **Arm**, **Release** and **Activate**. Note, however, that other events are applicable to contexts of the Push Button type; you would display them by clicking on other buttons in the
row.

See "STRONG TYP-ING", 3.5, page 47.

Arm is a mouse button click; **Release** is a mouse button release; **Activate** is click and release.

If you start drag-and-dropping any event such as these, the pebble will have the shape **I** corresponding to the event hole on the lower-left. (As usual, left-click anywhere if you want to cancel the drag-and-drop.)

To build a behavior, you are simply going to drag-and-drop event-command pairs: bring an event to the Event hole; bring a command to the Command hole; the two fall into the table, forming one row of the behavior; you will have specified that we wanted your system to execute the chosen command for every occurrence of the chosen event in the chosen context. Let us explore this key mechanism in detail.

12.7.3 Dropping an event

For **OPEN** we will define the command associated with the **Activate** event. Drag-and-drop that event to the Event hole. The event is displayed next to the hole:

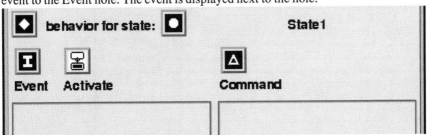

Nothing else happens yet; we must also obtain a command, to be associated with the chosen event for the context under study — the **OPEN** button.

12.7.4 The command catalog

We need a command whose execution semantics will be to open a file. To obtain it, turn to the Command Catalog. Its window is probably not displayed at this point; go back to the Base Tool, and check the corresponding box to bring up the Command Catalog on the screen:

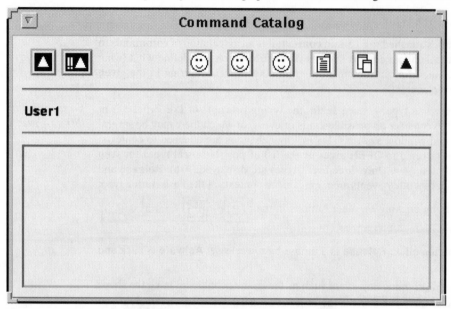

The Command Catalog offers predefined commands in a number of different areas; as your usage of EiffelBuild grows you will be able to add more and more of your own commands, or commands obtained from colleagues, to the catalog. Such a visual form of reuse will, I believe, play a central role in the evolution of the software field.

The catalog offers a number of categories, which you can explore using the Focus Area. Click on the button ▤ representing File commands. They include in particular **Save** and **Open**:

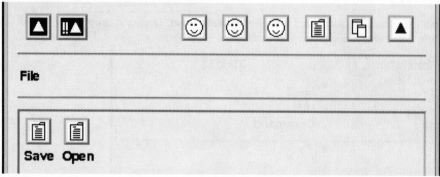

Open, as we shall soon check, is exactly the command that we need. This predefined command allows users (of your system, not of EiffelBuild, of course) to open a file and display it in a text area, prompting them to enter the file name through the File Selector.

If you right-click on **Open** and start dragging it, you will see that the pebble represents the Command Type type: ▲. So it is natural to drag it to the Command hole ◮ that we noticed earlier in the Context Tool, so as to associate the Open command to the Activate event for the **OPEN** button.

12.7.5 Command types and command instances

Not so fast! The two shapes, ▲ and ◮, almost match but not quite. The first is a pebble representing a command type, the second a hole for a command instance. So if you try to drop the pebble into the hole nothing will happen.

Why distinguish between command types and command instances? Before you can derive an actual command from a command type you need to instantiate it, and usually to give it one or more arguments. This is exactly like an Eiffel class, which will give an object only if you execute a creation instruction such as

!! x.make (a, b, ...)

For commands such as the one in our example the pragmatic reason to require instantiation is clear: to obtain a usable **Open** command, you must specify what part of the interface will serve to display the text of the file that the command opens during a session of the system.

Let us then instantiate the **Open** command. Drag-and-drop **Open** from the command catalog to the instantiation hole ‖◮. In this graphical symbol the !!, as you have guessed, is a discreet reference to Eiffel creation instructions, and the triangle is big enough this time for the command type pebble to fit.

The result is to bring up a Command Instance tool:

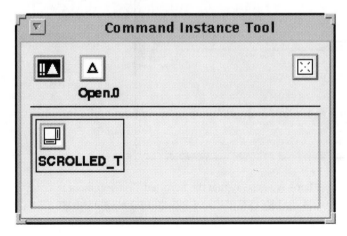

As the **SCROLLED_T** hole indicates, the Open command expects one argument, of type Scrolled Text. What an apropos request! We just happen to have such an object — the Text Area scroll text that we put at the bottom-right of our window:

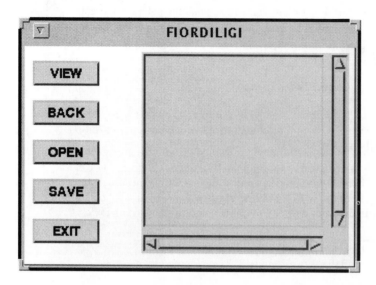

Drag-and-drop the Text Area to the **SCROLLED_T** hole of the Command Instance Tool. (Remember that if the above interface is not immediately visible, you can also pick the Text Area in the Context Tree; the result is exactly the same. Semantic consistency!)

As a result the command now instantiates itself:

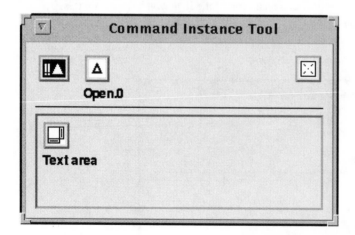

In the terminology of the rest of this book we can say that the Scrolled Text argument is now targeted to a particular Scrolled Text — the Text Area of our editing system under development.

12.7.6 Building a behavior pair

Now we have a real command. It is visually represented by the **△** button labeled **Open.0** at the top of the Command Instance tool (next to the tool hole). Note that the shape now exactly matches that of our command instance hole **▲**.

Indeed, drag the command (starting from the button labeled **Open.0**) into the Command hole that has been waiting for it in the Context Tool:

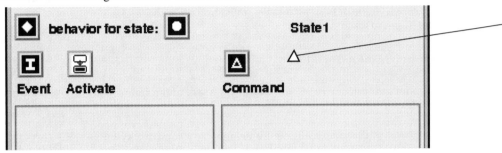

The other hole, the Event hole, had already been filled: earlier on you dropped the Activate event into it. So everything is ready to define an association between an event and a command. The event and the command fall into place, linked to each other, for better or worse, in the definition of the behavior for the current context:

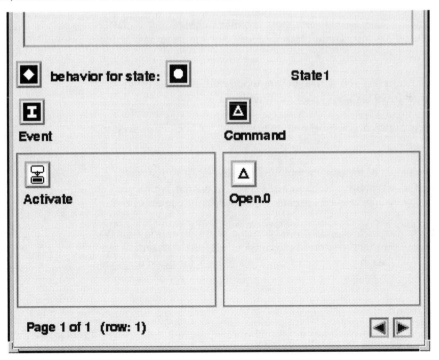

We were not, by the way, required to drop the event before the command. The reverse order would have worked just as well. The only requirement is that we drop one event pebble and one command pebble, each into the matching hole. The first drop does not cause any immediate action other than a visual record (shown above by the name of the event, **Activate**, displayed next to the **Event** hole); the second one will cause the association.

We now have our first behavior. It is very simple, consisting of just one event-command pair that associates a predefined command (Open File) with a simple mouse click. A more complete behavior will have several such event-command pairs: you may want to define what happens when a user clicks a button or releases it in the context, when the mouse cursor leaves the context, or enters it, and so on.

12.7.7 Building system by visual association

Simple as it is, the first behavior that you have just built shows the power of the EiffelBuild paradigm for building applications.

Note in particular the power of the visual support for defining an interactive system: you associate reusable commands with standard events for graphical contexts; for the whole process you use a simple interaction technique: **visual association** — bringing things together through typed drag-and-drop.

This method of software construction follows from a full application of object-oriented principles and the other ideas developed in this chapter. In particular:

- The reusability goal means that you can work from command classes such as **OPEN** drawn from the command catalog. These classes cover common cases and include ready-made semantics for these cases.

- The extendibility goal means that you will be able to modify these classes if you need to, simply by editing their Eiffel texts in Command Type Tools.

- You can alternate freely between graphical and textual forms of interaction with the environment.

- To define the overall structure of the application, the graphical mode is best, thanks in particular to the powerful and intuitive technique of visual association, which you can use to build an application by linking events to commands for specific contexts.

- Visual mechanisms are also well adapted to support the reuse of existing catalog components — contexts, events and commands to consider only the abstractions seen so far — which you will include in your systems using, once again, the typed drag-and-drop mechanism.

12.7.8 A complete command class

The text of class **OPEN** follows on the next three pages.

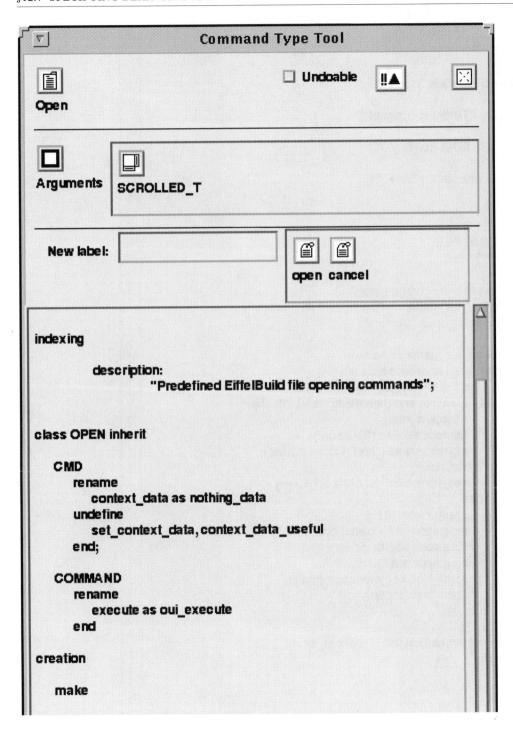

```
feature

    open_label: STRING is "open";

    cancel_label: STRING is "cancel";

    argument1: SCROLLED_T;

    asked_for_name: BOOLEAN;

    execute is
        local
            file: UNIX_FILE;
            msg: STRING
        do
            if not asked_for_name then
                asked_for_name := True;
                file_box.popup (Current)
            else
                asked_for_name := False;
                if not file_box.canceled then
                    !!file.make (file_box.selected_file);
                    if file.exists and then file.is_readable then
                        file.open_read;
                        file.readstream (file.count);
                        argument1.set_text (file.laststring);
                        file.close;
                        set_transition_label (open_label)
                    else
                        !!msg.make (0);
                        msg.append ("Cannot open: %"");
                        msg.append (file.name);
                        msg.append ("%"");
                        error_box.set_message (msg);
                        error_box.popup;
                    end
                else
                    set_transition_label (cancel_label);
                end;
            end;
        end;
```

```
    make (arg1: SCROLLED_T) is
        local
            Nothing: ANY
        do
            argument1 := arg1;
            !!file_box.make ("File Box", argument1.top);
            !!error_box.make ("Alert", argument1.top);
            error_box.hide_help_button;
            error_box.hide_cancel_button;
            error_box.add_ok_action (Current, Nothing);
            error_box.set_exclusive_grab;
        end;

    file_box: FILE_BOX;

    error_box: ERROR_D;

    oui_execute (argument: ANY) is
        do
            error_box.popdown
        end;

end
```

This command example gives a good idea of the style used to write commands for EiffelBuild.

There is seldom a need to write such a command text from scratch. Usually you will imitate the text of a catalog class such as **OPEN** or, better yet, adapt it through inheritance as explained next. All command classes will inherit from the EiffelVision class **COMMAND**.

12.7.9 Defining a command by inheritance

To complete the semantics of our example we need a few more behaviors.

Let us look at the behavior associated with the **VIEW** button. Here too only the Activate event is relevant, at least in a first step. In fact the **View** command is very similar to the **Open** command. In object-oriented software construction we know that such observations should never be allowed to rest unexploited: they form the basis for reuse *cum* adaptation through inheritance.

Create a new command instance by clicking on the Command buttonhole of the Command Catalog:

Command buttonhole

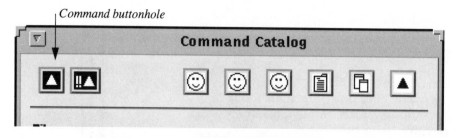

This adds a new command type, temporarily called **Command1**:

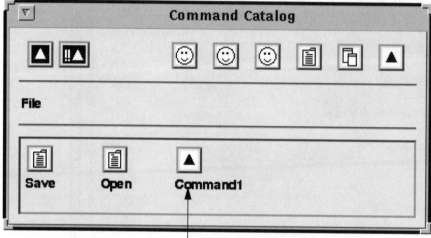

The new command type

This is not a very evocative name; use the Namer facility (through the Namer hole and the Namer field in the Base Tool) to rename the command:

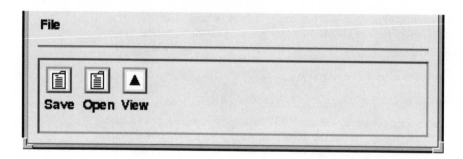

Drag-and-drop it the command by its pebble ▲ into a Command Type Tool (reuse the earlier one, or drop into the Command Type hole of the Base Tool). The text of the command is a simple template:

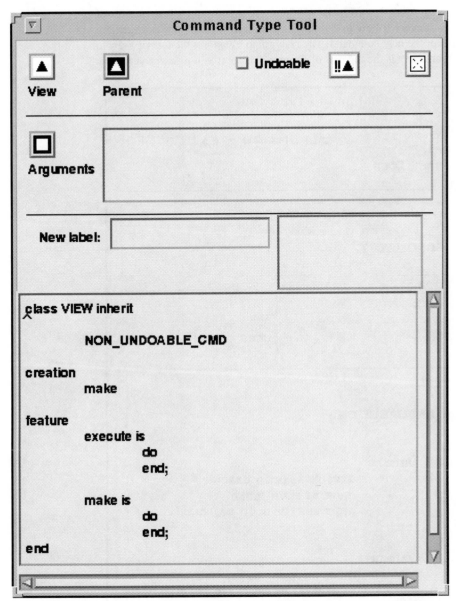

This command will need a transition label , which will make it possible (as explained in more detail later) to add flexibility to the application by distinguishing between various states. To include this label, which we will call **view**, type it in the **New label** field in the middle of the window, and press Enter.

The top row includes a Command Type hole ▲ whose label reads **Parent**. This hole enables you to build a command by making it inherit from another.

Here we can use this possibility to make our new command type, **View**, an heir of **Open**. You have certainly guessed how to do this: drag-and-drop the pebble representing **Open** to the Parent hole of the new command. The result is to transform the text of **View** to make it inherit from **Open**. Here is the top part of the new class text as it now appears in the Command Type Tool :

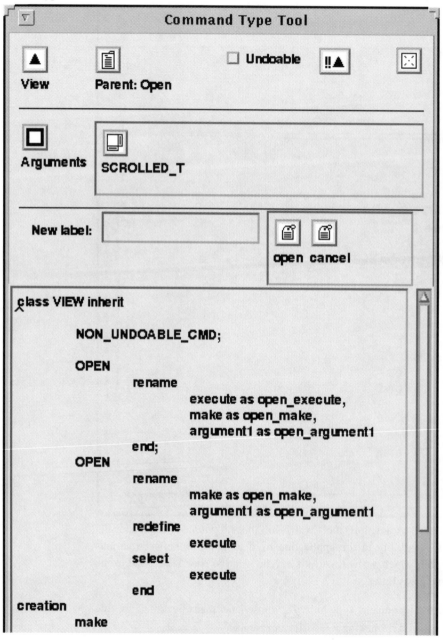

Notice how the transformation has generated an inheritance clause that includes all the appropriate Rename, Redefine and Select subclauses to satisfy all the validity rules regarding inheritance. Also, the command has three transition labels, appearing next to the **New label** field; two of the transitions, **open** and **cancel**, come from the parent command, **OPEN**; the third, **view**, corresponds to the transition that you have just added.

The transformation has also generated an attribute corresponding to this transition label:

```
view_label: STRING is "view";
```

To get the full **View** command with its own semantics you need to redefine one feature: procedure **execute**, which describes the command's action. As generated by EiffelBuild when you specified the inheritance relation, it just calls **open_execute**, the version of the procedure inherited from class **OPEN**. Here is what you should write for the redefinition:

```
execute is
   do
      if not asked_for_name then
         shared_text.wipeout;
         shared_text.append (argument1.text);
         asked_for_name := true;
         file_box.popup (Current)
      else
         open_execute;
         if equal (open_label, transition_label) then
            open_argument1.set_read_only;
            set_transition_label (view_label)
         end
      end;
```

It is also convenient to make **VIEW** inherit from a class **SHARED**. Just add **SHARED** to the list of parents of **VIEW** and include the following class text:

```
class SHARED feature
   shared_text: STRING is
      once
         !! Result.make (0)
      end
end -- class SHARED
```

Now that you have the **VIEW** class, define the behavior of the **View** button exactly as you did for **Open**: instantiate the command, give it an argument (the same Text Area, since it is used both for editing the primary file and for viewing others), and associate the resulting command instance **with the Activate** event in a Context Tool targeted to the **VIEW** button and displaying under the **Behaviors** format.

12.7.10 Making a command undoable

To provide your system with an undo-redo mechanism similar to that of EiffelBuild itself, you would need to make the commands undoable. To achieve this, simply click on the box labeled **Undoable** at the top of a Command Type Tool (as on the previous page) targeted to the command. This will make the command inherit from the EiffelVision class **UNDOABLE**, rather than directly from its parent **COMMAND**. You must then provide a procedure **undo** which cancels the effect of the command as described by procedure **execute**.

*See "THE HISTORY MECHANISM", 12.6, page 200. For the commands of this example, which can modify files, no simple **undo** procedures are available.*

12.8 THE STATES

Our system will need a few more behaviors and commands, built along the earlier lines. But let us first take a global look at the system; this will bring up the last three concepts — the last development abstractions not yet seen: State, Transition and Application.

12.8.1 The concept of state

A state is the definition of certain behaviors associated with certain contexts. Since a behavior is itself an association of certain commands to certain events, another way to express this definition is to note that a state includes the following elements:

- A set of contexts.
- For each context, a set of events that can occur within the context.
- For each context and each event applicable to the context, a command (which should be executed when the given event occurs within the given context).

A more complete presentation of this notion, based on the mathematical theory of functions and currying, may be found in the book *Object-Oriented Software Construction* (second edition).

Every interactive application has at least one state. Most applications have several, reflecting the property that at different stages through a session the context-event combinations available to the users may be different, and those combinations that are common may have different effects. As a simple example involving a textual system rather than a graphical one, if you are in the insertion state of a text editor and type the letter **y** followed by Enter the effect will be to insert the letter and a carriage return into the text, whereas the same action executed in response to a prompt (such as **Quit now [y|n]?**) will have a different result.

Such then is the nature of a state: defining the valid context-event combinations and the associated commands.

12.8.2 Are states bad?

Much of the early progress in interactive systems involved **limiting** the role of states: having few states in an application improves its consistency, makes it easier to learn (since there are fewer combinations to remember) and fosters user confidence. "Don't mode me in!" is a slogan often quoted by interface designers, "mode" being here a synonym for state.

The slogan "Don't mode me in!" originated with the design of the Smalltalk environment. On avoiding states, see "The perspective of the environment's user", 3.2.3, page 44.

In a complex system, however, it is generally impossible and in fact undesirable to get rid of states completely. For example an interactive operating system providing both a mail tool and a desk calculator will call for quite different contexts, events and commands in each case.

Once again we need to fresh look at accepted ideas. States are not necessarily bad by themselves; what is bad is **inconsistencies** between states. Different states and differences between states are legitimate when they cover the need to have different operations available at different times; but for those operations that are common to several states the interface should be as similar as possible.

Ignoring states would not be the right way to reach this goal. Instead we must make the notion of state explicit, and design our systems' state structures with care. Then with the help of object-oriented techniques we can build new states by modification and adaptation from existing ones, spot and correct unjustified differences, and achieve consistency.

EiffelBuild supports this approach by making the notion of state one of its principal development abstractions, and enabling developers to build and manipulate states visually like all other development objects of the ISE Eiffel 3 environment.

12.8.3 Taking the state into account

Simple applications may be quite happy with just one state. In fact it is possible to use EiffelBuild extensively and never to worry about states. By default there will always be a first state, called **State1**; this is the state with which we have worked so far, although we have been able to ignore it. All behaviors defined so far applied to **State1**; its name appeared in a hole of the Context Tool in Behavior mode, shown here again for the behavior of the **OPEN** which appeared in an earlier figure:

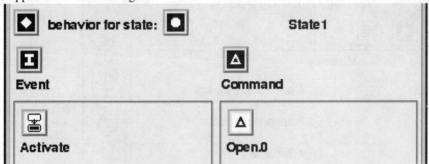

To take another state into account, drag its pebble, which will have the shape of a circular disk ●, into the corresponding hole ▣ as it appears above. Subsequent behaviors will apply to that state. This mechanism enables a context (for example an OK button) to have different behaviors in different states.

You may have noted another development abstraction on the above figure: **Behavior**, for which the hole is a diamond ◆. It is indeed possible to manipulate behaviors as full-fledged development objects, through Behavior Tools; we will not need to explore this possibility, as the Context Tool provides all that is needed to define the behaviors of this Tour.

Similarly, states can be edited through State Tools.

12.8.4 States for the editing system

Our example system provides a good illustration of why states are useful. To obtain the desired system we need to make sure that at each stage certain operations are available, and these operations only. More precisely we will need three states:

- **Basic**: this is the initial state, and users will return to it when it is safe to do so, for example after editing a file and saving the result of the editing. In this state the permitted commands are **Open** and **View**.

- **Editing**: in this state a user has started editing a document; the possible commands are **Save** and **View**.

- **Viewing**: in this state the user has requested a View. The possible command are **Back** (go back to editing mode) and **Save**.

This design, of course, can be criticized. But this is precisely the benefit of treating states as first-class development objects: making it possible to discuss important system architecture choices and to assess the respective merits of various approaches.

12.9 APPLICATIONS

An entire system consists of one or more states assembled into an application. The application will define transitions between the various states; its visual representation will be a transition diagram.

Let us define the transition diagram for our application; this will enable us to define its various states other than the first. Find the box for the Application Tool (also known as Application Editor) in the Base Tool window:

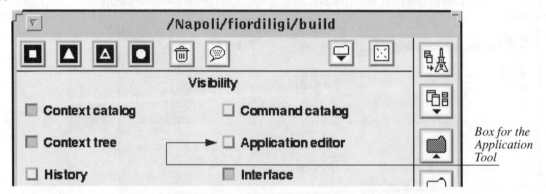

Box for the Application Tool

Click on the box to bring up the Application Tool :

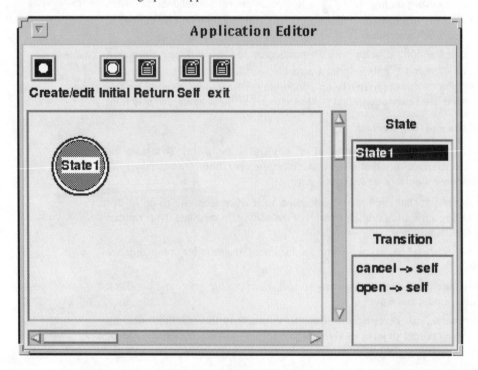

This shows the default state. Create two more, in each case by drag-and-dropping from the **Create/edit** button hole to the desired location. (As usual, you can use the mouse, left button kept down, to move the objects at any time.)

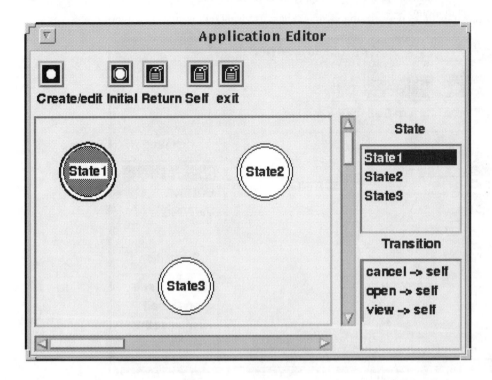

The state names are not very evocative. We should use the names suggested earlier: **BASIC** instead of **State1**, **EDITING** instead of **State2** and **VIEWING** instead of **State3**. As with any other type of EiffelBuild development object, you can use the Namer hole mechanism to rename a state; drag each state into the Namer hole and type the corresponding name. Here is the result:

12.9.1 The transitions

Now we need to define the transitions between states. To draw a transition simply drag-and-drop the source of the transition to the target. Apply this operation four times to produce the following transition diagram:

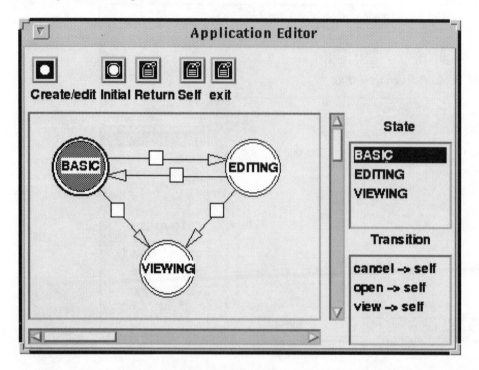

When you select a state (by clicking on its name, such as **BASIC** above) the Transition field shows the list of transition labels that have been defined for the commands in that state. Here command **Open** defined transitions **cancel** and **open**, and, as you will remember, we added a label called **view** when we created the **View** command. For all these labels the transition generated by default is **self**, which is no transition at all — it leaves the session in its current state.

Here is how to produce a real transition. The obvious example is what happens when a command in the **BASIC** state generate terminates with the **view** transition label. (Here the only command that can do this is the **VIEW** command, but in general two or more commands can share a transition label.) Such a situation should cause a transition to the **VIEWING** state; in fact this is the reason why we introduced such a state.

To implement this transition, click on the **BASIC** state name (if it is not already highlighted); click on the transition labeled **view**; and drag-and-drop it to the target state of the desired transition, **VIEWING**. (During the drag step, the pebble representing the transition label is ⬚.) The **Transition** table at the bottom-right shows the state now associated with transition label **view** for the currently highlighted state **BASIC** — no longer **self** as above but **VIEWING**:

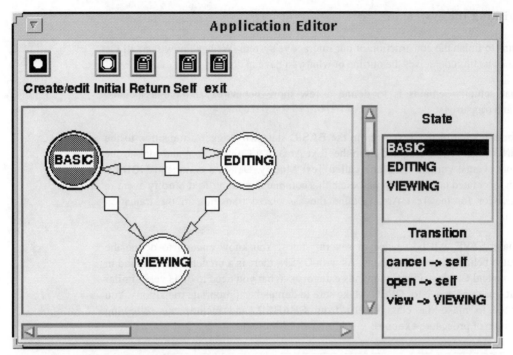

Apart from the transitions that you define yourself, such as the one labeled **view**, three special transition types are always available:

- **self**, the default as already seen, leaves the session in the current state.

- **return** brings the session back to the previous state in a last-in, first-out way.

- **exit** terminates the application.

Three transition label holes at the top of the Application Tool represent these special transition types. To apply them to any transition, drag-and-drop the transition into the corresponding hole.

The existence of **Return**, by the way, explains a property that may have left you wondering whether the above transition diagram was realistic at all: there is apparently no way out of state **VIEWING**! The reason is simply that **return** will serve our purposes: whenever a session leaves the **VIEWING** state, it should go back to the state that it encountered before **VIEWING** — to **BASIC** if the View command was requested from **BASIC**, to **EDITING** if it was requested from **EDITING**. This **return** transition will be triggered by the **back** transition label, itself one of the labels of the **BACK** command class.

Without the **return** transition, expressing the transition diagram for this system would require more states and significantly more complexity.

Mathematically, the presence of **return** means that the transition diagram structures of EiffelBuild applications are not finite-state automata but stack automata.

12.9.2 Finishing the system

There remains to finish the construction of our interactive system. We have now seen all the concepts, so let us limit ourselves the outline of what you have to do.

All that actually remains is to define a few more behaviors and the associated commands and transitions:

- Any modification of the Text Area in the **BASIC** state will trigger a transition to the **VIEWING** state. If you drag-and-drop the Text Area to a Context Tool and look at the available events, you will find one called Text Modify. Define a command **MODIFY** with an associated label **modify**; associate this command with the **Text Modify** event in the behavior for the Text Area. Define the associated transition in the transition diagram.

- Command **SAVE** will be needed in several states. You know enough to define the associated behaviors and transitions. As with **OPEN**, there is a predefined command in the Command Catalog (File Commands category). What you need to do is very similar to what was done above for **OPEN**. Make sure to define the appropriate transitions. You will need to make the class inherit from **SHARED**, and include the following redefinition of procedure **execute**:

```
execute is
   do
       argument1.set_text (shared_text);
       argument1.set_editable
       set_transition_label (back_label)
   end
```

- For the **BACK** command the semantics will be very simple: triggering the appropriate back transition.

- Finally, the semantics associated with the **EXIT** button will be to exit from the application.

12.10 GENERATING AND EXECUTING

With the system now fully specified, you are ready to generate the corresponding Eiffel system, and run it.

12.10.1 Generating an Eiffel system

To generate the Eiffel text simply click on the Generate button on the Base Tool:

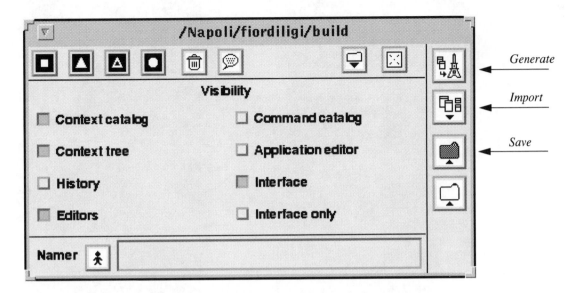

The Generate operation — which typically takes only a few seconds — produces classes in a subdirectory called **Classes** in the project directory. In turn **Classes** has its own subdirectories **Application**, **Commands**, **Groups**, **State**, **Widgets**, **Windows**.

If you take a look at the classes generated in these directories, you will note that they are simple and readable Eiffel texts. In accordance with the principles defined at the beginning of this chapter, there is no gap between what you specify visually and what you can program textually. You can edit one of the generated classes and modify it; the next session of EiffelBuild will take the changes into account. EiffelBuild uses an elaborate mechanism to integrate such textual changes with changes that you can make using visual techniques.

You can now compile your system using EiffelBench and the Melting Ice Technology.

If you are using precompiled EiffelBase and EiffelVision, as should normally be the case when developing a system using EiffelBuild, the compilation will be very fast, so that you can see the result of your development immediately, use EiffelBuild to change what you do not like, melt again, see the result right away, and so on — a comfortable development process. The combination of EiffelBuild and the Melting Ice explains why there is no need for a simulation mode: you want to run the real thing, not a simulation!

Index

abstract retargeting 143–145
Ace (Assembly of Classes in Eiffel) 11–13, 115–117
    creating for a new project 116–117
    for precompiled libraries 99
    specifying 11
    specifying under **es3** 166
ancestor version 106
Ancestor Versions format, see under format
Ancestors format, see under format
ANY 30, 134, 135
application 182, 218–222
application builder 178
Application Tool 218–221
arguments
    to a command (EiffelBuild) 205–206
    to a system's execution 91–92, 94–95
array
    direct array access 175
    high-performance array usage 175–176
ARRAY 26, 27, 28, 29, 143, 144, 145, 175, 176
ARRAYED_LIST 143–148
ARRAYED_STACK 148
assertions, effect on performance 110–112, 173–174
Attributes format, see under format
attribute, accessed less fast than local entity 176
automatic recompilation 82

BAG 134
Base Tool (EiffelBuild) 185–186, 198, 200, 201, 204,
    212, 218, 222
behavior 181, 201–204, 207–208, 217
    building 207–208
    definition 203
Behavior Tool 217
bin directories 6
binding, see static binding, dynamic binding
bitmaps directory 4

BON (Business Object Notation) xiii
BOOLEAN 137
Boucher 199
browsing 19–31, 140–148, 166–170
    from outside the graphical environment 166–170
    through run-time structures 164
    with Feature Tools 140–148
Bug_reports directory 4
button
    adding and modifying (EiffelBuild) 191
    areas 64
    End Run 91, 150
    Finalize 80, 169
    Font 64, 67, 141, 152
    Freeze 80
    Melt 14, 32, 33, 80
    Open 64, 70, 141
    Push Button (EiffelBuild) 203
    Quit 63, 64, 124, 141, 152
    Run 80, 91, 150, 163
    Save 32, 64, 69, 129, 141
    Save As 64, 70, 129, 141
    Search 64, 68–69, 141, 152
    Shell Command 31, 64, 65, 124, 141
    Special Operations 80
buttonhole 54, 79, 148, 150

C 83, 112, 171, 173, 179
    efficiency 171
    role in modern software development viii, 83
C-shell 2
C++ viii, 112, 171, 174, 179
    efficiency 171
callback 179
Callers format, see under format
CASE tools 81–82
catalog 182
    command 204

CHAIN 133, 134, 148

Chardin 199

class 42

creating a new class 127

"not in system" 121

class file 114

class hole, see under hole

Class Tool 16–24, 29–33, 123–138

formats 22, 30, 129–138

operations 123–128

using two Class Tools 30

click, synonym for left-click 16

see also middle-click, right-click

clickability vii, 20

see also clickable

clickable 20, 25, 30, 33, 35, 38, 39, 51, 59, 102, 103, 105, 106, 119, 121, 126, 130, 131, 133, 134, 135, 136, 137, 145, 147, 150, 152, 157

Clickable format, see under format

Clients format, see under format

cluster 114

creating a new cluster 127

Clusters format, see under format

COLLECTION 134, 144, 147

color 198–199

color names (EiffelBuild) 199

COMMAND 181, 201, 211, 215

command 181, 201–215

built by inheritance 211–215

catalog 204

complete class example 208–211

instance 205–206

type 205–206

undoable 215

undoing and redoing 200–201

Command Instance Tool 205–206

Command Type Tool 208, 212–215

command-line interface to the environment 89–90, 165–170

compilation 13–16, 81–112, 166–170

automatic mechanism 82

command-line interface 89–90

from outside the graphical environment 166–170

incrementality 82

messages 14, 15

performance 83, 172–173

role 82

using the three compilation modes properly 87–90

compilation modes 83–90

precise differences 85

configuration file 108–109

consistency vi, 41–42

constraint, see validity constraint

CONTAINER 137

context 181, 188–199

editing 192–194

resizing 189–190

tree, see Context Tree

Context Tool 181, 188, 192–194, 195, 196, 198, 201–203, 205, 207, 215, 217, 222

formats 193, 202

Context Tree 188, 194–195, 198

Context-Event-Command-State model of graphical interfaces 177, 180–182

control panel

EiffelBench, see Project Tool

EiffelBuild, see Base Tool

control-right-clicking 28

creating

a new class 127

a new cluster 127

a new project 10

curried function 181

data abstraction 42

principle 45

debugging 36–39, 139–164

Deferred format, see under format

degree messages 15, 32, 105

delivery directory, contents 4–6

delivery structure 4–6

Descendant Versions format, see under format

Descendants format, see under format

development abstraction 43, 180

EiffelBuild 180

development object 16, 43

applying operating system command 65–66

applying operations 65–70

editing 67–70

direct array access 175

direct manipulation 45–46

principle 46

directory 114

directory for a project

EiffelBench 76
EiffelBuild 185
    requirements and trouble-shooting 76–77
disk space
    needed for compilation 173
double-clicking, no special mechanism needed 25
drag-and-drop 16–18, 46, 48, 54–56, 59–62, 143–144
    a feature to a Class Tool 125–126
    keep-button-down 50
    why it works the way it does 59–62
dynamic binding 104, 174
    effect on performance 174

editing 19–28
    a class 65
effecting 28
efficiency of Eiffel 171–176
Eiffel
    organization of Eiffel software 113–115
EiffelBase x, 4, 15, 30, 223
    precompiled 15, 96, 223
EiffelBench x, xii, xiv, xvi, 4, 7–176, 223
    control panel, see Project Tool
    first steps 1–6
    guided tour 7–39
    starting 8–10, 75
    used with EiffelBuild 178, 223
EiffelBuild x, xiii, xvi, 4, 177–223
    applications 218–222
    concepts 178–182
    drawing the interface 188–199
    formats 193
    generating and executing 222–223
    history mechanism 200–201, 215
    setting up and starting 184–186
    specifying behaviors and commands 201–215
    states 216–217
    used with EiffelBench 178, 223
EiffelCase x, xvi, 4
EIFFELGEN directory 77, 109
EiffelLex x, 4
EiffelParse x, 4
EiffelShelf x, 4
EiffelStore x, xiii, xvi, 4
EiffelVision x, xiii, 4, 201, 215, 223
    precompiled for EiffelBuild 185, 223
EIFFEL3 environment variable 2, 184

End Run button 91, 150
ensure then 130
environment
    non-graphical 165–170
    principles, see user interface principles
environment variables 2, 101, 184
environment, setting up 2–3
ergonomics vi–vii
error handling 33–36, 49–51, 102–107
es3 command 90, 166–170
    –loop option 169–170
    options 167–170
event 181, 203
examples directory 4
exception 161–164
    catching an exception before it occurs 161–164
    handling 111
    recipient 162
    tracing 110, 162
execution 36–39, 90–95, 158–164, 166
    from the graphical environment 91
    of a finalized system 95, 166
    outside of the environment 92–95, 166
    specifying the arguments 91–92, 93–95
execution abstraction 42
execution object 42, 150–164
Execution Object Tool 17, 39, 150–164
exploration of run-time structures 164
extendibility 182
external software
    integrating in the compilation process 87
    wrapper classes 87
Externals format, see under format

feature
    callers 145
    history 145–148
feature hole, see under hole
Feature Tool 16, 17, 23, 24, 25, 26, 27, 29, 39, 140–148
    layout 140–141
File Selector 10, 70–73, 75, 129, 186, 205
Finalize button 80, 169
finalizing 14, 80, 89, 95, 107–112
    and assertions 110–112
    and precompilation 109
    execution of a finalized system 95

finalization directory 107–108
　　under the non-graphical interface 169
　　warning and confirmation panel 80, 89
FINITE 136
finite function 181
first steps with EiffelBench 1–6
first-time user 1–6
Flat format, see under format
Flat-short format, see under format
focus area 9, 10, 18, 63
font
　　adjusting 67–68
Font button 64, 67, 141, 152
format
　　Ancestor Versions 141, 146–148
　　Ancestors 22, 30, 128, 133
　　and retargeting 57–58
　　area 64
　　Attributes 30, 128, 135
　　Behaviors 201–203
　　Callers 141, 145
　　Clickable 30, 126, 128, 130–131
　　Clients 30, 128, 135
　　Clusters 19–20, 117, 119–121
　　Deferred 30, 128, 137
　　Descendant Versions 24, 25, 26, 141, 148
　　Descendants 22, 25, 30, 128, 134
　　Externals 30, 128, 138
　　Flat 30, 128, 130, 132, 141
　　Flat-short 30, 128, 132–133
　　for Class Tools 129–138
　　for System Tools 117–121
　　Implementers 141, 146
　　Once 128, 137
　　Routines 30, 128, 136
　　Short 30, 128, 132
　　Suppliers 30, 128, 135
　　Text 22, 23, 24, 26, 30, 117, 118–119, 128, 129,
　　　　130–131, 132, 141, 147
formats, EiffelBuild 193, 202
Fortran 171
Freeze button 80
freezing 14, 80, 85–88
　　warning and confirmation panel 80, 88
　　when necessary 87
function 181

garbage collection, effect on performance 174
GENERAL 56, 134
generic parameter, in Class Tool formats 136
Gotcha panel 49–51, 77, 143
graphical　interaction,　compared　with　textual
　　interaction 179–180, 223
guided tour
　　of EiffelBench 7–39
　　of EiffelBuild 183

history
　　window 200
history mechanism 200–201, 215
history of a feature 145–148
hole 16, 78
　　class 17, 18, 27, 29, 48, 124
　　class (in Feature Tool) 27, 140
　　empty or filled 18
　　execution object 152
　　feature 24, 27, 140
　　input 63
　　list of hole types 73
　　Project Tool 78
　　stop point 148–150, 157
human factors analysis vi, 59–60

iconifying the Project Tool window 79
identification number for execution object 152
Implementers format, see under format
include directories 6
incremental compilation 82
INDEXABLE 25, 134, 147
inheritance
　　repeated 104
　　used to build commands (EiffelBuild) 211–215
input hole 63
INTEGER 134
interactive mode of non-graphical interface 169–170
interface builder 178

keep-button-down dragging 50
keyboard entry 56–57, 126–128

label, see under transition
Lace (Language for the Assembly of Classes in Eiffel)
　　115
　　see also Ace

lib directories 6
library
    see precompilation
license manager 4
LINKABLE 151, 153
LINKED_LIST 30, 132, 135, 136, 137, 151, 153
local entity, accessed faster than attribute 176
–loop option of **es3** command 169–170

Make file 82–83
    adaptation for C compilation on different target
        platforms 83, 107–108
    no Make file necessary for Eiffel compilation 33,
        82–83
Melt button 14, 32, 33, 80
melting 13–14, 80, 84–88
    when not appropriate 87
Melting Ice Principle 84
Melting Ice Technology 13–16, 31–33, 81–112, 185,
    223
    applied to EiffelBuild 223
    definition 83–86
MELT_PATH variable 92, 94–95
messages, see compilation messages, error handling
Metaconfig 109
method support 41–45
Microsoft Windows xiii
middle-click 194
migration tools from Eiffel 2.3 4, 6
mode 45
    see also state
mode, see state
modifying software 31–33
Motif xiii
MVC model 183

Namer hole and field (EiffelBuild) 196–197
needed class 114
Nerson, Jean-Marc xiii
NEXTSTEP xiii
NONE 90, 135
non-graphical environment 165–170

object
    duplicating (EiffelBuild) 196
Objective-C viii
object, see development object, execution object

Once format, see under format
Open button 64, 70, 141
opening a project 75–77
optimization 110–112, 171–176

panel
    error, see Gotcha panel
path 3
pebble 16
    list of pebble types 73
performance 83, 109–112, 171–176
    how to assess 173–174
permanent window 188–189
platform (hardware-software architecture) 6
PLATFORM environment variable 2, 134, 184
polymorphism 28, 174
    effect on performance 174
precompilation 96–102, 168–169
    and finalizing 109
    concepts 97
    moving a precompiled library 101
    precompiling libraries at installation time 96
    producing precompiled libraries 100
    under the non-graphical interface 168–169
    using precompiled libraries 98–100, 168–169
precompiled library 15
    EiffelVision, for EiffelBuild 185
prevention, better than cure 49–51
principle, see user interface principles
project 10
    creating a new project 10
    directory 76, 185
    EiffelBuild 186–188
    opening 75–77
    retrieving 10
Project Tool 9–10, 32, 35, 75–80, 91
    iconifying 79
    layout 9, 78–79
    operations 78–80
    Stop Point hole 148–150
pseudo-Gotcha 51, 143
Push Button (EiffelBuild) 203

Quit button 63, 64, 124, 141, 152

redefinition 28
redemption principle 50

redoing 200–201
reinitializing text 70
Release_notes directory 4
repeated inheritance 104
require else 130
resizing (EiffelBuild) 189–190
resynchronizing a tool 15, 63
retargeting 20, 25, 54–58, 125–126
    a Class Tool 125–126
    a Class Tool to a feature 125–126
    a Feature Tool 142–143
    abstract 143–145
    and formats 57–58
    textual 143–145
    through keyboard entry 56–57, 126–128
reusability 182
right-click 16
root 114
Routines format, see under format
Run button 80, 91, 150, 163
running a system, see execution
run-time exploration 164

Save As button 64, 70, 129, 141
Save button 32, 64, 69, 129, 141
saving Class Tool formats 129
saving text 69–70, 129
scaffolding 179
Search button 64, 68–69, 141, 152
searching for a string 68–69
Select subclause 104–106
selector, see File Selector
semantic consistency 46–47, 195
    principle 47, 195
semantics of an interactive application 178
setting up your environment 2–3
    EiffelBuild 184–186
shell 2
shell command 65–66
    changing the default 65–66
    default 65
Shell Command button 31, 64, 65, 124, 141
Shneidermann, Ben 45
Short format, see under format
signature 132
simulation mode, none needed in EiffelBuild 179, 223
Smalltalk v, 183
    MVC model 183

spec directories 4, 6
SPECIAL 176
Special Operations button 80
speed, see performance
starting
    EiffelBench 8–10, 75
    EiffelBuild 185
state 45, 181, 216–217
    definition 216
    role in good system design 216–217
State Tool 217
static binding 174
stop point 97, 148–150, 155–161
    on routines of precompiled classes 97
    removing 149
    setting up 149, 157
STRING 25, 26
strong typing 47–49, 203
    principle 49, 203
Suppliers format, see under format
symbolic debugging, see debugging
symbolic link
    to driver of precompiled library 169
    to update file 94
syntax error 33–34, 102–103
system
    definition 113–114
    hole 11
System Tool 12–13, 19, 20, 113–121, 128
    formats 117–121
    layout 117
    operations 117–121

TABLE 22, 23, 25, 144, 145, 147
target 53
    primary 141, 142
    secondary 141, 142
    see also retargeting
targeted, see under tool
test mode, none needed in EiffelBuild 179
text area 189–190
text editing system 183–184
Text format, see under format
text window 64
textual interaction, compared with graphical interaction 179–180, 223
textual retargeting 143–145

Tool
    see also Application Tool, Base Tool, Behavior Tool, Class Tool, Command Instance Tool, Command Type Tool, Context Tool, Execution Object Tool, Feature Tool, Project Tool, State Tool, System Tool
tool 53–58, 62–64, 182
    creating 54
    general organization and layout 62–64
    resynchronizing 63
    retargeting, see retargeting
    targeted 53, 128, 142, 206
    tool-independent operations 64
    void 53
transition 181, 182, 213, 215, 220–221
    label 181, 215, 220
transition diagram 218
trouble-shooting 76–77
typed drag-and-drop, see drag-and-drop
typing, see strong typing

UNDOABLE 181, 201, 215
undoing 200–201, 215
universe 90, 114, 115
Unix xiii
UNIX_FILE 138
update file 93–95
user interface
    mechanisms 16–18, 53–73
    principles 16–18, 41–51, 177, 180
    principles, data abstraction 45
    principles, direct manipulation 46
    principles, EiffelBuild 177
    principles, redemption 50
    principles, semantic consistency 47, 195
    principles, strong typing 49

validity constraint 34–36, 83, 103–106
validity error 34–36, 103–106
variable, see environment variables
vi editor 31, 65, 124
visual association 208
visual interaction, see graphical interaction
VMS xiii
void, see under tool

Waldén, Kim xiii
WIMP (Windows, Icons, Menus, Pointing device) vi
window
    permanent 188–189
    text window 64
workbench code 86, 173
    performance 173
wrapper class (for non-object-oriented software elements) 87

X window system xiii

HOW TO OBTAIN

THE ENVIRONMENT DESCRIBED IN THIS BOOK

The tools presented in this book are available as part of ISE Eiffel 3, an object-oriented development environment for the production of quality software. The environment offers a number of components, including:

- EiffelBench, the graphical development environment (compilation, browsing, documentation etc.)..
- EiffelBuild,the graphical interface and application generator (see chapter 12).
- EiffelVision, the Graphical User Interface library.
- EiffelCase, the analysis and design workbench based on the BON method.
- EiffelStore, the general persistence library and uniform interface to Database Management Systems.
- And many more.

ISE Eiffel 3 is available on a great variety of platforms. Developed primarily for the needs of medium and large-scale industrial developments, it is also a good vehicle for teaching modern computing science and software engineering at all levels, from "Introduction to Programming" courses through Data Structures and Algorithms to advanced graduate seminars.

ISE Eiffel 3 is backed by an international network of distributors and by consulting services for both application and library development.

SEMINARS AND VIDEO COURSES

The Institute of Object Technology regularly offers courses in Santa Barbara, Paris and many other locations worldwide on the theory and practice of systematic object-oriented development. Topics include: *Object-Oriented Software Construction* (two or three days), *Object-Oriented Analysis and Design* (two or three days, with case studies), *Building Object-Oriented Libraries of Reusable Components* (one day), *Design by contract* (one day), *Building GUI applications* (three days, hands-on) and many other technical presentations. The Eiffel track includes *Introductory Eiffel* (three days, hands-on) and *Advanced Eiffel Development* (three days, hands-on). The management track offers *Object Technology: A Management Overview* (one day) and *Managing O-O projects* (one day). Seminars can be presented in-house for groups of 10 attendees or more.

Also available is the 6-hour video course ***Object-Oriented Software Construction*** by Bertrand Meyer (NTSC, PAL or SECAM).

FOR MORE INFORMATION

Return the coupon below to: Interactive Software Engineering Inc., 270 Storke Road Suite 7, Goleta CA 93117 (USA), Telephone 805-685-1006, Fax 805-685-6869, E-mail <info@eiffel.com>. If more convenient, you may also contact SOL, 104 rue Castagnary, 75015 Paris (France), Telephone +33/1-45 32 58 80, Fax 45 32 58 81, E-mail <info@eiffel.fr>.

Please send me information about how to obtain the environment presented in *An Object-Oriented Environment: Principles and Application.*

I am particularly interested in the following ISE Eiffel products: _____

My possible hardware-operating system platforms are: _____

Name: _____ Company: _____

Department, Mail Stop etc.: _____

Address: _____

City, State, Country, Postal Code: _____

Please send: Seminar schedules in my area ❑   Information about the OOSC video ❑